AFRICA
0 250 500 750 1000 miles
0 500 1000 1500 kilometres
Marseilles
Genoa
Naples
Lisbon
MEDITERRANEAN SEA
Algiers
Gibraltar
Oran
Casablanca
Madeira
Tripoli
Port Said
Suez
Canary Is
RED SEA
Port Sudan
Massawa
Aden
Socotra
Djibouti
Berbera
Bathurst
Freetown
Lagos
Port Harcourt
Monrovia
Abidjan
Accra
Takoradi
Mogadishu
ATLANTIC OCEAN
Equator
INDIAN OCEAN
Mombasa
Tanga
Zanzibar
Dar es Salaam
Ascension
Mtwara
Lobito
Mozambique
St Helena
Mauritius
Beira
Walvis Bay
Lourenco Marques
Durban
Mossel Bay
East London
Cape Town
Port Elizabeth

# THE CAPE RUN

By the same authors

BRITISH STANDARD SHIP SERIES
Empire Ships of World War II
The Oceans, the Forts and the Parks
British Standard Ships of World War I

AMERICAN STANDARD SHIP SERIES
The Liberty Ships
Victory Ships and Tankers
From America to United States
(in four parts)

MERCHANT SHIPS OF THE WORLD SERIES
Cruising Ships
Tankers

The Cunard Line—a Post-War History

# THE CAPE RUN

The story of the Union-Castle service to South Africa and of the ships employed

by

W. H. Mitchell
and
L. A. Sawyer

with drawings by
Nigel V. Robinson

TERENCE DALTON LIMITED
LAVENHAM . SUFFOLK

1987

Published by
TERENCE DALTON LIMITED

ISBN 0 86138 030 4

First published 1984
Revised edition 1987

*Text photoset in 11/12pt Garamond*

*Printed in Great Britain at*
*The Lavenham Press Limited, Lavenham, Suffolk*

# Contents

# Introduction

NOT long ago, if you had asked a seaman in a downtown Southampton pub what line he was with, or what service he was on, the answer would more than likely have been "on the Cape run", for ships to Cape Town—"Cape boats" in local idiom—sailed in regular service with passengers and cargo from the port for one hundred and twenty years. Now the passenger service is no more, ousted by the overwhelming odds of air competition, while high fuel and labour costs and the container, a revolution itself in world-wide shipping, have all contributed to the closure of the conventional cargo service.

It was the Portugese sailors in the fifteenth century who did much of the exploration of Africa's Atlantic seaboard and it was a Portuguese, Bartholomew Diaz de Novaes, who discovered the Cape in 1487. Diaz had reached the mouth of the Orange River in South West Africa when a northerly gale drove his ship southwards for thirteen days, far out of sight of land. Eventually the storm abated and he sailed northwards and found land, now known as Mossel Bay, having unknowingly rounded the Cape. Then, turning about and heading for home, he sighted the Cape which he called Cabo Tormentoso—Cape of Storms—later to be renamed Cape of Good Hope by King John II of Portugal.

Ten years later Vasco da Gama was sent to search for new trade routes. He rounded the Cape, sailed northwards and on Christmas Day, 1497, sighted land which he named Natal, in honour of the day. But he did not land, and instead sailed on northwards to Mombasa and Malindi and from there, with the monsoon behind him, north-east to discover the sea route to India.

Then to Africa went English, French and Spanish ships, making their ways along the coasts and, as was then the custom, claiming possession of newly discovered lands for their kings. The Portuguese, however, kept mainly to the east coast. Then followed the traders, their trading posts gradually becoming larger and more profitable as the years rolled by.

Early in the seventeenth century the East India Company was formed in London and ships bound for India and the East began calling at the Cape in increasing numbers, to take on fresh water and to trade for native cattle and herbs. There then started the habit of outward-bound sailors leaving letters under marked stones, called Post Office stones in later years, for homeward bound sailors to collect; the habit lasted until occupation of the Cape in 1652.

In that year the Dutch came, the first white settlement—virtually a trading post for the Dutch East India Company ships—being founded by the Dutch commander, Johann van Riebeeck, on the spot where Cape Town now stands, the settlement consisting of a few tiny huts clustered in the shelter of a fort at the mouth of the Zoeta (Sweet stream). The Dutch colony gradually spread inwards but in 1795, during the Napoleonic wars, Cape Colony was taken by the British, only to be returned to Holland after the Peace of Amiens in March, 1802. Within fourteen months, however, Britain and France were again at war and in 1806 the Cape was re-occupied by the British and finally ceded to Britain in the peace of 1814.

In the following year a Government-sponsored monthly mail packet service was started from Britain to the Cape, fast sailing ships leaving the Thames for the Cape, Mauritius and India. The inaugural ship took 114 days to reach the Cape via Madeira and Rio de Janeiro.

In 1820 the British government was again sponsor, this time of a mass experimental emigration scheme to South Africa. Members of the public were invited to settle along the eastern district of the Cape of Good Hope. A large number applied, 4,000 were chosen and sailed in a fleet of twenty-one chartered ships. About 3,000 landed at Algoa Bay, Port Elizabeth was born and the locally-given title of "The 1820 settlers" is as much revered in South Africa as is the "Pilgrim Fathers" in the United States. At the entrance to Port Elizabeth docks stands a campanile, a 170-foot square tower, erected in 1921 to commemorate the landing of the settlers one hundred years earlier.

At dawn on 13th October, 1825, there arrived in Table Bay the first steamer to sail between England and India. She caused great excitement when signalled from the hill known as the Lion's Rump and, before anchoring, she proudly steamed about the Bay in boastful demonstration of her manoeuvrability. The *Enterprise*, of the East India Company, had left Gravesend on 3rd August and from Falmouth, where she had called on the 16th, had taken fifty-eight days to the Cape. Of 464 tons, she was 122 feet long and had two small engines of 120 horsepower which contributed 7 knots: she had been built by Gordon & Sons, of Deptford.

The first company to attempt to provide some sort of regularity of service was the General Screw Steam Shipping Company, founded in 1848 and running ships through the Mediterranean to Turkey from the following year. In late 1850 the company contracted for a mail service to the Cape, the first sailing being taken by the auxiliary *Bosphorus*, which arrived at the Cape on 27th January, 1851, after a forty-day voyage from Plymouth, five days in excess of the contract time. The first five sailings were to the Cape but then, in the summer of 1852, the company extended its service to India, calling at Mauritius and Ceylon. Several new sisterships were built and used in this service, including the *Queen of the South*, *Lady Jocelyn*, *India* and *Calcutta*. But in March, 1854, with expensive fuel costs and a number of mishaps to their ships having contributed to monetary losses, the company abandoned the service.

The *Arundel Castle* (1921, as rebuilt in 1937-38) on Itchen Quays, Southampton, with B.O.A.C. flying boats moored in the River Test in the background.

The next attempt was by W. S. Lindsay's Line which acquired the mail contract in 1856 and with it a thirty-six-day voyage stipulation. The service again continued from the Cape to India. The first arrival at the Cape in the new service on 29th September, 1856, was the *England*; other ships used were the iron screw vessels *Robert Lowe* and *Tynemouth*; and the *Scotland*, *Ireland*, *James Hartley* and *W. S. Lindsay*. But after thirteen voyages the thirty-six-day schedule proved impossible to maintain and the service ceased after only one year, the last arrival at the Cape being the *Scotland*, on 23rd September, 1857.

Then there appeared the Union Line, followed, after a number of name changes, by the Castle Mail Packets Company Limited, and in 1900 came the merger of the two to form one of the world's great shipping concerns. South

Africa made Union-Castle and Union-Castle in turn contributed much to the development of the sub-continent. Settlers, emigrants and, in unfortunate times, soldiers have all been carried in countless thousands, many using the service time and time again as passengers in later years. Machinery to work the ground and to mine the ores, textiles, foodstuffs—a thousand and one items that are classified as general cargo—have all been shipped from Britain. In return the fruits of Africa have found their way to the British table, starting with trial shipments in experimental cold chambers and growing to full shiploads of hundreds of thousands of packages. Wool, ores, sugar, cereals—all have helped to fill the holds of homeward-bound ships. And it is recorded that at one time pedigree cattle were carried from the United Kingdom, free of freight in intermediate steamers, to stock the ranches of South Africa. South African interests were Union-Castle interests. And as trade grew the names became synonymous; those who have heard of South Africa must surely know of Union-Castle.

This book has been written as a record of Union-Castle services up to the last sailing of the mail service in 1977 and of the ships employed, for they will never be seen again. The early years have much of interest and the first part is devoted to the beginning of the Union Line, the later intervention of the Castle Line, and the eventual merger and formation of the Union-Castle Mail SS Company Limited in 1900. Then, in order to preserve continuity, Chapter Two starts at the beginning of the century and moves through the two World Wars. The third part, Chapters Three to Five, by far the largest part, brings the story up to the present.

Fleet lists at important times are given and histories of ships within living memory are more detailed. Greater detail of company history and personalities has not been recorded, for this has been perfectly covered in other worthy works of shipping history, in particular Marischal Murray's *Union-Castle Chronicle*, from which some source material is acknowledged. Acknowledgement is also made to Lloyd's Register of Shipping; The Corporation of Lloyds; *Marine News*, journal of the World Ship Society; Tom Rayner, of Ryde, IoW; to numerous magazines, journals and shipping guides; and to a host of items from many sources, far too numerous to list.

Statistics in the text have been restricted but, occasionally, a few have been allowed to creep in regarding trade.

Abbreviations used are: Length overall (oa), Length between perpendiculars (bp), Gross tonnage (gt), Deadweight tonnage (tdw).

Southampton and London
September, 1983

W. H. Mitchell
L. A. Sawyer

CHAPTER ONE

# The Building of Empires

IN June, 1853, Russian forces crossed the River Pruth and entered the trans-Danubian territories, and there followed a Turkish declaration of war on Russia. In January, 1854, British and French naval squadrons entered the Black Sea, and two months later these two powers entered the conflict on the side of Turkey. Allied armies landed in the Crimea in September, 1854.

On the face of it, these historical facts would seem to bear no relevance to a shipping service between England and South Africa, yet . . .

The Southampton Dock Company opened its nearly-completed tidal dock to shipping on 29th August, 1842, when two Peninsular & Oriental Steam Navigation Company ships, the 780-ton *Tagus* and the 500-ton *Liverpool*, were berthed. Of sixteen acres, it was known as the Outer Dock and was fully opened to general trade on 1st July, 1843. In 1851, a second achievement was a non-tidal basin, the Inner Dock, leading from the Outer Dock. Already the Royal Mail Steam Packet Company had its regular, expanding service from the port to South America while the P & O Company, trading to the Orient, was only a few months away from inaugurating a Southampton-to-Australia service. Cross-channel packets of the South Western Steam Navigation Company were contributing valuable links to the near-Continent, and services from Northern Europe to America included Southampton as a port of call. The future of the port was extremely promising.

These were steamship companies, operating in regular service; for the sailing ship, relying on the elements, could not compete and was already being ousted. But steamships needed coal, and so it was that in the summer of 1853 the Southampton Steam Shipping Company was formed, on 7th October changing and registering its title as the Union Steam Collier Company, to operate five small steamers of about 500 tons deadweight in the carriage of coal from the pits of South Wales to feed the furnaces of ships using the south coast port.

With the beginning of the Crimean War the P & O Company withdrew their ships operating between Southampton and Constantinople, these being used in war service, so with more remunerative cargoes offering the Union Steam Collier Company switched their fleet to run from Southampton to Constantinople and Smyrna. This arrangement did not last long, for after

*Windsor Castle* (1960). *Union-Castle*

only a few voyages they were chartered to the French and British transport services, the *Norman* sailing first from Southampton to the Crimea with a cargo of wooden huts on 3rd December, 1854.

In 1855 the fleet consisted of six ships:

| | | | |
|---|---|---|---|
| *Union* | 336gt | Completed | 6.1854 |
| *Briton* | 491gt | | 9.1854 |
| *Saxon* | 490gt | | 10.1854 |

All built by Samuda Bros., Poplar, London.

| | | | |
|---|---|---|---|
| *Norman* | 530gt | | 11.1854 |
| *Dane* | 530gt | | 3.1855 |

Built by Lungley, Deptford, London.

*Celt* 514gt ex *Gothenburg*, of the North of Europe SN Company.

Also built by Lungley and purchased in 1855.

In 1856 the war ended and the six ships were released from transport duties, but the original enthusiasm for carrying coal had waned and the company now had an eye to overseas trade. The word "Collier" was deleted from the title, offices were acquired in Oriental Place, Southampton, and an attempt was made to enter the Brazilian trade with the despatching of two vessels in 1856. This proved unprofitable and the idea was abandoned. Another scheme to run ships from Liverpool to Hamburg met with no more success. But better things were to come.

The British Admiralty had invited applications for a mail service to Cape Town and accepted the Union Line tender on 4th September. On 12th September, 1857, a five years mail contract was signed by the Union Steam Ship Company Limited for a service between England and South Africa. A monthly sailing was to be maintained in each direction and the passage was to take no more than forty-two days each way. The ships were not to be less than 530 tons, but the annual subsidy was a then attractive £33,000.

*Dane,* completed by Charles Lungley of Deptford in 1855.

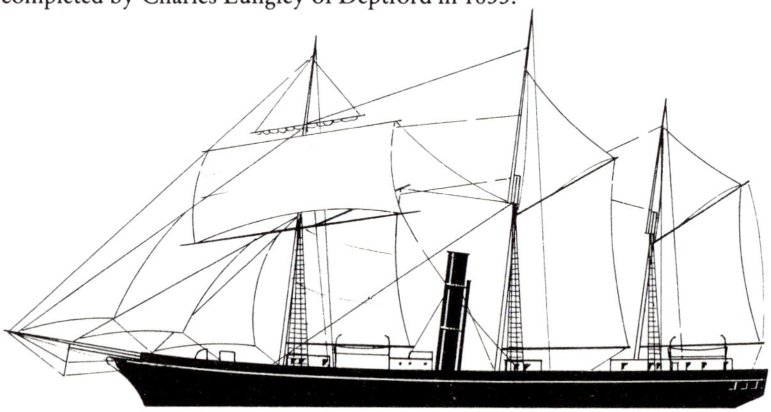

The *Dane* was at Liverpool and she hurried to Southampton, there to be drydocked, scraped and painted and made ready for her long voyage. Then, loaded with mails and a few packages of freight, she sailed down Southampton Water on 15th September, 1857, bound for the Cape of Good Hope, her crew and six passengers undoubtedly gazing with mixed feelings at the lush New Forest scenery passing by and certainly quite unaware that they were making history as the forerunners of the magnificent South Africa service that was to come. In the event the *Dane* took nearly forty-four days on the voyage, anchoring in Table Bay on 29th October, 1857. Income for the voyage was some £300, although homewards she made nearly five times as much. The *Norman* and *Dane* were rigged as three-masted schooners, square-rigged on the foremast, and in a favourable breeze and without steam assistance they could make 10 knots. The 40 hp engine alone could give the

Built by Alexander Denny at Dumbarton in 1851, the *Phoebe* was fitted with a vertical jet condensing engine.

ship 7 knots in fine weather. However, when they sailed against head winds they used about seven tons of coal daily and a 5 knot speed could not be kept up. Steaming against the trade winds was simply not practicable and they were put on a wind under all fore and aft sails and the steam reduced.

The *Briton*, on a voyage charter to Spain in 1857, had sunk in the Bay of Biscay while the *Union* and *Saxon* were sold in 1857-58, being too small for the long run. In place of these three ships the 613-ton *Phoebe* was acquired in 1857 and the 739-ton *Athens* in 1858. The second outward steamer in mid-October, the *Celt*, took forty-three days, in November the *Norman* took thirty-nine, and the *Phoebe* arrived at the Cape in January after a passage of thirty-seven days. On these regular monthly voyages the ships called at Plymouth, both outwards and homewards, with mails. In 1858 the Union Line ships commenced homeward-bound calls for mails at St Helena and Ascension.

About this time the chief, indeed, the only powers with any large stake in the African continent were Great Britain, France and Portugal. In the south, Great Britain had the Cape of Good Hope and Natal; on the east coast British influence was present at the Court of the Sultan of Zanzibar and on the west coast some ports on the Gold Coast had been acquired.

The *Cambrian* (1,055 gt), the first ship to exceed 1,000 tons to be designed and built for the mail service, entered the fleet in 1860. She had engines developing 120 hp, and on 13 tons of coal daily could make 8 knots in fine weather. She was joined in the following year by the 1,160 gt *Briton*, a brig-rigged flush-decker of the same power as the *Cambrian* and the first ocean-going vessel to be built by Lungley on the "unsinkable" plan, with the usual bulkheads plus three watertight decks.

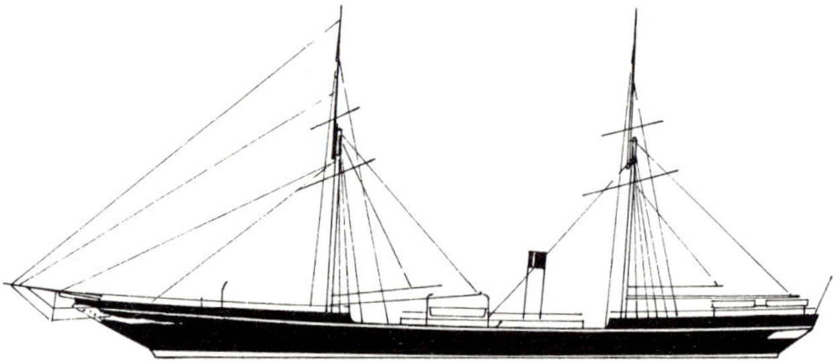

The brig-rigged *Cambrian* of 1860, another Lungley-built ship. Launched in April, 1860, she was towed to Southampton where her 130 hp engine was installed.

Table Bay was not very hospitable in those days. There were no docks or wharves, although the first stone of a breakwater had been laid by the Duke of Edinburgh in 1860. Aids to navigation were few. There was nothing on Robben Island at the entrance to Table Bay nor on Mouillie Point, but two fixed white lights gleamed from a small light tower on Green Point on the slopes of what is now known as Signal Hill. These, however, caused consternation at times when the lights of nearby houses were mistaken for the navigation lights. There were northerly gales in winter and south-easters in summer and the ships, anchored some five or six weeks in the Bay while loading and unloading by shore boats taking 10-ton loads, caused great anxiety. Heavy anchors and cables formed part of the ship's equipment and heavy coir springs were fitted to the cables in gales. The coir springs were put over a special bollard on deck, abaft the foremast, the other end being lashed to the cable, and they were capable of great stretching.

One of the worst storm disasters of Table Bay occurred in 1865. On 17th May a north-easterly gale, more vicious than usual, was blowing. There were many ships anchored there, barques, schooners, brigs and cutters, and there were also three Union Line steamers, the *Dane*, *Briton* and *Athens*.

As the gale increased in intensity some sailing ships began parting their cables and, without power, drifted helplessly. Two sailing ships drifted towards the *Dane*, whose engines were put full ahead so that danger was minimized. Even so she was holed below the waterline. Quickly the hole was stuffed with mattresses and the like and the ship suffered no further damage.

The *Athens* was not so lucky. In the evening she endeavoured to clear the bay but ran on to a reef near Mouille Point and was quickly lost with all hands. The strength of the storm can perhaps be gauged from the fact that no fewer than sixteen wrecks of sailing ships were strewn around the bay and there was great loss of life from those vessels as well as from the *Athens*. Among the sailing ships lost were six barques, including the *Star of the West* (386 tons), *Frederick Banil* (341 tons), and *Alacrity* (317 tons).

In 1863 the company introduced a coastal run from Cape Town to Port Elizabeth and Durban, with a call a little later at Buffalo River, where East London was then little more than a trading post. This replaced the John T. Rennie service which had started in 1857, but which was defeated by the loss of the two ships employed. Two old Union Line ships, the *Norman* of 1854 and *Dane* of 1855, were employed and a third, *Anglian*, acquired in 1864, was added. The *Dane* stranded near Port Elizabeth in late 1865 and was replaced by another ship of the same name, but with a larger tonnage at 788 gt.

At East London the coasters anchored well out, for only small boats of extremely shallow draught could cross the bar, even at high water. Lines were run from the anchored ships and the cargo boats were hauled out through the surf. The bar at Port Natal was almost as shallow—some 4 feet at low water, although some small ships, after lightening their cargoes, could be towed across at high water by a small Government tug named *Pioneer*. Coastwise cargo offering was light, some bananas and sugar being moved down the coast; occasionally small consignments of bales of wool were loaded for transhipment to England.

Meanwhile the main fleet was augmented by the *Saxon* and *Roman* in 1863 and the *Norseman* and *Celt* in 1866. Two years later the service was increased to two sailings a month.

Ocean freight mainly in the form of manufactured articles was, however, very light, and return cargoes presented even more of a problem. The small population of South Africa was employed in subsistence farming and little was left for export. Industries of any note had not yet begun. After fourteen years of service the Union Line fleet in 1870 comprised nine steamers:

| | Acquired | gt | | Acquired | gt |
|---|---|---|---|---|---|
| *Cambrian* | 1860 | 1,055 | *Norseman* | 1866 | 1,386 |
| *Briton* | 1861 | 1,164 | *Dane* | 1866 | 788 |
| *Saxon* | 1863 | 1,142 | *Celt* | 1866 | 1,439 |
| *Roman* | 1863 | 1,282 | *Northam* | 1869 | 1,330 |
| *Natal* | 1865 | 618 | | | |

But something of great importance had happened three years previously, for in 1867 diamonds had been discovered. However, until it had been determined that the discovery was no mere "flash in the pan" the news was not made public until 1869. By late 1870 diamond fever was endemic. Emigrant searchers for diamonds arrived in great numbers and as the industry developed machinery, railway equipment and ancillary imports began arriving in large quantities. During the following decade the value of diamond exports actually exceeded the value of the products of the agricultural and pastoral industries.

The Union Line took advantage of this upsurge in trade. The *Northam*, 1,330gt, built in 1858 for the P & O SN Company by Day & Co., Southampton, had been purchased in 1869 and the company now acquired the *Syria*, 1,959 gt, constructed by the same builders, also for the P & O. She was of paddle propulsion but when bought in 1871 was quickly converted to screw propulsion. In the same year the *Danube* (2,039 gt), built in 1866 for the Royal Mail Steam Packet Company, was purchased.

With the signing of another contract, effective from 1st January, 1873, three sailings a month from England and a reduction from thirty-seven to thirty days voyage time were called for. There was also to be a four-weekly service from Cape Town northwards up the east coast to Zanzibar. The contract prompted the acquisition of more and larger ships. Five mail ships and four coasters were added to the fleet in 1873 and in 1874 the *Nyanza*, ten years old, was bought from the P & O.

The first ship of over 3,000 gross tons came in 1876. She had a figurehead of a dark-skinned Nubian—as was her name—and was the first two-funnelled Cape mail steamer. When re-engined in 1891 she was demoted to the intermediate service and then only had one funnel.

But moves of great importance were taking place that were greatly to influence the Union Line. To the end of 1875 the company had owned twenty-four ships.

## Enter Donald Currie

Donald Currie, later to become Sir Donald Currie, was a colossus in the shipping world. Always living in close proximity to the sea, he moved from his birthplace of Greenock to Belfast at a very early age and lived in Castle Place. He returned to Greenock for his first job; joined Cunard in Liverpool and, in 1862, founded the Castle Line of sailing ships from Liverpool to Calcutta; two years later the line made London their home port. The ships took the names of castles, perhaps influenced by Currie's childhood address of Castle Place, and these names were destined to be perpetuated beyond the middle of the twentieth century. The first was the *Stirling Castle* (1,165 gt) of

1863; the *Roslin Castle*, *Warwick Castle* and *Pembroke Castle* followed the same year; the *Arundel Castle* and *Kenilworth Castle* were completed in 1864; *Tantallon Castle* in 1865; *Carnarvon Castle* and *Carisbrooke Castle* in 1867-68. The last Currie sailing ship was the four-master *Cluny Castle* of 1883. In 1864 Currie also founded the Liverpool & Hamburg Steamship Company, which as the name implies marked a turn to steam propulsion.

Meanwhile the Cape & Natal Line, sailing from London, which had been formed when the diamond discovery caused a boost in shipping, was struggling to compete with the Union Line and Currie was approached to charter two ships to them. He arranged for the *Iceland* and *Gothland* to be

Currie's full-rigged iron ship *Carnarvon Castle* of 1867, built for the London-Calcutta run.

chartered from the Leith, Hull & Hamburg Steam Packet Company, in which he also had interests. Departing from Dartmouth on 25th January, 1872, the *Iceland* was not halfway on her voyage when the Cape & Natal Line collapsed.

Currie was immediately pressed by important businessmen and merchants to continue the Cape service and the *Dover Castle*, the first of four steamers ordered for the India run and completing in Barclay, Curle's yard on the Clyde, was turned over to the Cape sailing schedule. Now committed to the Cape service, Currie at first chartered steamers and then in an evidently lucrative arrangement, chartered out the first of his new quartet, *Dover Castle*, to the Pacific S.N. Company for a voyage—a maiden one—to South

America. She never came back, being lost by fire off the Chilean coast, and the *Westmoreland* was switched from Currie's Liverpool and Hamburg Line to be the first Currie-owned vessel to sail to the Cape.

The second of Currie's quartet of "Castle" steamers, *Walmer Castle* (2,446 gt), arrived in Table Bay on 4th October, 1872, in just under twenty-four days and was the first "Castle" in the service. The others, *Edinburgh Castle* (2,678 gt) and *Windsor Castle* (2,670 gt), were switched to the Cape run in 1873.

The new service was at first called The Regular London Line, the ships sailing from London and calling at Dartmouth for a few hours. The schedule was set for them to sail from Dartmouth two days earlier than the Union liner from Southampton, to go direct to the Cape without calling at wayports and thus to arrive at the Cape seven or more days earlier than the Union ship.

The name was soon altered to the Colonial Mail Line, and in 1876 the Castle Mail Packets Company came into being as a private company, becoming a limited company in 1881. The renaming of the company in 1876 coincided with the expiry of the mail contract held by the Union Line and the new contract was divided between the two companies. The maximum voyage time was now to be twenty-six days and for the first time in the history of the Cape Colony a weekly mail service was possible, ships of each company sailing alternate weeks. This arrangement heralded a period of twenty-five years of intense competition between the two companies, each striving to provide better and faster ships than the other. The period was to be an

*Conway Castle*, built 1878, was wrecked off Madagascar in 1893. *Tom Rayner collection*

exciting one, not only because of the continuing struggle between the two companies but because of happenings in South Africa itself.

Currie augmented his Castle Line in 1876 with the *Dunrobin Castle*, just under 3,000 gt, which easily sailed within the twenty-six days contracted voyage time. So did the Union Line's *Nubian* of the same year. With spare tonnage a monthly "extra" service was inaugurated in November, 1876, direct from Southampton to Port Elizabeth, the first sailing being by the ex P & O steamer *Syria*.

Five more "Castles" were added to the Currie fleet in 1877-78. The *Balmoral Castle* and *Dublin Castle* came from Robert Napier's yard at

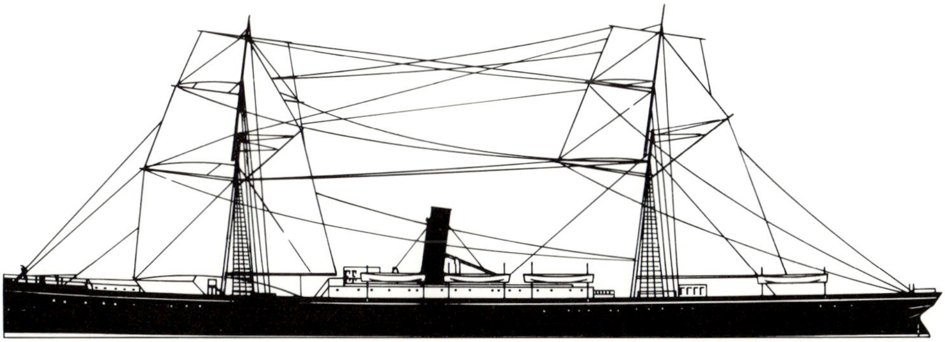

Built by Wm Denny and Bros., Dumbarton, in 1877, the *German* sailed for twelve years in the mail service and was eventually sold to Italy in 1896.

Glasgow, the *Taymouth Castle* from Barclay, Curle & Company. These ships were just under 3,000 gt. Two sisterships were the *Warwick Castle*, the first ship of the fleet measuring over 3,000 gt, and the *Conway Castle*, which came in 1878. Both were from the Napier yard. The *Taymouth Castle* arrived at the Cape on her maiden voyage with smallpox on board and swung to her anchor in quarantine in Saldhana Bay for six weeks. When the *Dublin Castle* was completed, the *Taymouth Castle* became the company's first "extra" steamer.

The Union Line's reply to these ships was the 2,875 gt *Durban*, from Laing's at Sunderland, the *German* and *Pretoria* of 3,200 gt in 1877-78 and the *Arab* in the following year. All these ships were making passages within the contracted time.

Here then was absolute competition, each company endeavouring to obtain more and more of the trade. In turn the ships became larger, accommodation was improved and the passage time reduced. In 1880 the

*Kinfauns Castle* and *Grantully Castle* appeared, carrying 120 First, 100 Second and 160 Third class passengers. The ships reached the 3,500 gt mark. The first-named was built of steel but was not regarded as successful and was sold within three years. The *Grantully Castle*, built of iron, sailed for sixteen years under the "Castle" flag.

In this same year the Union Line disposed of the *Nyanza.* Originally of paddle propulsion when built in 1864 for the P & O, she was acquired by the Union Line in 1874, then being converted to screw propulsion and losing one of her two funnels. The *Nyanza* was one of four steamers demoted from the mail run to operate in the 2,700-mile service between Cape Town and Zanzibar. Her buyer was the Sultan of Zanzibar and she lasted until 1904 before being broken up. The largest ship of the Union Line fleet, the *Trojan*, 3,650 gt, was also completed in 1880, an innovation being electric lighting in the saloon.

Two slightly larger "Castle" near-sisterships were delivered by John Elder & Company in the following year, the *Garth Castle* and *Drummond Castle*. Both ships were of 3,700 gt. The early service of the *Drummond Castle* was marred when, on two consecutive voyages, she arrived at Cape Town with smallpox on board and was quickly diverted to Saldhana Bay to discharge her passengers. Both were mail ships until the early 'nineties. The *Drummond Castle* was lost in 1896 when, homeward bound, she struck rocks on the island of Molene, East of Ushant, on 17th June and sank in deep water with severe loss of life.

*Garth Castle*, built in 1881, served for twenty years on the South Africa service before being sold to Elder Dempster. *Tom Rayner collection*

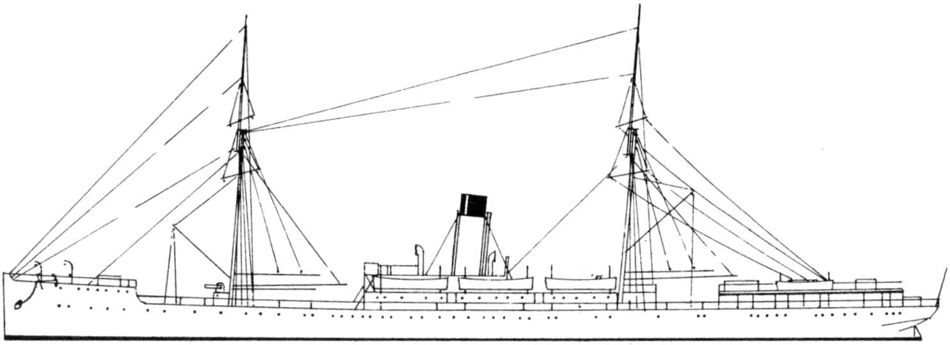

*Garth Castle,* named after the estate in Perthshire owned by Donald Currie.

Back came the Union Line with the *Athenian* (3,877 gt) and *Moor* (3,700 gt) in 1882 and the *Mexican* and *Tartar* of 1883, the latter two of 4,600 gt. In these four ships the company reverted to the three-mast, pre-1860 style. They were generally similar, with only minor differences in design, each carrying 350 passengers spread over three classes. On 22nd October, 1882, the *Athenian* had the distinction of being the first ship to use the Robinson Graving Dock at Cape Town.

The graving dock, named after Sir Hercules Robinson, Governor of South Africa, was of 500 feet bottom length and was built of Paarl granite. The dock was not eclipsed in size at Cape Town until the opening of the Sturrock Dock of 1945. The North Quay at Cape Town was the berth for both mail and intermediate ships and accommodated the dock offices of the Castle Line, with the rival Union Line using the opposite East Quay.

The *Moor* was completely remodelled in 1893-94, being bisected and having a new piece, 55 feet long, inserted. New engines and new masts were fitted and another funnel was added. All this raised her tonnage and she sailed as a mail steamer until she became too slow for the service.

At Southampton the Union Line ships had been using what was then known as the Southwest Quay and sheds in the Inner Dock (later to become Berths 14-16), these having become more or less the recognised home of the inward and outward South African cargoes carried by Union Line steamers.

In 1875 the old Southampton Dock Company had shown foresight in constructing an extension quay along the River Itchen, adjacent to the Outer Dock. This Itchen Quay had been planned for four berths, Nos 1-4 (later, Berths 30-33), and Berth No 1 (30) was used at times as a Union ship loading berth. Coupled with this, an adjacent drydock (No 4) was opened in 1877.

The developing trade with South Africa necessitated larger vessels. By 1883 ships had reached 4,600 gt with the *Mexican* and *Tartar* and the berths at the

Southwest Quay of the Inner Dock were no longer suitable. From 1884 Extension Berth No 2 (31) became the homeward berth, the ship, when discharged, moving to the adjacent drydock when necessary, and then out to Extension Berth No 1 (30) for loading. This pattern continued until the mid-1890s (except for the *Scot*), the drydock being used almost entirely by the Union steamers and becoming known, locally, as the Union Graving Dock. The tidal Empress Dock, opened by Queen Victoria in 1890, accommodated the *Scot*. Just after the opening of the Empress Dock the Southampton Dock Company, unable to raise capital for urgent expansion, opened negotiations with the London & South Western Railway Company and the docks changed hands on 1st November, 1892. The first works by the new owners were yet more berths along the River Itchen. These were named Prince of Wales Extension Quay (Berths 34-36) and accommodated the ever-larger ships on the Cape run and their cargoes.

The first "Castle" ships measuring over 4,000 tons came in 1883. There were three, all similar, the *Hawarden Castle* (4,380 gt) from Fairfield, the *Norham Castle* (4,240 gt) from John Elder & Company at Govan, and the *Roslin Castle* (4,267 gt) from Barclay, Curle & Company. They were a reply to the Union Line's *Athenian*-type.

In these early years of the 1880s there occurred a downturn in trade, several factors combining to make it so bad that many ships had to be laid up or used in other areas. This slump lasted until 1886, when there came the discovery of gold in the Rand. Reaction was immediate. The demand for shipping space became acute. Steerage accommodation was packed with fortune seekers. Shipping companies issued tickets at times endorsed "to

sleep where any space can be found by the Chief Steward". Holds became full of mining machinery and general cargo of all kinds. The gold rush was on. Gold fever prevailed.

But homewards the cargo lagged. Gold and diamonds, although of immense value, did not make full cargoes. In 1887, however, an attempt was made to increase homeward freight when a deputation of fruitgrowers met Currie in South Africa and urged him to have ships fitted with refrigerated space. In the following year a small amount was provided in the *Grantully Castle*, which loaded an experimental consignment of grapes on her return voyage from Cape Town early in 1889; unfortunately the consignment was received in poor condition.

In 1888 another mail contract came into effect, with higher speeds stipulated, and many ships of both fleets were re-engined with triple-expansion sets in 1888-89. The *Roslin Castle* was lengthened by 15 feet and given a new stern, being re-measured at 4,485 gt. From this alteration she became the fastest ship on the Cape run, making a homeward voyage to Plymouth in late 1889 in just under seventeen days. The other two ships of the *Hawarden Castle*-type were re-engined in 1891, and all three lasted in the fleet for twenty years before being sold for further trading. However, the turnover from compound to triple expansion engines for increased speed to fulfil the new contract was not completely successful, fines being imposed on the companies for late arrivals. New ships were required.

When the mail contract was divided in 1876, the two companies each contributed two sailings a month, a weekly service thus being provided. Increasing trade, however, brought "extra" steamer sailings, these being

**Right:** Union liner *Mexican* in drydock at Southampton, showing scrollwork at the bow and catted anchors.

**Opposite:** Union Line's *Moor*, of 1882, after rebuilding in 1893-94.

*Tom Rayner collection*

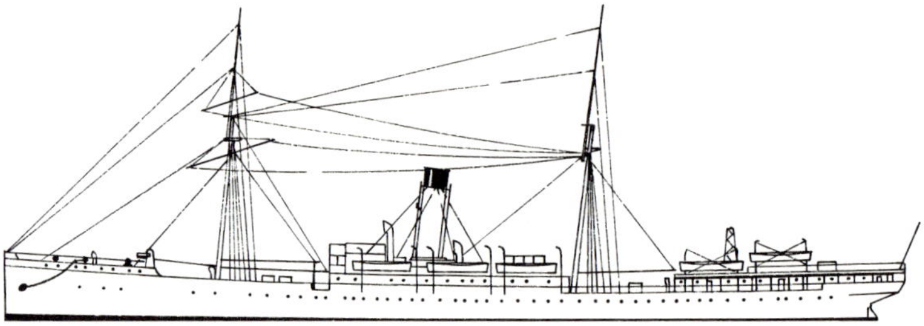

*Roslin Castle*, built 1883.

interpolated between one mail ship sailing and the next. The first "Castle" extra steamer was the mail ship *Taymouth Castle* of 1877 which began "extra" sailings only a year later. Another was the *Duart Castle* (1,839 gt), purchased in 1879. By 1881 both companies were operating these "extra" sailings.

There followed a short depression, but with the discovery of gold "extra" sailings were re-introduced in 1889, although from this date the term "intermediate" seems to have superseded the old title. The usual practice was to demote a mail ship which had lost her speed through obsolescence and age to the extra—or intermediate—service at reduced fares. Other "Castle" ships of that period were the singular *Pembroke Castle*, purchased while on the stocks of the Barrow Shipbuilding Company in 1883, and the sisterships *Dunbar Castle* (2,837 gt) and *Methven Castle* (2,681 gt), both completed in 1883. The *Pembroke Castle* also took sailings in the mail service and was the

Intermediate steamer *Lismore Castle* of 1891.

first four-masted ship of the Castle Line, square-rigged on fore and main. The yards were removed when the funnel was heightened and a sun-deck added. An innovation in this ship was that the main dining saloon was placed amidships, and a midships dining saloon was also a feature of the later intermediate ships *Doune Castle* and *Lismore Castle* of 1890-91, the first ships to be specially designed for the intermediate sailings with Second class passengers housed in the poop; and of the *Arundel Castle* of 1895, *Tintagel Castle* and *Avondale Castle* of 1896-97. No mail steamer, however, was to have this arrangement until the *Carisbrook Castle* of 1898.

Rivalry between the two companies was at its height in the last decade of the century and at this period some notable ships were constructed by both concerns, the two most outstanding ships coming in the early years.

In 1890 Currie produced his greatest challenge to the Union Line, the *Dunottar Castle* (one n). Launched by Lady Currie on 22nd May, 1890, she was ready for service by the following September. On her maiden voyage in October she made a record passage from Dartmouth of 17 days 19 hours 50 minutes and lowered that several times before being eclipsed by the *Scot* in 1891. The *Dunottar Castle* came from the Fairfield yard, Glasgow, had three masts and was the first two-funnelled ship built for Currie. She was designed to carry about 360 passengers in three classes. On measurements of 432 feet length oa, 420 feet length bp, and a breadth of 49 feet 4 inch she grossed 5,625 tons. Machinery was triple-expansion and, with a single screw, gave 17 knots. Mail ships of this era were being built with twin screws, yet the *Dunottar Castle* had yards on her foremast and barquentine rig. Another legacy of the sail age was the accommodation of her First class passengers under the poop. She was 1,000 gross tons more than any previous "Castle" ship and the horsepower was almost double that of her predecessor.

The fifth day of June, 1891, was a somewhat sad day for Dartmouth, for the sailing of the *Roslin Castle* was the last sailing of the Castle Line from that port, where the company had taken on mails for the previous twenty years. The Castle Line now made Southampton their first port of call from London to pick up mails and, undoubtedly with an eye towards publicity, it was their

*Dunottar Castle.*

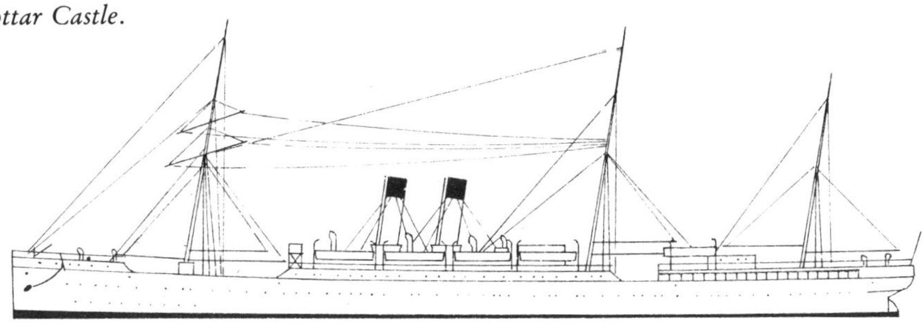

flagship, *Dunottar Castle*, that inaugurated the service from Southampton on 20th June, 1891. In a speech there, Sir Donald Currie said that this was the beginning of an era in the history of Southampton—and so it was.

The *Dunottar Castle* had a major refit in 1897 when the funnels were lengthened and her yards removed. Withdrawn in 1904, she lay at Netley for some three years. Then, chartered as a cruising ship, she cruised in connection with the Delhi Durbar in 1911, and in 1913 joined the fleet of the

The yacht-like *Scot* of 1891 was the most famous ship on the Cape run in the 1890s.
*Tom Rayner collection*

Royal Mail Steam Packet Company as the cruising ship *Caribbean*. In 1914 she served as a transport for a time and then as an armed merchant cruiser under Admiralty control from late 1914 until May, 1915. Turned into an accommodation ship, she foundered off Cape Wrath on 27th September of the same year in extremely heavy weather on a voyage to Scapa Flow.

At the time she was built the Union Line was watching intently and an order was given to William Denny of Dumbarton in 1889 for a ship which was to eclipse the *Dunottar Castle* and make the Union Line supreme on the Cape run.

The new ship was christened *Scot* and launched on 30th December, 1890, by Miss Giles, a daughter of the chairman of the Union Line. The length of

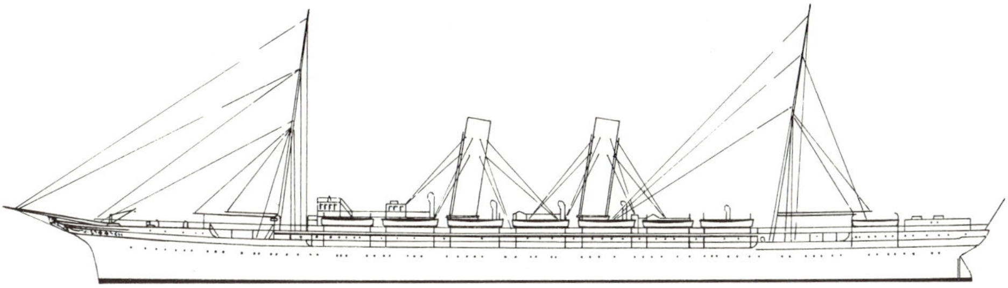

*Scot*, built 1891.

the ship was 500 feet oa and 477 feet bp, the breadth 54 feet 8 inches and the gross tonnage 6,844—half as much again as the *Mexican.* She had two triple-expansion engines driving twin screws—the first Union liner to be so provided—which gave 18½ knots. She also had a magnificent yacht-like sheer to her hull, a clipper stem and a graceful counter stern. Scotland's national hero, Sir William Wallace, with hand on sword, sternly defied the seas as a figurehead, with scrollwork winding away in a curve on either side. On either quarter were the Royal Arms of Scotland and of Great Britain.

Accommodation was fixed for over 400, divided into 200 in First, 100 in Second and 100 in Third class. She could also carry emigrants after a 'tween deck conversion, if required. A new style was set in that First class accommodation was placed amidships.

The builders had her finished in June, 1891, and she moved to Southampton, stored and sailed on 25th July from No 5 Berth in the newly-opened Empress Dock, arriving in Table Bay on 10th August in a passage time of 15 days 9 hours 52 minutes. On her first voyage she had lowered the record of her main rival by over a day, and the return leg was also the fastest home voyage ever.

Hitherto, the Union Line ships had had black funnels, black boats and

*Scot*, after lengthening in 1896.

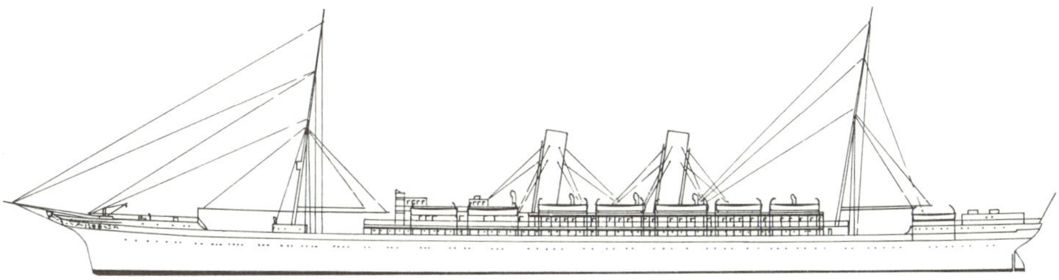

black hull with a white band, but after one voyage the lines of the *Scot* were enhanced by painting her hull white, her funnels cream and upperworks fawn. Other mail ships were also changed to those colours.

The best run of the *Scot* was in March, 1893, when she arrived in Table Bay on the 19th in a time of 14 days 18 hours 57 minutes, a record that stood until broken some forty years later by the *Stirling Castle*, which made the passage in 13 days 6 hours 30 minutes.

By this time the *Scot* had become a ship on which to travel. Fast and luxurious, she was "the" ship of the Cape run—a status symbol, perhaps. But all was not well for her owners. Accountants were producing figures showing losses incurred by the *Scot*. She was burning fuel at the rate of 170 tons each day. Her coal bills were enormous, her cargo capacity small. Late in 1895 she suffered engine trouble, put in to Vigo and from there went to Harland & Wolff at Belfast for repairs. At the same time, in an endeavour to make her more economical, she was cut in two just forward of the bridge and a new 54 feet section inserted, giving her a length of 531 feet b.p. with a tonnage increased to 7,815 gt. She resumed the mail service from Southampton in July, 1896, and with her added accommodation became ever more popular. But she was still hardly economical.

The *Scot* was withdrawn from service on arrival at Southampton on 12th September, 1903, and placed in reserve off Netley for the next two years. In September, 1905, she was purchased by the Hamburg Amerika Line for a Mediterranean link service but, in 1906, was converted for cruising for the

One of three G-class intermediate steamers delivered in 1893, the *Gaul*, with the *Greek*, was transferred to the Royal Mail S.P. Company in 1906. *Tom Rayner collection*

next three years. She then went to the American flag and finally sailed under the Spanish flag until she was laid up at Cadiz in November, 1925. In February, 1927, the old *Scot*, the most outstanding ship of the nineteenth century Cape run, went to Italian breakers.

Another attempt to ship fruit was made in 1892, this time in the *Drummond Castle*. The Castle Line had been urged by South African farmers to fit cold chambers in some vessels and with the realisation of the faults of the previous attempt, this shipment of peaches, made in different packing and at a different temperature, was a success. Statistics and conditions were carefully noted and the trade, at least in the deciduous type of fruit, grew.

Another Union ship, the *Moor* of 1882, was lengthened by 55 feet in 1893, a second funnel was added and she was remeasured at 4,664 gt. She became a seventeen-day ship and lasted until 1901, but by then had become too slow for the new service and was sold to the Royal Mail Steam Packet Company, who renamed her *La Plata*. In 1908 she began cruising under the name *The Viking*, finally being scrapped at Zwijndrecht, Holland, in 1913.

The early intermediate ships, as previously mentioned, were mail ships that for one reason or another had passed their prime, but in 1890-91 the 12½ knot sisterships *Doune Castle* and *Lismore Castle* were completed by Barclay, Curle & Company at Glasgow specifically for the intermediate service to the Cape and on to Mauritius. Of 4,045 gt, they carried thirty First, forty Second and eighty Third class passengers.

In 1891, the year of the *Scot*, the Union Line sent William Pirrie (later Lord Pirrie) of Harland & Wolff to South Africa in a consultative capacity, to study South African trade and harbours and to design a ship able to cross the restrictive bars at East London and Durban and to carry passengers and freight not in record times but with profit. His recommendations were accepted, plans were drawn up and three ships ordered in 1892, all three being delivered in the following year. Although the mail ships had been repainted, these three retained the old colours of black, white-banded hull with the new yellow funnel.

They were named *Gaul*, *Greek* and *Goth*, 400 feet in length bp, 47 feet in breadth and with a tonnage of 4,745 gt. The draft was light enough for them to cross the bars at East London and Durban. They were three-deck, twin-screw steamers with triple-expansion engines. One peculiarity of note was that the First class saloon was placed on the promenade deck. The Second class saloon was on the upper deck, over the engine room and on the port side of the vessel. Third class accommodation was aft, the saloon in the centre of the poop on the upper deck with cabins either side. There was no lounge or smoking room. The ships were economical in coal although slow and the passage, at about 11 knots, took twenty-one days from Southampton to Cape Town. But they were profit makers in cargo carrying.

The intermediate G-class steamer *Gascon* of 1897 at Southampton.

The *Guelph* (Queen Victoria's family name) of 4,900 tons and the first G-class three-master, came in the following year, this time with the First class saloon placed on the boat deck. Accommodation on these ships was for fifty First, sixty Second and sixty Third class passengers, but a 'tween deck conversion could give further open accommodation for 500 emigrants.

The next batch of three were larger by 30 feet in length and by 5 feet in breadth, with a resultant gross tonnage of about 6,290. Named *Gaika*, *Goorkha* and *Gascon*, they were three-masted and all were completed in 1897. Another difference was a straight stem instead of a raked bow. Two, *Gascon* and *Goorkha*, served as hospital ships in the First World War.

The final three G-class ships, *German*, *Galeka* and *Galician*, reverted to two masts. These ships were larger again, by 10 feet in length and by 1 foot in breadth, and tonnage increased to 6,770 gt. The last of the class, the *Galician*, never flew the Union Line flag, for she was not completed until well into 1900. In 1914, in the fever of war, the Teutonic names of *German* and *Galician* were dropped, the ships taking the names *Glengorm Castle* and *Glenart Castle* respectively.

This series of ships were all entrusted to Harland & Wolff, and at the same time the builders undertook the lengthening of the *Scot* and orders for four more mail ships.

Although the Castle Line had been the first company to operate intermediate ships, they had nothing as successful as the Union Line's G-class. The small *Harlech Castle* (3,620 gt) came in 1894 from Barclay, Curle & Company at Glasgow, the *Arundel Castle* (4,590 gt) from the Fairfield yard in 1895 and the *Tintagel Castle* and *Avondale Castle* (sisterships of 5,500 gt) also from the Fairfield yard in 1896-97. In 1897 came the sisterships *Dunolly Castle* and *Raglan Castle*, very slow ships which rolled heavily and which were disposed of after only eight years of service. All these ships carried First and Third class passengers, but a considerable demand came about for a Second class for those who wished to avoid the severely austere conditions of the Third class accommodation, but who could not afford First class fares. This was answered when the 15-knot *Braemar Castle* (6,266 gt) was put in commission in 1898. She was the last four-masted intermediate ship. Built by Barclay, Curle & Company, she was given quadruple-expansion engines and was of single-screw propulsion. Accommodation was provided for First and Second class passengers. A great deal of her time was spent as a troop transport and she was repainted with a white hull and with her tall funnel yellow. She was a successful ship and would most likely have been followed by further ships of the same type had the Union and Castle merger not taken place.

Following the success of the G-class intermediate design the Harland & Wolff yard was given orders for the construction of a new mail ship to their own design. Based on the very successful North Atlantic ships they had built for the White Star Line, she was launched at Belfast in 1894 and christened *Norman*. She had measurements of 507 feet oa, 491 feet bp, a breadth of 53 feet and measured 7,392 gt. Two sets of triple-expansion engines to twin screws gave her a speed of 17 knots with great economy and, like all Union and Castle ships, she was built in consultation with the British government as regards her role in time of war.

The accommodation of the *Norman* was excellent. She carried passengers in three classes, First and Second amidships and Third class on the main deck,

Intermediate steamer *Arundel Castle* of 1895.

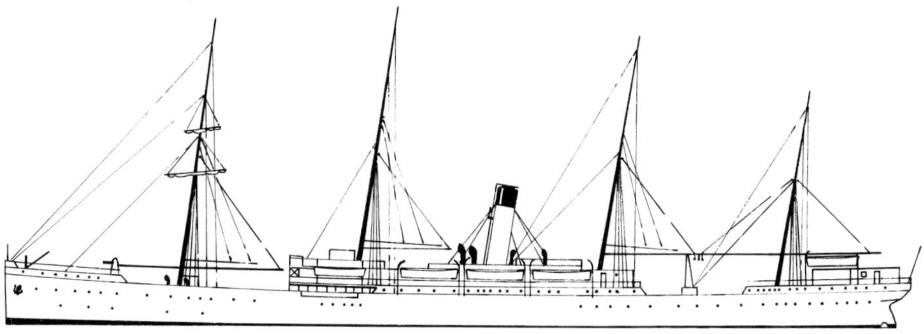

Sold in 1905, the *Arundel Castle* changed her national flag several times before being broken up in 1924.
*Tom Rayner collection*

Intermediate steamer *Braemar Castle* of 1898 became a troopship in 1909. Later she became a hospital ship, serving at the Dardanelles and then at Murmansk in 1918.
*Tom Rayner collection*

Launched at Belfast in July, 1894, the *Norman* was the first of an entirely new type of mail steamer from which a further seven mail vessels evolved.
*Tom Rayner collection*

The intermediate ships *Raglan Castle,* seen here, and *Dunolly Castle* were big cargo carriers as well as having accommodation for some 150 passengers. *Union-Castle*

forward and aft. Some space was also provided for open berth passengers. An innovation was an early form of air-conditioning connected to the refrigeration plant, but able to be controlled by the passengers. One of the first showings of moving films on ships was made on a southbound voyage of the *Norman* in March, 1896.

Her maiden voyage was from Southampton in November, 1894. First and Third classes of accommodation were extended in the following year and Third class was further extended in 1904. Until 1910 the *Norman* sailed in the mail service but was then made reserve ship, anchored off Netley. After a short period as a transport in August, 1914, she continued through the war in the mail service from Tilbury, Southampton having become a military port. From May, 1918, she was trooping for a year, then again served the mail service for a time before moving to London for the intermediate service.

In 1922 she was on the East African run and in 1923 on the eastabout "Round Africa" service. Eventually laid up at Tollesbury in the Blackwater in 1925, she was sold in 1926 for breaking up. The *Norman* was considered one of the finest and most handsome of Union ships and proved very economical. She had two funnels, two masts and a vertical stem, the design being followed and improved in the *Briton* of 1897 and *Saxon*, launched in 1899. All subsequent liners for the Union Line were built by Harland & Wolff.

The *Briton* was a giant compared with the *Norman*. She measured 549 feet oa, her length bp was 530 feet 3 inches and her breadth 60 feet 3 inches. At 10,248 gt she was the first Union ship to exceed the 10,000-ton mark and was the last Union liner to be completed before the amalgamation. She carried 280 First, 182 Second and 190 Third class passengers, with further space available for Steerage. The First class accommodation was amidships. Propulsion was by two sets of triple-expansion engines to twin screws, giving 17½ knots. She was the largest liner trading between any ports of the British Empire.

It is perhaps fitting to quote a description of her public rooms from a contemporary handbook:—

> Her accommodation is the finest yet seen on the mail route and reached by a superb Entrance Hall is the First Class Library, a noble room 34 ft by 28 ft. The furniture is of rich and choicely-inlaid mahogany, and the panels are of polished teak, relieved by satinwood, while overhead is a magnificent dome on a square base. Fitted in this room are splendid bookcases containing a choice selection of books.
>
> The First Class Smoking Room, which is about the same size as the Library, is fitted in a style worthy of its magnificent surroundings. The floor is of rubber tiles, the lounges are upholstered, as are the chairs, in figured morocco leather, while the ceiling is in cream and gold. From the centre of the lofty ceiling rises a dome of stained glass. Provision is made for ventilation, the large panels at the four angles being filled with *repoussé* work in brass.
>
> The First Class Dining Saloon is 60 ft by 40 ft—furnished in solid oak, with handsome and appropriate carved work. At one seating this Saloon will accommodate 172 persons. It contains a splendid piano by Broadwood, and also a very fine organ. The large dome which lights it is made of mahogany painted white, and the rich mouldings relieved by gold produce a very handsome effect.
>
> The First Class Cabins are all roomy and spacious apartments fitted in rich mahogany, and with patent spring wire-wove berths.

The *Briton* had two, long, open decks. She was two-funnelled, had three masts and a vertical stem. Launched on 5th June, 1897, she sailed on her maiden voyage on 4th December of the same year and, with her fine accommodation, quickly became popular. August, 1914, saw her at Cape

The first Union Line ship over 10,000 tons, *Briton* of 1897. *Tom Rayner collection*

Town and she was one of a convoy of six Union-Castle ships with a two-cruiser escort which sailed on 27th August, bringing home the Imperial garrison. Most of her war service was spent in trooping, but eventually she returned to the mail service in 1920, continuing until 1925 when she arrived at Southampton on 30th November for the last time. She was scrapped in Italy in the following spring.

The *Athenian* and *Tartar* were now surplus to requirements and were sold in 1897 to the Canadian Pacific Railway Company to help in the rush to the Klondyke goldfields. Both left Southampton in February, 1898, sailing via Cape Horn full with prospectors. They were scrapped in Japan in 1907 and 1908 respectively.

The first quadruple-expansion engined ship of the fleet, the *Tantallon Castle* was wrecked after only seven years of service.
*Tom Rayner collection*

In the closing years of the century the Castle Line had five mail ships completed for them. The first, the *Tantallon Castle*, came in 1894 from the Fairfield yard. Her tonnage of 5,636 gt was on measurements of 456 feet oa, 440 feet bp length and 50 feet breadth, and she was similar in appearance to the *Dunottar Castle*, but had only one funnel. She carried 500 passengers and the Castle Company still persisted in placing First class aft. Propulsion was by quadruple-expansion engines to a single screw, giving 17 knots. She was, in fact, Currie's attempt to answer the *Scot*, but was quickly outclassed by the *Norman*. She lasted only seven years, for in the afternoon of 7th May, 1901, she ran on a shoal just west of Robben Island in thick fog. Passengers were taken off by lifeboat and tugs from Cape Town endeavoured to pull her free. The next morning it must have been quite a sight to see the *Braemar Castle*, *Avondale Castle* and *Raglan Castle* all trying to tow her off, but she was firmly ashore, listing heavily, and was quickly smashed by the pounding of heavy seas.

In 1896 came another similar ship, the *Dunvegan Castle*, longer by 10 feet and of 5,960 gt. She, too, carried some 500 passengers. However, like the *Tantallon Castle* she was a little behind in design and when, after eight years, the *Kenilworth Castle* appeared, *Dunvegan Castle* was withdrawn and swung at anchor off Netley until placed on the East African run in 1910. After war service as a troopship and then a hospital ship, she made a few voyages via Suez to East Africa before laying up again in 1921, being scrapped in Germany two years later.

In fact, both the *Tantallon Castle* and *Dunvegan Castle* were, surprisingly, almost of the same design as the *Dunottar Castle*, which itself was regarded as being behind the times when constructed.

The last "Castle" ship in this group was the *Carisbrook Castle* (7,594 gt) of 1898. She also had a single screw and, as with the others, had three masts with

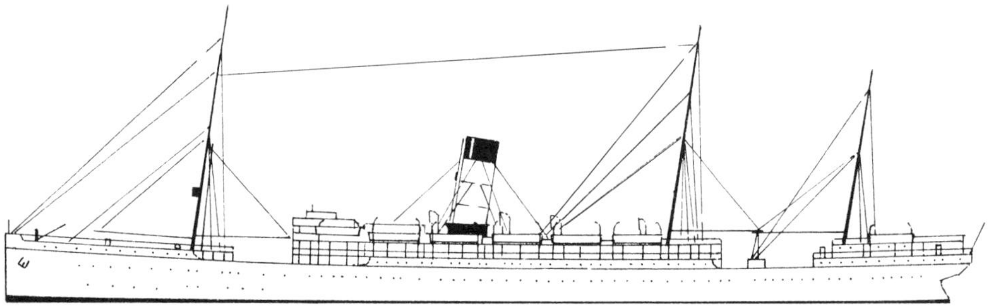

The mailship *Carisbrook Castle* of 1898 had First class accommodation amidships. Second class was placed aft and Third class forward.

yards on the foremast, although these were never used and were later removed. There was a difference though in that at long last a Castle mail liner had First Class accommodation amidships. She was taken off the mail run in 1910 and placed in the East African service, going into reserve in 1914. After service as a hospital ship she filled in on the mail service until scrapped in 1922.

But these ships were always overshadowed by the *Norman* and *Briton* of the Union Line, and not until the *Kinfauns Castle* and her sistership *Kildonan Castle* of 1899 could the Castle Line compete with the latest ships of their competitors. These two were also built by Fairfield and were just under 9,700 gt. The *Kinfauns Castle* was the first twin-screw liner in the Castle Line and the *Kildonan Castle* was the last mail steamer of the Currie fleet. They measured 533 feet length oa and 59 ft breadth. The *Kinfauns Castle* was the first away from Southampton on her maiden voyage in September, arriving at Cape Town just after the Boer War had started. The *Kildonan Castle* was, in

The last single-screw mailship, the *Carisbrook Castle* of 1898 was to have been named *Crookston Castle.*

*Tom Rayner collection*

Launched on 22nd August, 1899, the *Kildonan Castle* was completed as a troop transport for the Boer War. She was the last Castle Line mailship.

*Tom Rayner collection*

The *Dunvegan Castle* of 1896 was one of the first ships to land British troops in France on 10th August, 1914. By mid-August eleven Union-Castle ships had been requisitioned for war service.

*Tom Rayner collection*

fact, completed for troop transport duties, which she performed for some two years. Many Union-Castle ships, particularly the intermediate fleet, were continually employed in trooping and military service during the conflict.

The *Kinfauns Castle* was stranded on the Isle of Wight for several days in April, 1902, and from 8th August, 1914, served for a year as an armed merchant cruiser in African waters. It was the seaplane of HMS *Kinfauns Castle* that spotted the German cruiser *Koenigsberg* in the Rufiji Delta in German East Africa; the *Koenigsberg* was later destroyed by the 6-inch guns of the monitors HMS *Mersey* and HMS *Severn*, brought specially from Britain. The *Kinfauns Castle* then returned to trooping duties. In 1921-22 she was displaced by the new four-funnellers coming into service and lay at Netley, later making several emergency voyages during the shipping strike. Her last voyage was from Cape Town on 17th November, 1925, then she spent another short period at Netley before being scrapped in Holland in September, 1927.

Her sistership, *Kildonan Castle*, did not make her maiden commercial voyage from Southampton until 7th December, 1901. She, too, was an armed merchant cruiser from 1916 to 1917 and then operated on the mail run from 1920 until 1926 when she was placed in reserve. Eventually in May, 1931, the *Kildonan Castle* went to Stavanger, Norway, for breaking up.

These ships were very similar to the successful *Norman*-design and, indeed, had a strong resemblance to the *Briton*. Both had two funnels and three masts and accommodation for some 600 in three classes.

Castle Line's *Tantallon Castle* and the Union Line's *Norman* at Cape Town docks just prior to the merger. They are dressed overall for the departure of the Governor of South Africa.
*Union Castle*

CHAPTER TWO

# United and Onwards

DURING the last quarter of the century continuous effort had been made by both the Union Line and the Castle Line to build ever-faster ships which would outclass those of its competitor, and this policy had caused intense rivalry.

Since the first joint contract of 1876 the Cape Government had not been in favour of an amalgamation of the two companies, urging competition and improvements to services with the negotiation of each new contract. There had already been four joint contracts and a new one was due to be effective in 1900. This time the Cape Government announced that it would be awarded to one company only and not in joint form as hitherto. However, neither

The Union-Castle houseflag.

company made application, and the Cape Government reviewed its terms so that an agreement with each company could be made and the contract divided. But the most significant point of the terms was that the clause forbidding amalgamation had been omitted.

The Castle Line being stronger financially, Sir Donald Currie seized his chance and approached the Union Line, and in December, 1899, the two boards came to an amicable agreement for a merger. On 13th February, 1900, the shareholders agreed terms and the Union-Castle Mail Steamship Company Limited (Managers, Donald Currie & Company) was registered on 8th March, 1900, with the new mail contract, signed by the new company, to date from 1st October, 1900.

It was also agreed that the fleet colours would be those of the Castle Mail Packets Company. The bright red funnel had been adopted by Sir Donald Currie as a compliment to his early employers, the Cunard Steam Ship Company. The hull colouring had developed from light grey, becoming slate by 1880 and by 1896 almost white. Just before the merger a lavender colour (French grey) was introduced which was to become the familiar recognition symbol of the ships. The new flag cleverly combined the flags of the two companies. The red diagonals of the Union Line were superimposed on the white saltire of the Castle Line, the blue ground of the Castle Line flag providing the ground of the new houseflag.

The ships involved were:

Union Steam Ship Co. Ltd.

Acquired:

Built as mail ships

| Year | Ship | gt: |
|---|---|---|
| 1879 | *Arab* | 3,192 |
| 1880 | *Trojan* | 3,652 |
| 1881 | *Spartan* | 3,487 |
| 1882 | *Moor* | 4,664 |
| 1883 | *Mexican* | 4,661 |
| 1891 | *Scot* | 7,815 |
| 1894 | *Norman* | 7,537 |
| 1897 | *Briton* | 10,246 |
| 1900 | *Saxon* | 12,385 |

(The *Saxon* was ordered and launched before the amalgamation)

| Year | Ship | gt: |
|---|---|---|
| 1902 | *Celt* | 12,546 |

(Ordered by the Union Line. Completed in 1902 as the *Walmer Castle*)

Intermediate ships:

| Year | Ship | gt: |
|---|---|---|
| 1893 | *Gaul* | 4,745 |
| 1893 | *Goth* | 4,738 |
| 1893 | *Greek* | 4,747 |
| 1894 | *Guelph* | 4,917 |
| 1897 | *Gascon* | 6,288 |
| 1897 | *Gaika* | 6,287 |
| 1897 | *Goorkha* | 6,335 |
| 1898 | *German* | 6,763 |
| 1899 | *Galeka* | 6,772 |
| 1900 | *Galician* | 6,575 |

(The *Galician* was ordered by the Union Line but not completed until after the amalgamation)

Cargo ships:

| Year | Ship | gt: |
|---|---|---|
| 1898 | *Sabine* | 3,809 |
| 1898 | *Susquehanna* | 3,712 |

Castle Mail Packets Co. Ltd.

Acquired:

Built as mail ships

| Year | Ship | gt: |
|---|---|---|
| 1881 | *Garth Castle* | 3,704 |
| 1883 | *Hawarden Castle* | 4,389 |
| 1883 | *Norham Castle* | 4,241 |
| 1883 | *Roslin Castle* | 4,487 |
| 1890 | *Dunottar Castle* | 5,625 |
| 1894 | *Tantallon Castle* | 5,636 |
| 1896 | *Dunvegan Castle* | 5,958 |
| 1898 | *Carisbrook Castle* | 7,626 |
| 1899 | *Kinfauns Castle* | 9,664 |
| 1899 | *Kildonan Castle* | 9,692 |

Intermediate ships:

| Year | Ship | gt: |
|---|---|---|
| 1883 | *Pembroke Castle* | 4,045 |
| 1890 | *Doune Castle* | 4,045 |
| 1891 | *Lismore Castle* | 4,046 |
| 1894 | *Harlech Castle* | 3,624 |
| 1895 | *Arundel Castle* | 4,588 |
| 1896 | *Tintagel Castle* | 5,531 |
| 1897 | *Avondale Castle* | 5,531 |
| 1897 | *Dunolly Castle* | 4,167 |
| 1897 | *Raglan Castle* | 4,324 |
| 1898 | *Braemar Castle* | 6,266 |

Practically all Castle Line ships had been built in Scotland, for Sir Donald Currie was a Scot, the Fairfield yard accounting for all the ex-'Castle' mailships which continued in service after the amalgamation.

On the amalgamation, Southampton became the base for the mail ships, the intermediate service using East India Dock, Blackwall, London. In this service cargo was loaded at Antwerp, Rotterdam and Hamburg, the ship then completing loading at London for her fortnightly sailing to South Africa.

The last steamer to sail for the Cape in Union Line colours was the *Moor*, on 10th March, 1900, and the new flag of the Union-Castle Mail SS Company Limited was first broken from the masthead of the *Dunottar Castle* which left Southampton a week later, on Saturday, 17th March. The next sailing was by the *Briton*, repainted in the red, black-topped funnel and French grey hull. The new era had begun.

At that time, ships of the mail fleet arrived early Saturday morning from the Cape, the outward bound ship leaving in the afternoon. The merger caused considerable redundancies of ships in the two fleets and a number were laid up in the Thames and in Southampton Water pending disposal.

The *Saxon*, the last liner ordered for the Union Line, was launched ten days before the turn of the century and was completed just after the merger.

The last mailship built to carry a Union Line name was the *Saxon*. Her livery for her maiden voyage was with Union-Castle funnels and Union Line white hull.
*Tom Rayner collection*

She was another improved ship of the *Norman*-type, although much bigger at 12,385 gt. Her length was 586 feet oa, 570 feet bp, her breadth was 64½ feet and she had quadruple expansion engines giving 17½ knots through twin screws. Passenger accommodation was for 310 First, 203 Second and 132 Third class. On 16th June, 1900, a month after trials, she left Southampton on her maiden voyage, continuing in the mail service until 1917 when she became a transport. The *Saxon* returned to the mail service in 1919 and continued until June, 1931, when she was laid up off Netley as a reserve ship. In 1935 she was sold for breaking up at Blyth.

The first new mail ship under the Union-Castle banner was the *Walmer Castle**, which had been building when the merger took place. She was almost identical to the *Saxon* and was to have been named *Celt*. Her measurements were similar, although the tonnage was 12,546, and she had the

*Walmer Castle, Kent, was built by Henry VIII and was the official residence of the Lord Warden of the Cinque ports.

same type of machinery. Accommodation was again in three classes, although the numbers at 336, 174 and 244 were different. Her maiden voyage began on 15th March, 1902. She also became a transport in 1917, returning to normal service after the war and continuing in the mail service until steamers were superseded by the motorship. She was broken up at Blyth in 1932.

The Castle Line had never owned any cargo steamers, as distinct from ships that carried passengers and cargo. Neither had the Union Line until

Laid down as Union Line's *Celt*, the hull was launched on 6th July, 1901, and then renamed *Walmer Castle*, to become the first new mailship under the Union-Castle houseflag. *Tom Rayner collection*

**Opposite:** Deck quoits. The length of the pitch was twelve paces (one less for ladies) from the centre of the marked score rings, and the game was played with four quoits. *Union-Castle*

Deck billiards at the turn of the century. Six wooden discs and four sticks broadening out at the ends were used in this game, played on a pitch that had a length of ten paces (one less for ladies). *Union-Castle*

1898. Trade with the USA had been negligible until the discovery of gold in the Rand in the mid-1880s, but from then on mining machinery and allied products from industrial America flowed increasingly to South Africa. Both Castle and Union companies inaugurated steamer services from the United States to South Africa in May-June, 1893, the Castle Line running in conjunction with Bucknalls under the title American & African Line and the Union Line in joint service with the Clan Line, all using chartered tonnage.

In 1898 the Union Line purchased its first true cargo ships, only one, *Sabine*, conforming to Union Line nomenclature, the others bearing American names. They were:

| | | |
|---|---|---|
| *Sabine* | 3805 gt. | Built by Harland & Wolff, 1894, as Elder Dempster's *Marino* |
| *Sandusky* | 6336 gt. | Built 1891 as *Ionia* for the City of Liverpool SN Co but renamed *Montezuma* in the following year when purchased by Elder Dempster |
| *Susquehanna* | 3712 gt. | Built by Barclay, Curle in 1896 as *Mount Sephar* for Smith & Service of Glasgow. |

The purchase of the *Sandusky* was evidently a mistake, for she was resold in the same year to the Dominion Line who renamed her *Englishman*. She was torpedoed in the North Atlantic on 24th March, 1916.

An unusual task was given to the *Sabine* in 1909. Lund's Blue Anchor liner *Waratah* had disappeared between Durban and East London. No trace could be found, but with hundreds of human lives at stake the Australian Government financially supported a search to try to find the missing liner. The *Sabine* was chosen for this, hurriedly fitted out and for three months searched the South Indian Ocean to no avail. Eventually she moved on to

Intermediate ships in the East India Dock, London, in the early days of the century. Left to right are *Goth, Arundel Castle, Gascon, Raglan Castle, Braemar Castle* and *Gaika*.
*Shipbuilding and Shipping Record*

Bullard, King & Company in 1921. The *Susquehanna* also left the fleet in 1921 and, renamed *London City* by her new owners, Denaby & Cadeby Collieries Limited, spent the rest of her life as a coal hulk at Brixham.

The merger in 1900 made no difference to the services from the USA, both continuing separately. However, four black-hulled cargo ships of between 4,500 and 5,000 gt, *Aros Castle*, *Corfe Castle*, *Gordon Castle* and *York Castle*, were added to the merged fleets in 1901. All were three-island design, the first two by Barclay, Curle, the third by C. Connell & Company, and the fourth by Laing of Sunderland.

With the end of the Boer War the term "extra" steamer was revived when six ships were ordered for an anticipated rush of emigrants to South Africa. The emigrant boom never really materialised but all the ships were completed by 1903. To their schedule were added the ports of Walvis Bay and the terminal of Mauritius in a monthly service which lasted until the outbreak of war in 1914.

The first two, *Alnwick Castle* and *Berwick Castle* of some 5,900 gt, were by Beardmore of Glasgow. The first was lost in 1917. The *Berwick Castle* had

The cargo ship *Aros Castle* was a war loss in 1917. Cargo ships of the fleet were given black hulls.
*Tom Rayner collection*

two unfortunate incidents in her life. The first was on a voyage from Southampton to Hamburg when, in the afternoon of 18th March, 1904, off the Nab lightship, she rammed HM submarine *A1*, which sank with all hands. The incident caused much comment in the press and questions were raised in Parliament, for the A-class vessels, only 100 feet long, were the first British-designed submarines intended for the new developing underwater arm of the Royal Navy. The *A1* had, indeed, only been completed the previous year. The second incident which involved the *Berwick Castle* was a fire she suffered in Port Reitz, Kilindini, in October, 1919. After laying up at Durban for a year she was sold to Italy, lasting until scrapped at Spezia in 1925.

The other four ships were by Barclay, Curle & Company of Glasgow—

The *Alnwick Castle* was one of six similar "extra" steamers ordered for an anticipated emigrant trade increase just after the merger.

the *Cawdor Castle* and *Newark Castle* in 1902; *Cluny Castle* and *Comrie Castle* in 1903. The first pair of sisterships, larger editions of the *Alnwick Castle*, were of 6,200 gt and twin screw. Both were lost by grounding, the *Cawdor Castle* in Conception Bay, South West Africa, on 30th July, 1926, and *Newark Castle* near Port Durnford on 12th March, 1908. The *Cluny Castle* and *Comrie Castle* were also twin-screw steamers with upright masts and funnels but, at 5,160 gt., were smaller than the others.

In the decade prior to the outbreak of war, no fewer than ten intermediate ships were built. The first three, the D-class, were all completed in 1904:

| | | |
|---|---|---|
| *Dover Castle* | 8,271 gt. | built by Barclay, Curle & Co. Ltd., Glasgow |
| *Dunluce Castle* | 8,114 gt. | built by Harland & Wolff Ltd., Belfast |
| *Durham Castle* | 8,217 gt. | built by Fairfield SB & Eng Co. Ltd., Glasgow |

They were elegant ships with a tall funnel and were the first true intermediate ships of the Union-Castle era. The length was 475 feet, the breadth 56 feet and accommodation was for 220 First and 250 Third class passengers. There was no Second class, which allowed more deck space for the Third class. However, there was room to carry about 300 passengers in

**Above:** A D-class steamer, *Durham Castle* of 1904. Her unusual lapped plating clearly shows.
*Tom Rayner collection*

**Left:** A later *Norman*-type design, the *Armadale Castle* began her maiden voyage from Southampton on 5th December, 1903.

**Below:** Sistership to the *Armadale Castle*, the *Kenilworth Castle* was launched on 15th December, 1903, and completed in the following May.
*Tom Rayner collection*

open-berth accommodation. On 21st March, 1904, the day of the maiden voyage of the *Durham Castle, Lloyd's List* said:

> A striking illustration of the advances that have been made of late years in the facilities for ocean travel, particularly in the provision made for passengers of limited means, is afforded by the case of the new *Durham Castle*, which leaves Southampton today on her maiden voyage. Within very recent time the third-class passenger would have been voted a dreamer for ever imagining that accommodation for him and his fellows would soon include a handsome dining saloon with comfortable revolving chairs, a large smoking room, a lounge for the ladies, closed cabins for two, four or six passengers, baths, electric bells, pianos, a well stocked library and various other accessories of undoubted value on ship-board. The provision for first-class passengers is of a most luxurious character and up to date in every particular.

Propulsion was by quadruple expansion engines to twin screws with a speed of 14 knots. These successful ships were slightly larger and faster than the G-class of the Union Line.

In 1887, the incorporation by Royal Charter of the German East Africa Company had been the first step in the development of the territory. In the following year the Arab rebellion took place and in 1889 a German Protectorate was proclaimed over the territory, with a garrison at Dar es Salaam. The boundary line of German East Africa and British East Africa was agreed in 1890. The German Government took over the Administration from the German East Africa Company in 1891 and development of the territory got under way. Along the coast some navigational aids were introduced, a dockyard for small craft was built at Dar es Salaam in 1902 and in 1905 a railway line began stretching westwards from the port. And with the railway came port development, for until then export cargo handling facilities had consisted of chutes in which packages were trundled down, and stone steps from the beach up which were manhandled imports. A small jetty, followed by a quay, was constructed and Germany began to take more and more interest in East Africa.

The Union-Castle Company kept an eye on this development and, although no British Treasury subsidy was forthcoming for a shipping service to East Africa, Union-Castle decided in 1909 to extend the intermediate service from its terminal port of Delagoa Bay northwards to Mombasa, where the ships turned south again.

The new service started in January, 1910, with the *Dunluce Castle*, competing with the subsidised German companies running to German East Africa, and by the summer, after good results, agreement was reached with the British Government for the establishment of a route from Britain via the Suez Canal and Aden to Mombasa. Southwards the ships terminated at Durban, there connecting with the mail steamers before turning north again. Outward Government cargoes were promised and the Government also gave support for homeward freight.

On 13th September, 1910, the *Guelph* inaugurated the modified service from London via Suez, titled The Royal East Africa Service of the Union-Castle Line, the ships loading at Antwerp, Rotterdam and Hamburg before the final departure from London. The *Dunvegan Castle* and the *Carisbrook Castle* were brought from reserve and used on this run when the *Guelph* and *Goth* were sold to the Royal Mail Steam Packet Company in 1913.

Two more mail steamers evolving from the *Norman* design of 1894 were delivered in 1903 and 1904. The *Armadale Castle* was completed by the Fairfield yard in November, 1903, and six months later Harland & Wolff delivered the *Kenilworth Castle* at Belfast. Both ships measured 570 feet bp in length and 64½ feet in breadth and were registered at 12,975 gt. They lasted until 1935-1936 before being broken up.

The *Armadale Castle* (named after a castle on the Isle of Skye) was the first ship to be ordered by the new Union-Castle company and quickly made history. On 26th June, 1904, at 11 am she hove in sight around the Bluff, the commanding headland of green hills which screens and protects Durban Bay from southerly squalls, and, drawing well over 20 feet of water, steamed slowly across the bar, moved through the narrow harbour entrance and, watched by thousands of people, berthed alongside a quay in the inner harbour. She was the first mail ship to do so, and the frustrations and difficulties of tendering passengers to and from liners which could only anchor in the bay, and then transferring them from deck to deck in a specially designed basket for six standing passengers, became a thing of the past.

Although the British flag had been first hoisted on the Bluff in 1824, Durban settlement (named after Sir Benjamin D'Urban, then Governor of Cape Colony) was not founded until 1835. As it slowly grew to town status great efforts were made over the years to make the small seaport more efficient, clearing a large sandbank, building breakwaters and quays, dredging and introducing navigational aids to shipping. By 1904 the population had grown to 75,000 and the 26th June, the day that the first mail steamer berthed alongside a Durban quay, was indeed a day for rejoicing. From then Durban grew enormously; now, with a population of some 700,000, it rates as a major port.

The *Armadale Castle* continued in the mail service until the war came. She was then quickly taken up as an armed merchant cruiser, given eight 4.7-inch guns and served from 2nd August, 1914, until 11th September, 1919, first in South African waters, then in the North Atlantic and in the 10th Cruiser Squadron in the North Sea.

Her sistership *Kenilworth Castle* saw war service as a transport and, although no Union-Castle mail ships were lost during the war, had a narrow escape from destruction. Just after midnight on 4th June, 1916, she was in

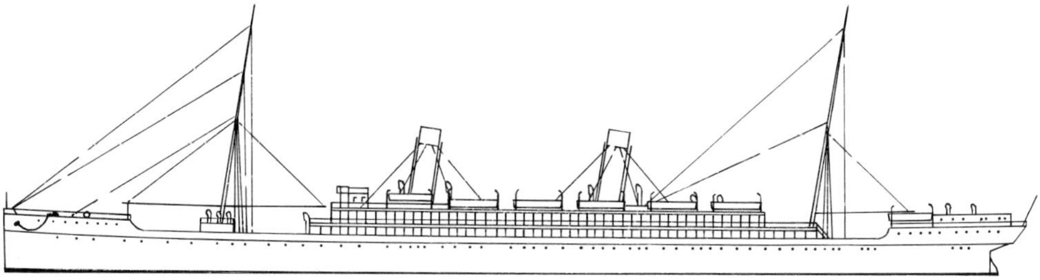

*Norman*, built 1894

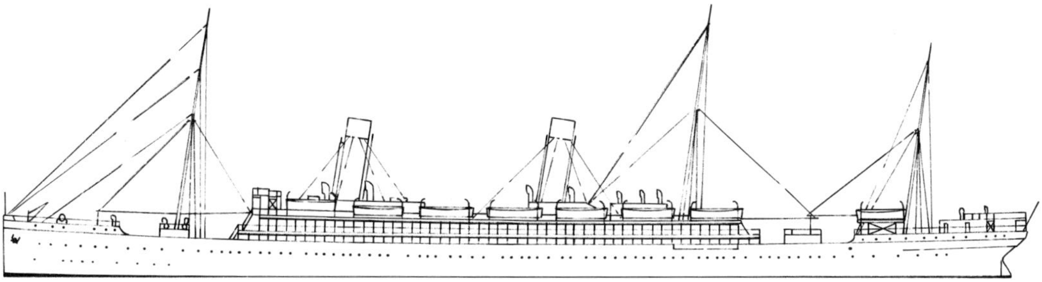

*Briton*, built 1897

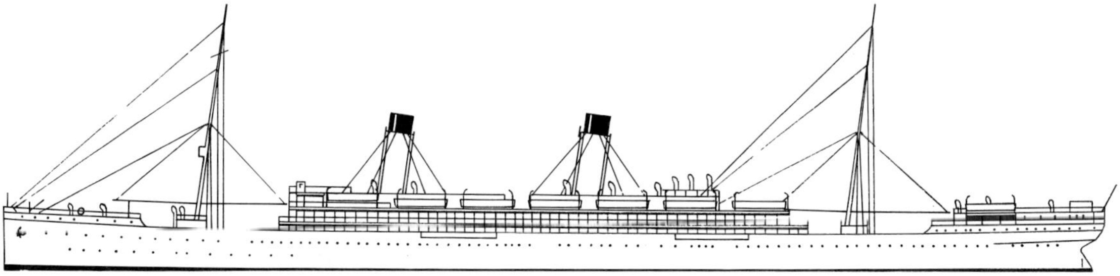

*Saxon*, built 1900
*Walmer Castle* (similar), built 1902

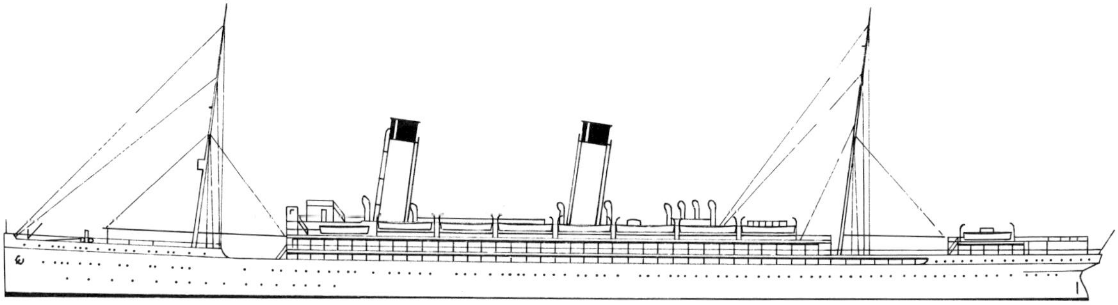

*Edinburgh Castle*, built 1910
*Balmoral Castle*, built 1910

Note: *Armadale Castle* of 1903 and *Kenilworth Castle* of 1904 differed slightly from *Edinburgh Castle*, the promenade deck not being joined to the poop as in the later pair. The funnels were closer and slightly thinner.

The *Edinburgh Castle* of 1910 served the Royal Navy throughout two world wars.
*Tom Rayner collection*

convoy in the English Channel and while swinging to avoid a collision hit the stern of the M-class destroyer HMS *Rival*. Depth charges on the destroyer's stern exploded and holed the liner, but she managed to reach port.

The last two ships of the *Norman*-type arrived in 1910. As with the earlier vessels, they were slim, elegant ships with two thin funnels. Their names were *Balmoral Castle* (13,661 gt.) and *Edinburgh Castle* (13,330 gt.). The first ship was constructed at the Fairfield yard, the second at Belfast. Both measured 591 feet oa, 570 feet bp in length and 64½ feet in breadth, making them the largest ships of the fleet. Propulsion was by quadruple-expansion engines driving twin screws and giving 17½ knots. Accommodation was for 800 passengers in three classes. The *Balmoral Castle*, the first ship on the South Africa run to be equipped with wireless telegraphy, arrived for service in February, 1910, and her sistership in April, replacing the *Carisbrook Castle*—then the only single-screw ship in the fleet—and, in the following year, the *Norman*.

On 31st May, 1910, the four provinces of South Africa, Cape Province, Transvaal, Orange Free State and Natal, united under one government to become the Union of South Africa. It had been planned that the Prince of Wales would open the first Union parliament in the following November and the *Balmoral Castle* was chosen by the British government to take the Prince and Princess Mary to Cape Town. The choice was admirable. She was the

The First class dining saloon of the *Balmoral Castle* of 1910. *Union-Castle*

largest ship in the fleet and her name, with its associations with the Royal House, could not have been bettered. Given yellow funnels and masts, manned by Naval personnel and wearing the White Ensign at her stern, she sailed from Portsmouth on 11th October, 1910, as HMS *Balmoral Castle*. But not with the Prince and Princess on board, for in the meantime King Edward VII had died and the Prince of Wales was now King George V. Instead, the Duke and Duchess of Connaught were the Royal passengers.

The *Balmoral Castle* spent some time trooping in the war, then returned to the mail service, being sold for breaking up at Newport, Mon., in 1939.

The last ship of the Currie regime was the *Edinburgh Castle*, for Sir Donald Currie had died in 1909 at a time when the fleet had reached a total of forty-seven ships. The *Edinburgh Castle* had a long and distinguished career. She was taken up as an armed merchant cruiser on 4th September, 1914, and spent most of the war off the east coast of South America, returning to the Cape run in 1919. She was reprieved from the shipbreakers in August, 1939, when she was bought by the Admiralty to give a further six years of war effort as a base ship.

These, then, were the last of the *Norman*-type ships which covered a period from 1894 until 1945. The six mail steamers, each over 12,000 gt., completed the voyage in sixteen and a half days. Arrival at Cape Town was early on Tuesday and the ship left for Durban the next day at 3 pm, returning

Two Union-Castle vessels which served as hospital ships. **Above:** The *Grantully Castle* of 1910 seen as a hospital ship in the First World War. **Below:** Taken over in 1917 as a hospital ship, the *Llandovery Castle* was sunk in June, 1918, with the loss of 234 lives.

*Both Tom Rayner collection*

on the Monday week and sailing for Southampton at 4 pm on the Wednesday.

The old G-class ships of the Union Line were beginning to age in the early 1900s and to replace them in the intermediate service five 13-knot G-Castle-class ships were built. Two were completed in 1910, three in the following year:

| Name | gt. | Built |
|---|---|---|
| *Garth Castle* | 7,612 | Barclay, Curle & Co. Ltd., Glasgow. |
| *Grantully Castle* | 7,617 | Barclay, Curle & Co. Ltd., Glasgow. |

Measurements: 450 feet bp length, 54 feet breadth.

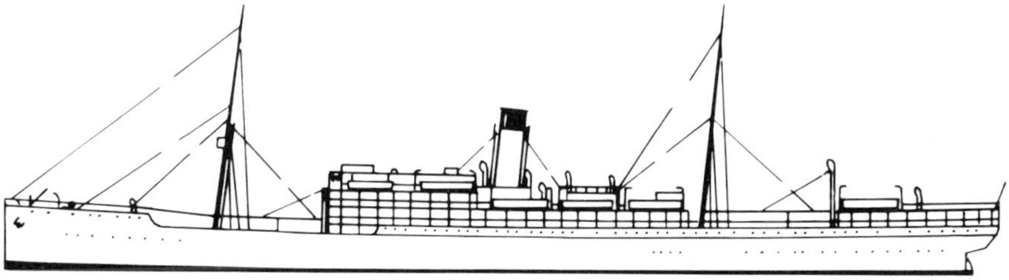

The intermediate steamer *Galway Castle,* built in 1911.

| | | |
|---|---|---|
| *Galway Castle* | 7,988 | Harland & Wolff Ltd., Belfast. |
| *Gloucester Castle* | 7,989 | Fairfield SB & E Co. Ltd., Glasgow. |
| *Guildford Castle* | 7,995 | Barclay, Curle & Co. Ltd., Glasgow. |

Measurements: 450 feet bp length, 56 feet breadth.

In the first pair, Second class accommodation was reintroduced for about 100 passengers out of the 400 carried. Quadruple-expansion engines gave 13 knots, slower than the earlier D-class ships. The three later ships were improved inasmuch as they were given a short upper promenade deck. They were also two feet wider.

The *Guildford Castle* was in collision with the Blue Funnel liner *Stentor* in the River Elbe and sank on 1st June, 1933. The *Gloucester Castle* had a longer life span. In 1914 she was torpedoed on the last day of March while serving as a hospital ship, but was towed into Southampton and repaired. She was later to be sunk in the Second World War.

Meanwhile, in 1911 some speculation as to the future control of the company was followed by a joint bid from the Royal Mail Steam Packet Company and Elder, Dempster & Company Limited. This was accepted in April, 1912, and control handed over, Donald Currie & Company Limited relinquishing their managership. Another era had begun.

The first two ships after this change of ownership were the largest intermediate ships to date. Of some 11,300 gt., they came out in the year of the war, 1914, the *Llandovery Castle* from Barclay, Curle's yard in January and the *Llanstephan Castle* from Fairfield in February. The names were Welsh and the ships specifically designed for the east coast of Africa service. Quadruple-expansion engines driving twin screws were again used and the speed was 14 knots. Accommodation was for 450 in three classes and the ships had two long promenade decks as a feature of their design. These were the last Union-Castle passenger ships completed before hostilities, and the *Llandovery Castle* was the last Union-Castle ship to be sunk in the four-year conflict.

The Union-Castle fleet in 1914 (excluding tugs, tenders and launches)

| Acquired | Name | gt. | Acquired | Name | gt. |
|---|---|---|---|---|---|
| **Mail ships** | | | | | |
| 1897 | *Briton* | 10,248 | 1903 | *Armadale Castle* | 12,973 |
| 1899 | *Kinfauns Castle* | 9,664 | 1904 | *Kenilworth Castle* | 12,975 |
| 1899 | *Kildonan Castle* | 9,692 | 1910 | *Balmoral Castle* | 13,361 |
| 1900 | *Saxon* | 12,385 | 1910 | *Edinburgh Castle* | 13,326 |
| 1902 | *Walmer Castle* | 12,546 | | | |
| **Intermediate ships** | | | | | |
| 1894 | *Norman* | 7,537 | 1904 | **Dover Castle* | 8,271 |
| 1896 | *Dunvegan Castle* | 5,958 | 1904 | *Dunluce Castle* | 8,114 |
| 1897 | *Gascon* | 6,288 | 1904 | *Durham Castle* | 8,217 |
| 1897 | *Gaika* | 6,287 | 1910 | *Garth Castle* | 7,612 |
| 1897 | *Goorkha* | 6,335 | 1910 | *Grantully Castle* | 7,617 |
| 1898 | *Carisbrook Castle* | 7,626 | 1911 | **Galway Castle* | 7,988 |
| 1898 | *Braemar Castle* | 6,266 | 1911 | *Gloucester Castle* | 7,999 |
| 1898 | *German* | 6,763 | 1911 | *Guildford Castle* | 7,995 |
| 1899 | **Galeka* | 6,772 | 1914 | **Llandovery Castle* | 11,423 |
| 1900 | **Galician* | 6,575 | 1914 | *Llanstephan Castle* | 11,346 |
| **Extra ships** | | | | | |
| 1901 | **Alnwick Castle* | 5,893 | 1903 | *Cluny Castle* | 5,152 |
| 1902 | *Berwick Castle* | 5,883 | 1903 | *Comrie Castle* | 5,167 |
| 1902 | *Cawdor Castle* | 6,235 | | | |
| **Cargo ships** | | | | | |
| 1898 | *Sabine* | 3,809 | 1901 | *Corfe Castle* | 4,592 |
| 1898 | *Susquehanna* | 3,712 | 1901 | *Gordon Castle* | 4,406 |
| 1901 | **Aros Castle* | 4,460 | 1901 | *York Castle* | 5,517 |
| **Feeder ship** | | | | | |
| 1906 | *Hansa* | 880 | | | |

*Denotes war loss. The eighth ship lost was the *Carlisle Castle* (4,325 gt.), acquired 1916, sunk 1918.

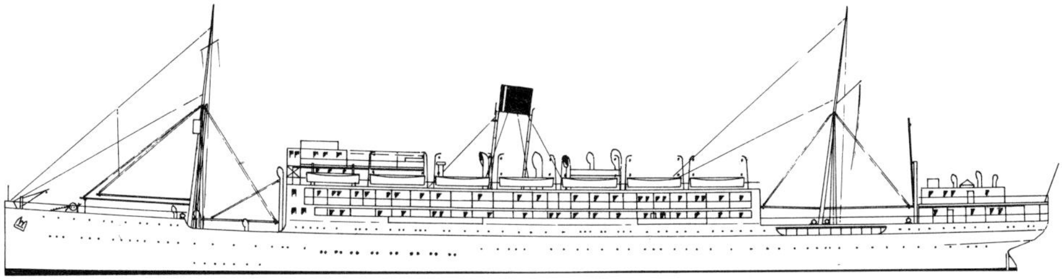

The *Llanstephan Castle* and *Llandovery Castle,* completed in 1914, were specially designed for the service to East Africa via Suez.

Southampton was taken over as a military port in September, 1914, and the mail service was transferred to Tilbury. The *Armadale Castle* and *Kinfauns Castle* were taken up as armed merchant cruisers in August, 1914, the *Edinburgh Castle* in September, 1914, and the *Kildonan Castle* in July, 1916. Most of the other liners were used for periods as troopships, but the *Norman* ran throughout the war as a mailship until May, 1918, when she began trooping for one year in the Indian and Mediterranean areas. None of the mailships was lost, although eight other ships of the fleet failed to return.

At the start of the war there were forty-one ships in the fleet and at one time only three small cargo ships maintained the service, all other vessels being requisitioned for war duty. Union-Castle also managed a munitions factory and, at Admiralty request, undertook the stevedoring of war supplies at Southampton between March and June, 1917, moving nearly 80,000 horses, 6,000 guns and half a million tons of war equipment. All this took 600 ship voyages.

During the years of war and through to 1920, thirteen cargo ships came under Union-Castle ownership while another fourteen ships were placed under the company's management by the Government. The largest of these managed ships was the war-built 21,000 ton *Cap Polonio* of the Hamburg South America Line; she made but one voyage in 1919 to the Cape in Union-Castle colours before being transferred to the Peninsular & Oriental S.N. Company.

Of the remainder of the managed ships, twelve had been captured or seized in various ports at the outbreak of war, and of these six had been on African routes. Three were Woermann Line ships and three were of the German East Africa Line. The Woermann Line steamers were *Eduard Woermann* (5,619 gt.), *Professor Woermann* (6,078 gt.) and *Erna Woermann* (4,878 gt.), all built in 1902-1903. After the war the *Erna Woermann* became the German East Africa Line's *Sultan*.

The *Feldmarschall* (6,181 gt.), a twin-screw ship of the German East Africa Line, built by Reiherstieg in 1903, had put into Dar es Salaam at the outbreak of war and was seized when the port was taken in 1916. Under Union-Castle management she was renamed *Field Marshal.* After the war she was sold to China as the *Ling Nam* and then to the Ho Hong SS Company of Singapore in 1928, becoming the *Hong Kheng*. It is interesting to record that she survived the Second World War but was finally lost when she went ashore at Chilang Point on 17th July, 1947, on a voyage from Rangoon to Swatow. The similar *Prinzessin* of 1905 (6,387 gt.) and the cargo ship *Rufidji* of 1911 (5,442 gt.) were also under Union-Castle management, the latter being given the prefix "Hun" in her new name of *Huntscliff*, as were so many seized ships thus prefixed when renamed by the Shipping Controller. She foundered in heavy weather a month before war ended, in October, 1918.

The Norddeutscher Lloyd ships *Derfflinger* of 1907 (9,060 gt.) and *Lutzow* of 1908 (8,818 gt.) were seized in eastern waters in 1914, later renamed *Huntsgreen* and *Huntsend* respectively, and sold back to the Norddeutscher Lloyd after the war. Another capture by a British cruiser was the Doxford-built *Sudmark* (built 1913) of the Hamburg Amerika Linie. She became *Huntscraft* and remained under the British flag as *Clan Mackay* from 1919 until wrecked on 19th October, 1934, on Carpenters Rock, Sierra Leone, on a voyage from Cairns to Montreal.

A twin-screw steamer, the *Koerber* (5,400 gt.), built by the Austriaco, Trieste, in 1903 for the Lloyd Austriaco was seized and renamed *Huntspill.* Italy had taken over the North Adriatic coast of the Austro-Hungarian empire and with it the bulk of their merchant marine, and after the war the *Huntspill* was turned over to Italy, later on being employed in the Trieste-Durban service under the name *Asia.*

Two Hansa Linie ships were seized, the first of these being the *Tannenfels*, a 5,480 gt. steamer which had been converted to a German naval auxiliary. She was taken in the Basilan Strait, Philippine Islands, and was used as a Royal Navy auxiliary under the name *Basilan* for a time before becoming *Hunslet.* In 1917 she was under Union-Castle management; she returned to the German flag in 1921 as the Woermann ship *Waganda*. The other was *Reichenfels* (4,712 gt.), built by Swan, Hunter in 1903. Seized at Colombo on 5th August, 1914 (the day after war broke out), she was placed under British management and later came under Union-Castle control, being renamed *Polglass Castle* (after a castle on Loch Broom in Ross and Cromarty), although she never went to the Cape under that name. She returned to the Hansa company in 1921 and sailed under her old name until 1933, when she was broken up at Bremen.

The other ship given a "Castle" name was the *Leasowe Castle* (a castle built in 1593 by the Earl of Derby in the Cheshire village of that name). She had not been captured but was being built by Cammell Laird at Birkenhead as the *Vasilissa Sofia* for Embiricos Brothers when she was taken over by the British Government in 1916. In the following year she was completed as an 18-knot troopship of 9,737 gt. and given a new name. The *Leasowe Castle* was serving as a hospital ship when she was torpedoed and sunk 104 miles from Alexandria on 26th May, 1918.

All these ships were allocated for management by Union-Castle on behalf of the British Government and, from December, 1916, through the Shipping

A rare picture of the *Leasowe Castle*, acquired by the British Government while building for Greek owners in 1917 and placed under Union-Castle management. She was lost in May, 1918.
*Tom Rayner collection*

Controller, whose appointment was made under the New Ministries and Secretaries Act of that time.

Ships owned by Union-Castle and lost during the war

| | | |
|---|---|---|
| *Galeka* | 28th October, 1916 | Mined and abandoned, 5 miles NW from Cape La Hague, drifted ashore, total loss. A hospital ship. |
| *Alnwick Castle* | 19th March, 1917 | Torpedoed and sunk while in commercial service, 310 miles from Bishop Rock (Voyage: Plymouth (17 March) for Cape). |
| *Dover Castle* | 26th May, 1917 | Torpedoed and sunk by *UC.67*, 50 miles north of Bona while serving as a hospital ship. |
| *Aros Castle* | 21st November, 1917 | Torpedoed and sunk, 300 miles west of Bishop Rock. |
| *Carlisle Castle* | 14th February, 1918 | Torpedoed and sunk, 8 miles E by N from Royal Sovereign lightvessel. |
| *Galician* | 26th February, 1918 | Renamed *Glenart Castle*. Torpedoed and sunk by *U.56* 10 miles west of Lundy Island in the Bristol Channel while serving as a hospital ship (voyage: Newport, Mon., to Brest). 95 lost. |
| *Galway Castle* | 12th September, 1918 | Sailing under the name *Rhodesia*, was torpedoed and sunk by *U.82*, two days out from Plymouth, 160 miles SW from Fastnet while in commercial service. A tow was attempted by tugs from Plymouth but she sank on 15th September. |
| *Llandovery Castle* | 27th June, 1918 | Torpedoed by *U.86* 116 miles west of Fastnet Rock on a voyage as a hospital ship from Halifax, NS, to Liverpool. The worst disaster in the fleet, 234 lives being lost. |

Of all the cargo ships acquired by Union-Castle in the period from the outbreak of war in 1914 until the end of the decade, only two were ordered by, and built for, the company.

The two-year-old flush-deck steamer *Anglo Brazilian* (7,494 gt.) was acquired from Lawther, Latta & Company in 1915 and quickly renamed *Chepstow Castle*; the *Holtye* (4,325 gt.) of the same age and *Hova* (4,264 gt.) of 1910 were acquired from F. S. Holland in 1916-17 and renamed *Carlisle Castle* and *Crawford Castle* respectively, while the standard type flush-deck *Carlow Castle* (5,833 gt.) was acquired direct from the Northumberland SB Company, Newcastle, in 1917.

From the war disposal scheme of Government-built standard ships Union-Castle took over three straight-framed N-type vessels. Two, on the stocks at Armstrong, Whitworth, Newcastle, were taken up and completed in 1920 as the *Bratton Castle* and *Bampton Castle*, with cruiser sterns instead of the designed prefabricated transom sterns; the third, *Banbury Castle*, came from the Swan, Hunter yard. This ship was actually the first N-type vessel built and carried the name *War Climax* until renamed *Glenstrae* for the Glen Line in October, 1919. She became *Banbury Castle* ten months later. The National or N-type of fabricated ship, with all frames straight and none curved, was introduced to simplify the construction of standard ships and to utilise the capacities of the inland bridge-building companies and land engine works who had little of their normal work to do during the war and who were therefore able to develop this class of mass-production.

The *Windsor Castle*, completed by John Brown & Company, Clydebank, in 1922. She and her sistership *Arundel Castle* were the only four-funnelled ships in the fleet.

From the Government's National shipyards at Chepstow, a quantity of surplus materials was purchased by Harland & Wolff Limited of Greenock (formerly Caird & Company) and these materials were worked into two standard B-type cargo ships of 5,240 gt. The ships were modified to Union-Castle requirements with extra kingposts and a 'tween deck in No. 1 hold. The *Dromore Castle* was completed in November, 1919, and the *Dundrum Castle* in the following month. Both were lost in the Second World War.

Other war-built purchases were the *Ripley Castle* (7,521 gt.) and *Rosyth Castle* (4,328 gt.). The first was built by the Kawasaki Dockyard Company in Japan in 1917, a twin-screw, three-island type standard steamer with a 9,000 tons carrying capacity of a type which Japanese builders were developing before the war. She was launched as *War Soldier*, one of a batch under British

The twin-screw cargo ship *Ripley Castle,* built in Japan in 1917, is seen leaving Cape Town.
*Tom Rayner collection*

Government purchase. The second named was a war standard ship from Canadian Vickers, Montreal, built as the *War Earl.*

Finally came orders in 1920 for the *Sandown Castle* and *Sandgate Castle*, two larger ships of 7,600 gt., from Short Brothers Limited, Sunderland. They were the first geared turbine ships in the fleet.

Only the *Llanstephan Castle*, *Durham Castle* and three cargo ships were left to continue commercial service when war ended, but by October, 1919, enough tonnage had been received back from the yards after refits and conversions to recommence the mail service, which still included the *Llanstephan Castle.* New timings were now effective: Friday at 4 pm was the new Southampton departure time instead of 5 pm on Saturday. The same departure time was fixed from Cape Town instead of 1 pm on Saturday. Arrival at Southampton was at 6 am on Monday.

In April, 1921, something of a shock was given to those people welcoming the new *Arundel Castle* when she appeared at Southampton and later at Cape

Town, for this new 19,000 gt. ship, the largest ever owned by Union-Castle, had four funnels (one a dummy). The *Arundel Castle* had originally been laid down in 1915 at Belfast as the *Amroth Castle*, but she lay on the stocks for several years until launched on 11th September, 1919, as the *Arundel Castle*. There was also a sistership, the *Windsor Castle*, two feet longer at 632 feet bp, which was delivered from John Brown's yard at Clydebank in April, 1922.

The ships were driven by geared turbines and the hull design incorporated a cruiser stern—both features new to mail ships. They were, however, to be the last mail steamships to be built until 1948.

Extracts from a contemporary booklet describing the *Windsor Castle* help to illustrate the accommodation provided in a mailship of those immediate post-war years.

> . . . The First class passengers are berthed on the Bridge and Upper Decks, and a few on the Main Deck, forward of the Saloon, in one, two and three-berth rooms. The rooms are all large, and, with the exception of 26 rooms on the Upper and Main Decks, are all porthole cabins. They have wardrobes, chests of drawers, folding wash basins, mirrors, and reading lights over all beds. The beds are all of the "cot" type, of white enamel, fitted with sanitary spring mattresses, and in certain cabins with Pullman beds.
>
> Private Suites have been arranged on the Upper Deck, and these contain all the

*Arundel Castle* as built in 1922.

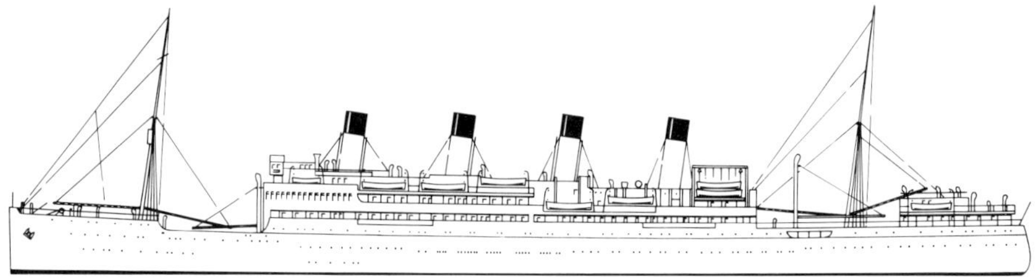

*Arundel Castle* after reconstruction in 1937-38.

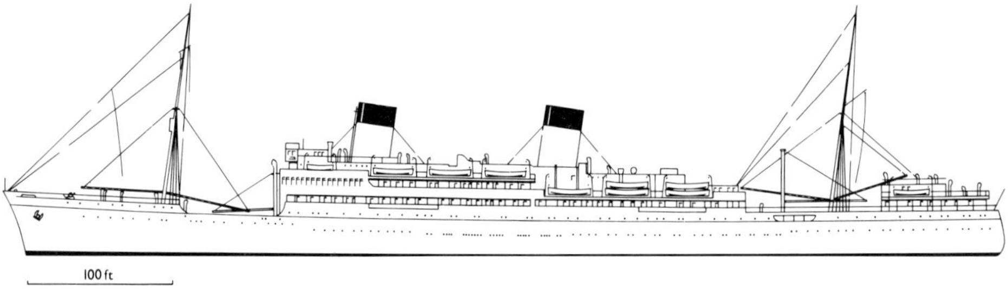

requirements one could desire. They consist of Sitting Room, Bedroom, Bathroom and Maid's Room. The Sitting Room on the Port Side of the vessel is panelled in oak of a simple character in the Louis XVI Period, and is furnished with table, comfortable Pullman couch, easy chairs, and small chairs upholstered in blue material. There is also a writing desk and a bookcase cabinet. The Pullman couch can be transformed into a bed. A carved gilt clock of the Period is fixed in a centre panel at the side of the room. The floor is covered with parquet linoleum, overlaid with rugs. The bedroom has a large wardrobe, fitted in the mural panelling, two single brass bedsteads, a chest of drawers, toilet table, writing table and chairs, a comfortable settee, and a marble washstand, with hot and cold water. The furniture is of white sycamore and the upholstery of this room is carried out in a delicate rose-coloured material.

All rooms are lighted from the ceiling, and from shaded electric light brackets placed in convenient places around each room. Provision is also made for heating if desired, and the vapour radiators can be operated at will by the passengers.

The First class Dining Room is a spacious apartment seating 254 passengers. It is panelled in simple Georgian fashion, with a note of richness in a few prominent positions—especially marked in the floral wreaths which decorate the ceiling, and also in the fine oil paintings by Maurice Randall, which adorn the walls and which remind the passengers of the fair county of Berkshire, where the stately Castle of Windsor rears its ancient towers on the banks of the Thames. The mahogany furniture is of an early Chippendale character, rather plain and massive in style. The dining chairs are reversible, so that in hot climates a cane seat replaces the stuffed morocco. The floor is covered with inlaid linoleum, reminiscent in colour of the rose coloured carpets, which came from France in the time of Mdme. du Barry, and from the walls and ceiling the soft glow of the electric light shines through milky glass and pink shades. The ventilation of the room is carefully thought out, and fresh air, either warm or atmospheric, is distributed by means of trunkways on the ceiling, without the annoying accompaniment of draughts.

The First class Smoking Room on the Promenade Deck is a long oak panelled room of the type that prevailed from the middle of the sixteenth to the middle of the seventeenth century, the type that is so familiar and homely, for example, in the halls and rooms of some of the Oxford and Cambridge Colleges, and in many of the delightful old houses scattered about Great Britain. Daylight is admitted through latticed windows with the flat arched top traditional from Tudor times, and at night the light comes soft, glowing and warm, from the electric sconces of oxidised silver, which hang on the walls. The ventilation is modern and it is unnecessary to open a single window to keep the air of the Smoking Room perfectly fresh and sweet.

Forward of the Smoking Room is the First class Lounge, a pleasant bow-windowed room with white Louis XVI panelling delicately touched here and there with gold. This is the Ladies' domain, the Drawing Room of the ship. The pretty sea-green curtains to the windows, the gay velvet coverings of the chairs and settees, the pictures hanging on the walls, and the palms and flowers scattered about the room, all give so pleasant an air of a home on shore that it is difficult to realise that one is on board a ship. Here ladies can do their work, write their letters, read, entertain their friends with Bridge and coffee, and play the piano. For comfort in colder latitudes a cheerful fire burns in the bronze grate.

The Reading and Writing Room on the Boat Deck is panelled in Sycamore wood, selected for its fiddle-back graining. Through a pair of swing doors, one is faced with a chimney piece of Campan Vert marble, the soft greyish green in harmony with the surroundings. The fireplace is lined with iron cheeks and back and there is an oval fire basket. Above is a gilt mirror.

The Second class public rooms are large and the comfort and convenience of the passengers have been considered with much care. The ventilation, heating and furnishing

**Above:** The Second class smoking room and First class saloon of the *Windsor Castle* of 1922. **Below left:** A Union-Castle poster. **Below right:** Reception hall and Suite Z bedroom of the *Windsor Castle.* *Union-Castle*

**Opposite:** Completed in 1925, the *Llandovery Castle* was the first postwar "Round Africa" liner. She is seen here at Cape Town.

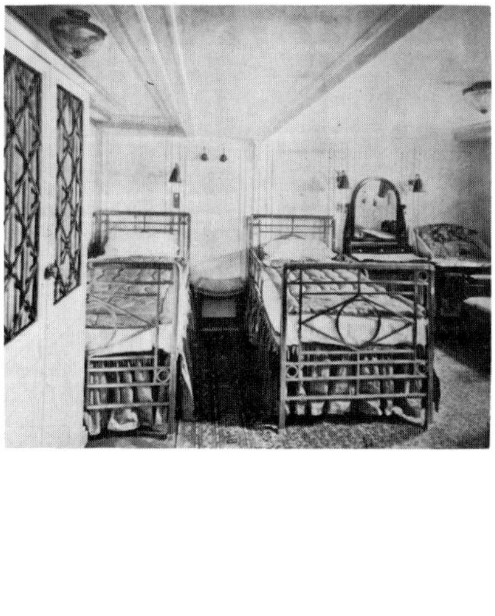

are most satisfactory. The Second class Dining Saloon is well lighted and cheerful, capable of dining 232 passengers; the Third class Dining Saloon is a large, airy apartment, occupying the full width of the ship. The Promenade Decks are available for dances and open air concerts and are most spacious. The Third class passengers are fortunate, for by arranging the hatchways on the Bridge Decks with flush covers, they have the whole extent of their deck from side to side for recreation.

And finally to the Ventilation system. Fresh air is discharged into every cabin, first, second and third class, and into all the Dining Saloons. The Lavatories and all the Galleys, Pantries and other offices have powerful suction fans, so that there is a continuous flood of pure air throughout. The air can be heated before being distributed in cold weather, maintaining thereby an even temperature throughout. In addition all Public Rooms are fitted with overhead fans . .

Since the amalgamation one of each pair of ships built for the mail service had been allocated for building to a Clyde yard and one to Harland & Wolff. The four-funnellers were, however, the last ships to be allocated in this way, and from then on Harland & Wolff at Belfast were allocated all the mailship orders until the new *Windsor Castle* was ordered from Cammell, Laird & Company at Birkenhead in 1957.

The war had caused changes in the political map of East Africa. The most important port was Mombasa, where Union-Castle opened its own office in

1917. In 1919, under the Treaty of Versailles, German East Africa became known as Tanganyika, a mandated territory placed under British Administration; and in 1920 the protectorate of British East Africa was formally annexed and received the name Kenya.

The intermediate run to East Africa had restarted in 1919 with the 8,000 gt. *Gloucester Castle* and *Guildford Castle* and the old *Norman*, the *Llanstephan Castle* also switching to this service in the following year. Then, in 1922, the Round Africa fortnightly service was inaugurated, with two ships sailing out via Suez and home via the Cape and two sailing in the reverse direction. The same four ships at first operated this service, but in 1925 the *Norman* was withdrawn and laid up at Tollesbury in the Blackwater estuary, being sold for breaking up early in 1926.

Coincidental with the opening of the new service, Second class was dropped in some intermediate ships; but not until 1934 did the smaller intermediates come into this arrangement, all Third class being regraded to Tourist class.

The *Norman* was replaced by the *Llandovery Castle*, built in 1925 and followed in 1926 by a sistership, the *Llandaff Castle*, which replaced the

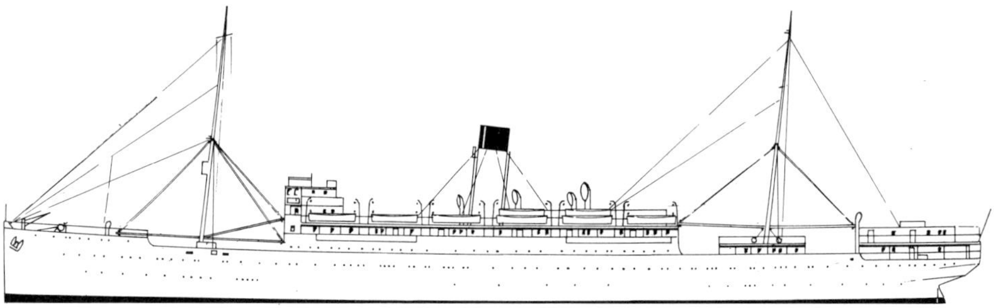

The *Llandovery Castle* of 1925.

*Gloucester Castle*, transferred to the west coast intermediate service. The *Llandovery Castle* came from Barclay, Curle & Company, Glasgow, the other from Workman, Clark at Belfast. They were two-class ships, carrying more than 400 passengers, and both had similar measurements. The *Llandovery Castle* sailed for many years after the Second World War, but the *Llandaff Castle* was lost in November, 1942, off the East African coast.

The motorship era of Union-Castle started in 1926 and lasted until after the Second World War, the first result of the decision taken in 1924 to adopt diesel propulsion being the appearance in 1926 of the twin-screw *Carnarvon Castle* with two squat funnels. Between 1922, when the turbine steamer

*Windsor Castle* was completed, and the building of the turbine-driven *Pretoria Castle* in 1948, twenty-five motorships were constructed. Six of these were mailships and one a cargo-feeder vessel, all based at Southampton, seven were intermediate London liners and eleven were refrigerated fruit ships.

Fruit exports from South Africa had been building up over the years and with the signing of a new Freight Agreement, operative from January, 1929, the company arranged that more refrigerated cargo was to be carried by the regular service liners. This was arranged in two improved motorships, *Winchester Castle* and *Warwick Castle*, which appeared in 1930-31, the former with 216,000 cubic feet of refrigerated space, the *Warwick Castle* with 207,000 cubic feet.

The maiden voyage of the *Winchester Castle* began on 24th October, 1930. She replaced the *Walmer Castle*, which arrived at Southampton for the last time on 5th January, 1931. The *Warwick Castle*, which departed from Southampton on 30th January, 1931, replaced the *Saxon*, which sailed on her last voyage from Southampton on 2nd January, 1931, arriving home on 23rd February. Both displaced ships lay at Netley for a time, the *Walmer Castle*

The *Carnarvon Castle* as built in 1926.

The elegance of the 1930s. *Union-Castle*

being broken up at Blyth in February, 1932; the *Saxon* went to the intermediate service for a time before she too went to the breakers in 1935.

The mail fleet in 1931 consisted of:

| | |
|---|---|
| *Kenilworth Castle* | *Edinburgh Castle* |
| *Windsor Castle* | *Winchester Castle* |
| *Warwick Castle* | *Armadale Castle* |
| *Balmoral Castle* | and |
| *Carnarvon Castle* | *Arundel Castle* |

At this time world trade was in a deep depression and the finances of the Royal Mail group of companies were greatly weakened. In 1931 the Kylsant empire collapsed and the Chairman of the group, Lord Kylsant (Sir Owen Philipps, Chairman of the Union-Castle Company from 1912), resigned. Union-Castle was left with heavy financial commitments, and only after long and involved financial arrangements, lasting several years, did the company achieve recovery and become an independent concern.

A further Freight Agreement, effective in 1934, called for yet more refrigerated cargo lift. Two more mailships were ordered from Belfast in February, 1934, *Stirling Castle* and *Athlone Castle*, each with 336,000 cubic feet of refrigerated space. With these ships, Union-Castle introduced a Cabin class of accommodation in place of Second and Tourist classes. Orders were also placed for the first two of a line of fast refrigerated motorships. These were named *Roslin Castle* (south of Edinburgh) and *Rothesay Castle* (on the Isle of Bute) and were designed with 402,000 cubic feet of refrigerated space.

The two liners *Stirling Castle* and *Athlone Castle* were designed for speeds enabling them to make the voyage between Southampton and Cape Town in under two weeks. Evidently this was done with a great deal of foresight for in 1936 a ten-year mail contract was signed whereby the voyage to Cape Town was to be reduced to fourteen days with arrivals at Port Elizabeth, East

*Athlone Castle* and *Stirling Castle* of 1936.

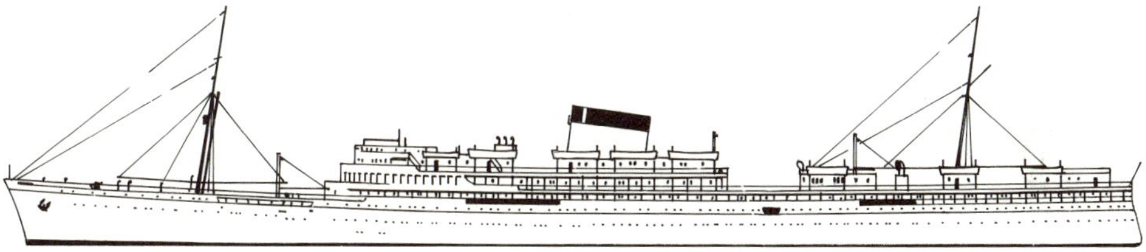

London and Durban in each case four days earlier from Southampton than hitherto. This service was to start in December, 1938.

To enable this to be achieved, however, many alterations had to be made to the existing fleet, and in March, 1936, a programme was drawn up for five ships to be fitted with new and more powerful engines and some related reconstruction work undertaken. All this to be done at Belfast. The *Armadale Castle* and *Kenilworth Castle* were to be withdrawn and broken up.

The oldest ships in the planned service, the four-funnelled steamers *Arundel Castle* and *Windsor Castle*, had to be given another three knots in speed; not only were they equipped with new watertube boilers and turbines of increased power but the hull form was necessarily lengthened. They were so altered that, with two rakish funnels in place of the four, they were almost unrecognisable when they returned to service; they were now really handsome ships.

So were the three earlier motorships, for they also returned with one large stylish funnel in place of their original two, adding to the impression of power. Each was given new engines. The *Warwick Castle* and *Winchester Castle* retained their original hull form, with upright stem and cruiser stern, but the *Carnarvon Castle* was also lengthened and given a curved stem.

Eight ships were required for the new service and in March, 1936, orders were placed with Harland & Wolff Limited not only for the re-engining of

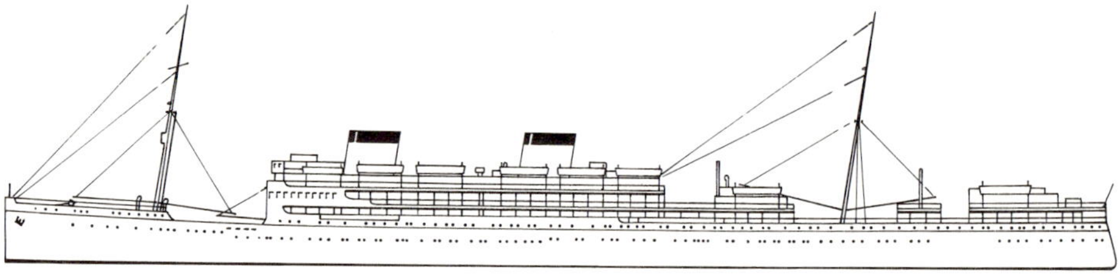

*Winchester Castle,* as built in 1930.

the five older ships but for a new liner, even larger than the recently-built *Stirling Castle* and *Athlone Castle*; in September, 1937, she was christened *Capetown Castle*. Repeated requests had been made by South Africans for a ship to be so named, but these had always been rejected on the grounds that the castle was actually a fort. After many arguments, however, it was accepted as being a castle and the tradition of naming the ships after ancient castles and residences of Britain was broken. The builders completed her in April, 1938. She was one of the largest motorships in the world.

Three days before Christmas, on 22nd December, 1938, the new service was inaugurated with the sailing of the *Athlone Castle* from Southampton, the sailing day being brought forward to Thursday.

Meanwhile the London-based service from the South West India Dock and Tilbury Landing Stage had not been ignored. The first of many motorships had been introduced with the *Llangibby Castle* for the "Round Africa" service in 1929, replacing the *Guildford Castle* which returned to the west coast route. The *Dunbar Castle* (after a castle in East Lothian), slightly smaller and slower, followed in June, 1930. These ships, each with two stubby funnels, were not sisterships, although both were built at the same Harland & Wolff yard at Govan on the Clyde. One recognition point was an extra promenade deck on the *Llangibby Castle*. In 1931 two more ships, *Durham Castle* and *Dunluce Castle*, were transferred to the "Round Africa" service.

*Winchester Castle,* after rebuilding in 1938.

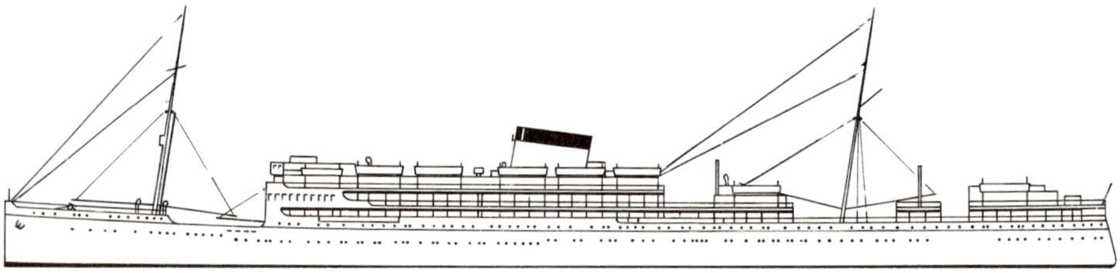

Single funnels were reintroduced in the next two motorships, the *Dunnottar Castle* (after a castle near Stonehaven, Kincardine) and the *Dunvegan Castle* (on the Isle of Skye). These 15,000 gt. ships both came from Belfast and immediately on completion helped out on the mail run while the larger ships were being altered.

So successful were these two that a further pair were ordered from the Belfast yard. These were of slightly different design, omitting the lower First class promenade deck and with cabins extended to the full width of the ship. The *Durban Castle* was completed in 1938 and the *Pretoria Castle* in 1939. Improvements were also made to the coal burners *Llanstephan Castle*, *Llandaff Castle* and *Llandovery Castle*, these being converted to burn oil.

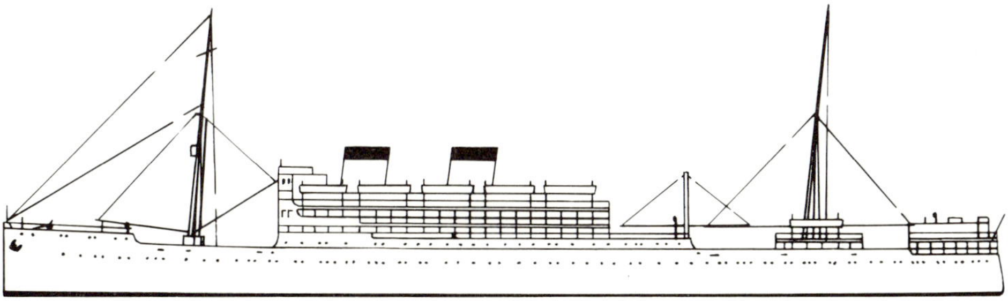

The first motorship in the "Round Africa" service, *Llangibby Castle* of 1929.

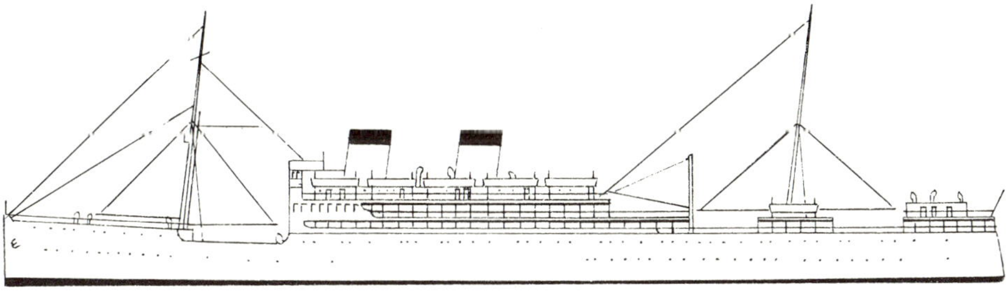

Built in 1930 for the west coast intermediate service, the *Dunbar Castle* was similar to, but smaller than, the *Llangibby Castle*.

But this was not all of this huge building programme, for another four 16-knot refrigerated motorships joined the fleet shortly before the war—*Rochester Castle* (in Kent), *Roxburgh Castle* (Scotland), both in 1937; *Richmond Castle* (Yorkshire) and *Rowallan Castle* (a 16th century residence just north of Kilmarnock) in 1939. Each had over 400,000 cubic feet of refrigerated space.

The smallest ship in the building programme was the *Walmer Castle*, a 906 gt. motorship delivered from Belfast in 1936 for the feeder service between

Bremen and Hamburg and Southampton, carrying transhipment cargoes for the mail ships. This feeder service had started in 1906 as a fortnightly run maintained by the *Hansa*, from Donald Currie's Liverpool-Hamburg Line. She became a Union-Castle ship in 1907 and was joined by the *Eider*, from the Royal Mail Steam Packet Company, which eventually became a Union-Castle ship in 1926. Both these ships were replaced by the *Walmer Castle*, whose maiden voyage took place from Southampton on 5th December, 1936.

At Southampton the ship berthed at No. 37 berth, known as Dockhead, being conveniently placed between the inward Cape ship at No. 36 berth and the outward loading vessel at No. 38 berth. The service was not restarted after the war.

Ships employed:

| | |
|---|---|
| *Hansa* | 880 gt. Built by AG Neptun, Rostock, 1904.<br>Measurements: 215 feet length bp × 31 feet breadth.<br>Triple expansion engines.<br>1937: Sold to Stanhope SS Co., renamed *Stanray*. |
| *Eider* | 1,236 gt. Built by Campbeltown SB Co., 1900.<br>Measurements: 230 feet length bp × 33 feet breadth.<br>Triple expansion engines.<br>1936: Sold to Stanhope SS Co., renamed *Stanhill*. |
| *Walmer Castle* | 906 gt. Built by Harland & Wolff Ltd., Belfast 1936.<br>Measurements: 236 feet length bp × 39 feet breadth.<br>1941: War loss. |

The motorship *Warwick Castle*, as built in 1931. *Tom Rayner collection*

In the summer of 1937 the company lost one of its cargo ships. The *Sandgate Castle* had left New York on 23rd June, bound for Cape Town with general cargo. Some 800 miles south-east of New York, 350 miles north-east of Bermuda (approximately 36.51N 60.05W) she radioed that she was on fire in her 'tween decks. The distress call was picked up by the Dollar SS Company's liner *President Pierce*, which went to the scene and picked up all the crew, who had taken to the boats. She reported the *Sandgate Castle* as lying low in the water and then, on 28th June, the Imperial Oil Company's tanker *Canadolite* reported she had passed the ship, which was still burning. A similar report was made by the Norske Amerikalinje ship *Idefjord* the next day, and on 30th June the Italian liner *Conte di Savoia* reported the same, adding that the stricken ship, now in position 38.06N 59.11W, was derelict, still burning, drifting north-east with the Gulf Stream and a danger to navigation. The liner circled the *Sandgate Castle* for forty-five minutes and the captain was confident no one was left aboard the hulk. There being no further reports, it was assumed that she had sunk.

At the end of the huge building programme the company had a large amount of tonnage for disposal and in 1939 several ships left the fleet. Some of their later histories are worth recording.

Both the *Balmoral Castle* and *Edinburgh Castle* of 1910—the last coal-burning mailships—were sold, the former to Cashmores at Newport, Mon., for breaking up. The *Edinburgh Castle*, which had been laid up at Netley on Southampton Water since her final voyage to South Africa in December, 1938, was purchased by the Admiralty and sent to Freetown, Sierra Leone, as a base ship, wearing the Pennant F.83 of the Freetown Escort Force. From 1940, she spent five hot years as an accommodation ship. When the war ended it was considered that the cost of towing her back to the United Kingdom would exceed her scrap value, so on 25th September, 1945, she was towed to sea by the Castle-class corvette HMS *Launceston Castle* and the tug *Empire Lawn*. Some 60 miles off Freetown she was raked by gunfire and depth charges from the River-class frigate HMS *Fal*, the trawlers *Arran* and *Buttermere* and other coastal craft and after capsizing was finally despatched by HMS *Portchester Castle*. The *Edinburgh Castle* had survived two wars, having been converted at Tilbury in 1914 to an armed merchant cruiser, served off South America until April, 1918, then became a troopship, and returned to the mail service in July, 1919.

Four London-based ships also left the fleet. Both the *Garth Castle* and *Grantully Castle* were sold for breaking up, and the two remaining ships of the D-class of 1904 were sold for Admiralty use as base ships. Unfortunately, the *Durham Castle* was mined off Cromarty on 26th January, 1940, and sank. The *Dunluce Castle*, however, served through the war, being finally broken up at Inverkeithing in July, 1945.

Built in 1936 for the Southampton-Germany feeder service, the *Walmer Castle* was lost in 1941 while serving as a convoy rescue ship. *Tom Rayner collection*

This, then, was the state of the Union-Castle fleet as war broke out on 3rd September, 1939:

| | |
|---|---|
| Mail liners | 8 |
| Intermediate liners | 10 |
| Refrigerated cargo ships | 6 |
| General cargo ships | 4 |
| East Africa coaster | 1 |
| Passenger tenders | 2 |

The requisitioning of ships for war service began early. On the day after war broke out the tender *Falcon*, so long based at Southampton as a general runabout for the mail fleet, was requisitioned and sent to Cowes for the use of the Senior Naval Officer. It is worth recording more details of this small ship. She was built by Day, Summers & Company at Northam, Southampton, in 1896 for the Union SS Company, was 41 gt. on measurements of 70 feet length and 13 feet breadth, had a saloon and burned coal. After the merger in 1900 she was given shining brasswork, a white dodger forward of a tall, slim funnel and Union-Castle colours. Her duties included taking the pilot down Southampton Water to meet the incoming mail ship and to deliver the ship's mail, and she was also used in storing the reserve ship off Netley. In September, 1940, she returned to Southampton, then quickly moved off to the West Country for service and was disposed of in 1942.

The first liners to go to war as HM ships were the *Dunnottar Castle*, *Dunvegan Castle* and *Pretoria Castle* from the London service and *Carnarvon Castle* from the mail fleet. All were converted to armed merchant cruisers of the Freetown Escort Force, but the *Pretoria Castle* was later purchased by the Admiralty and in 1943 converted to an aircraft carrier.

In January, 1940, the *Dunbar Castle*, outward bound from London to Beira, was sunk by magnetic mine off Deal.

The Liner Requisition Scheme was introduced this same month and very soon all ships were in war service. The ports of Southampton and London were virtually closed to liner shipping and the ships and shore staffs moved to Liverpool and Glasgow.

The almost new motorship HMS *Dunvegan Castle* was lost at the end of August, 1940. Launched on 26th March, 1936, she had made her maiden voyage from London in the "Round Africa" service in the September but was quickly taken up at the outbreak of war and armed with eight 6-inch and two 3-inch guns for service as an armed merchant cruiser. She was torpedoed by submarine *U.46* off the West coast of Ireland on 27th August and sank the following day in position 55N 11W.

HMS *Pretoria Castle* after conversion to an aircraft carrier, used for training purposes.
*Wright and Logan*

The *Walmer Castle* was the next casualty. She had been taken up in August, 1940, as an armed supply ship and then, in 1941, became a convoy rescue ship. She was sailing in a convoy to Gibraltar when, on 21st September, 1941, she was bombed while rescuing survivors from sunken ships. Fire broke out and she was eventually sunk by British naval gunfire.

The twin-screw cargo ship *Dunbar Castle* became a war loss early in 1940.
*Tom Rayner collection*

In July, 1942, the *Gloucester Castle* went missing; not until the end of the war was it known that she was the victim of a German raider, the 4,740 gt. motorship *Bonn*, taken over from Norddeutscher Lloyd by the German Navy and converted into a raider. Renamed *Michel*, the raider was armed with six 5.9-inch and eight smaller guns. She herself was torpedoed and sunk off Yokohama on 17/18th October, 1943, by the submarine USS *Tarpon*. Four more Union-Castle vessels were lost in that disastrous year of 1942, including the liners *Llandaff Castle* and *Warwick Castle*, the latter being the largest Union-Castle ship lost.

A twin-screw motorship, the *Warwick Castle* (20,107 gt.) was launched by

Harland & Wolff at Belfast on 29th April, 1930, and made her maiden voyage on 30th January, 1931, from Southampton. Re-engined in 1938, she became a troopship on the outbreak of war; her loss occurred off the coast of Portugal.

Completed in November, 1926, by Workman, Clark & Company, Belfast, the *Llandaff Castle* made her maiden voyage in January, 1927, in the "Round Africa" service. She carried 224 First and 186 Third class passengers. She was taken up as a troopship in 1940 and was lost off Lourenco Marques in November, 1942.

Altogether, thirteen ships were lost during the war, of which two were marine casualties. One other vessel, the French cargo liner *Charles L-D*, owned by Louis Dreyfus et Cie and managed by Union-Castle for the Government, was lost in December, 1942, when torpedoed by *U.553* in position 59.02N 30.45W in the North Atlantic.

Ships owned by Union-Castle and lost during World War II.

| | | |
|---|---|---|
| 4th January, 1940 | *Rothesay Castle* | Ashore at Sanaig Point, Islay, in position 55.53N 6.21W (Voyage: New York/Clyde—general cargo). |
| 9th January, 1940 | *Dunbar Castle* | Mined and sunk 2 miles NE of the Goodwin Sands, in position 51.23N 01.34E. |
| 28th August, 1940 | *HMS Dunvegan Castle* | Torpedoed and sunk by *U.46*, west of Ireland, in position 55N 11W. |
| 21st September, 1941 | *Walmer Castle* | Bombed and sunk in Gibraltar convoy OG 74, in position 47.16N 22.25W. |
| 12th December, 1941 | *Dromore Castle* | Mined and sunk 20 miles SSE of Humber. |
| 14th February, 1942 | *Rowallan Castle* | Bombed by enemy aircraft, in position 34.54N 19.40E. Sunk by British naval gunfire. |
| 16th July, 1942 | *Gloucester Castle* | Sunk by German auxiliary cruiser *Michel* in (estimated) position 08S 01E. |
| 4th August, 1942 | *Richmond Castle* | Torpedoed and sunk by *U.176* in position 50.25N 35.05W. |
| 14th November, 1942 | *Warwick Castle* | Torpedoed and sunk by *U.413* in convoy MFK 1 in position 39.16N 13.25W. |
| 30th November, 1942 | *Llandaff Castle* | Torpedoed and sunk by *U.177*, southeast of Lourenco Marques, in position 27.20S 33.40E (Voyage: Suez/Durban). |
| 22nd February, 1943 | *Roxburgh Castle* | Torpedoed and sunk by *U.107*, off the Azores, in position 38.12N 26.22W. |
| 23rd March, 1943 | *Windsor Castle* | Torpedoed and sunk by aircraft of KG 26 (Bomber group) north of Cape Tenes, in convoy KMG 11, in position 37.28N 01.10E. |
| 2nd April, 1943 | *Dundrum Castle* | On fire, explosion, sank in Red Sea in position 14.37N 14.23E (Voyage: Liverpool and Aden/Alexandria). |

CHAPTER THREE

# Return from War

AT LAST came the summer of 1945 and the world breathed a sigh of relief. Men of armies in every corner of the globe laid down their arms, celebrated the coming of peace and then turned their thoughts to the promised bright new world.

After years of deprivation, the desire to return to their homelands and to their families was paramount in the minds of millions of servicemen everywhere. With logical foresight, schedules for demobilization had long been drawn up, but not only had servicemen to be transported, albeit with the preference they deserved, but there were countless numbers of displaced persons to be considered and hundreds of thousands of prisoners of war to be moved.

This was the rundown of the war machine. But the immediate future also demanded old trade routes to be re-established and new ones opened. And quickly. Of major interest to Union-Castle was the fact that during hostilities, with the Suez route closed, convoys had necessarily to travel via the Cape of Good Hope, calling at Cape Town and other major ports in South Africa, to take on bunkers, stores, water and ammunition. Nor was this all, for the early voyage repairs made by South African ship repairers quickly grew into larger jobs as British and Allied yards became strained to capacity. All these servicing and repair jobs, in turn, caused great demand for

A survivor of the war was the *Winchester Castle,* built in 1930 and reconstructed in 1938.

tools, machinery, paint, stores and the thousand and one things required to keep ships moving, and South Africa looked to Britain to fulfil these orders. The need for ships remained as acute as ever.

As with most liner companies, Union-Castle had lost major units during the war, the fleet being decimated by the loss of eight passenger-carrying vessels, and ships that remained were serving in waters very different from those for which they were built. Nevertheless, there remained six mailships of the Southampton service and six of the London-based "Round Africa" ships, a good nucleus on which to rebuild. There also remained a number of refrigerated and cargo ships.

The fleet at the end of the war was thus:

| | (built) | | (built) |
|---|---|---|---|
| **Mailships** | | | |
| *Capetown Castle* | 1938 | *Winchester Castle* | 1930 |
| *Athlone Castle* | 1936 | *Carnarvon Castle* | 1926 |
| *Stirling Castle* | 1936 | *Arundel Castle* | 1921 |
| **"Round Africa" ships** | | | |
| *Durban Castle* | 1938 | *Llangibby Castle* | 1929 |
| *Pretoria Castle* | 1939 | *Llandovery Castle* | 1925 |
| *Dunnottar Castle* | 1936 | *Llanstephan Castle* | 1914 |
| **Refrigerated cargo ships** | | | |
| *Roxburgh Castle* | 1945 | *Rochester Castle* | 1937 |
| *Richmond Castle* | 1944 | *Roslin Castle* | 1935 |
| *Rowallan Castle* | 1943 | | |
| **Cargo ships** | | | |
| *Sandown Castle* | 1921 | *Rovuma* | 1927 |

On 2nd April, 1945, shortly before war ended, an Ocean Mail and an Ocean Freight Contract had been signed in Cape Town for a period of ten years, effective from 1st January, 1947. It was announced that orders for two 28,000 gt. liners, the largest ever in the company, were to be placed with Harland & Wolff Limited, Belfast. These would replace the two liners, *Warwick Castle* and *Windsor Castle*, lost during hostilities.

In March, 1946, the new refrigerated ship *Riebeeck Castle** was delivered from the Harland & Wolff yard, to be followed in June by the *Rustenburg Castle*†. They followed the *Rowallan Castle*, *Richmond Castle* and *Roxburgh*

*The *Riebeeck Castle* was named after Riebeeck 'Kasteel', once the frontier outpost of the Dutch East India Company's settlement at the Cape, some 100 miles north of Cape Town, founded in 1652 by Jan van Riebeeck for the purpose of victualling the company's vessels to and from the Indies.

†Rustenburg is a small town in the Transvaal and centre of a citrus fruit, tobacco and cotton growing district.

*Castle*, built during 1943-1945, but were slightly larger in tonnage, both being of 8,322 gt. with a deadweight capacity of 9,200 tons. For propulsion, single eight-cylinder oil engines were installed, driving single screws and giving 16 knots. Holds and 'tween decks, with a total capacity of over 400,000 cubic feet, were fully insulated for the carriage of fruit, meat and dairy produce. Including the two pre-war ships which survived the war, the *Roslin Castle* and *Rochester Castle*, this gave the company a fleet of seven refrigerated ships.

Cargo ships surviving the war were the *Sandown Castle* and the *Rovuma*, a coaster based at Beira and used in a feeder service with local ports. To augment the cargo ship section of the fleet three fast cargo liners were purchased in 1946 under the Government Ship Disposal Scheme. They belonged to a group of standard ships constructed during the war to fill a gap created when high speed cargo liners had been requisitioned early in the war. Not until late 1941 had marine engineers been able to turn their attention to providing suitable machinery for such a type but by mid-1942 plans had been completed for a 15-knot ship. A number were constructed for Government account and some licences to build were granted to private shipowners.

The length was 475 feet bp, the breadth 64 feet and the capacity 12,000 tdw. Some were propelled by steam turbines driving a single screw; some were given oil engines and a shorter but wider funnel. Lifting gear comprised one 80 ton, one 50, one 30, four 10 and seven 5 ton derricks.

The cargo ship *Good Hope Castle*, built 1945.

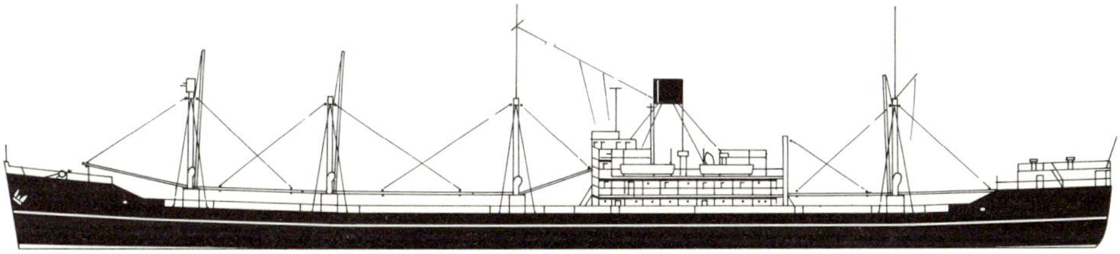

| Name | grt | Built | Renamed |
|---|---|---|---|
| *Empire Allenby* | 9,904 | J. L. Thompson & Sons Ltd., Sunderland 1945. Engines: two steam turbines. | *Drakensburg Castle* |
| *Empire Life* | 9,879 | Caledon SB & Eng Co. Ltd., Dundee 1945. Engines: two steam turbines. | *Good Hope Castle* |
| *Empire Wilson* | 9,916 | C. Connell & Co. Ltd., Glasgow 1944. Engines: Oil | *Kenilworth Castle* |

The *Good Hope Castle*, named after the Cape, was given passenger accommodation for fifty-four, the other two for thirty-six, a wartime expedient, but this was later reduced to twelve in each ship. Drakensburg is the name of a mountain range in Natal; Kenilworth Castle is in Warwickshire.

Under the ten-year Ocean Mail and Ocean Freight Contract certain cargo vessels were to be registered in the Union of South Africa. The first of these, the *Good Hope Castle*, was transferred from London to Cape Town registry at Cape Town on 14th July, 1946, when the flag of the Union of South Africa was raised at the stern prior to the ship sailing for the United States. The second ship, *Drakensburg Castle*, at first under Sunderland registry, was also later transferred to the South African flag. The ships were mainly for the USA-South Africa service. At first they were given the familiar hull colour, but in 1953 this was changed to black, the colour which had characterised the Union-Castle cargo ships of pre-war years.

At the turn of the year the mail service was resumed after a lapse of seven years when the *Roxburgh Castle* left Southampton on 2nd January, 1947. Although she was a refrigerated cargo vessel, this was an essential first step in restoring the service. The *Capetown Castle*, flagship of the fleet, which had already returned to Southampton at the end of 1946 after refitting by her builders following war service, took the first passenger ship sailing on 9th January, 1947, from Berth No. 38, which had been the outward "Cape" berth for so many years. Her passenger accommodation had been reconverted to the design of pre-war days and was arranged over six decks, provision being made for about 250 First and 550 Tourist class passengers. All the valuable fittings, so carefully stored when she was called to war service, were restored, including the painting of "The Castle, Cape Town", a gift from the Corporation of Cape Town, and the plaque presented by the garrison of the Castle.

This, then, was the first stage in the plan to restore the weekly mail service to South Africa, but until the liners returned from reconditioning the service had to be supplemented by fast refrigerated cargo ships of the R-type.

The second liner to join the mail fleet was the *Warwick Castle*. She had been built for the "Round Africa" service from London and when completed in 1939 was named *Pretoria Castle*. She served in the Royal Navy for much of the war and when reconverting at Belfast in 1946 was renamed *Warwick Castle*. Temporarily attached to the Southampton-Cape Town service while other mailships were refitting, she left Southampton on 13th March, 1947, on her first postwar sailing.

The third liner to be reconverted for the Southampton service was the *Athlone Castle* and again it was Harland & Wolff at Belfast which did the work. Some idea of the huge job in altering her from a troop transport to a passenger liner can be gathered from the fact that many cabins had been

The *Capetown Castle* leaving Cape Town. *Vic Young*

removed for mess deck "standee" berth accommodation, hospital wards, etc., while some public rooms had been stripped for tiers of bunks to be erected. The *Athlone Castle* left Southampton in April, 1947. Her sistership, *Stirling Castle*, was released from Government service in March, 1947, and the intention was that the *Winchester Castle*, *Carnarvon Castle* and *Arundel Castle* would follow at three monthly intervals.

It had been thought that the Southampton-Cape mail service would be back to normal by 1948, but the great development in South Africa during the war years, plus a further discovery of gold in March, 1946, at Odendaalsrus in the Orange Free State, a groundnut scheme in southern Tanganyika and general expansion in the Rhodesias, stirred the imagination of potential emigrants from Britain.

The Union government, with attractive sponsored schemes for urgently required artisans, caused great demand for shipping space and, after an approach by the Government, Union-Castle postponed the reconversion of two mailships, and later one other, so they could be employed on emigrant runs to the Cape. The *Carnarvon Castle* made the first sailing in June, 1947, her accommodation being rated at 1,283 passengers, and she was followed by the *Winchester Castle* (877 passengers) and *Arundel Castle* (846). These three ships continued carrying emigrants until more than 30,000 had been transported to South Africa by the time the service ended in May, 1949. To offset this arrangement as far as possible, the "Round Africa" liner *Durban Castle* was slotted into the service from Southampton when she became available in June, 1947, after reconditioning.

In 1939 nine ships had been employed in the London-based "Round Africa" service—*Dunnottar Castle* and *Dunvegan Castle*; *Durban Castle* and *Pretoria Castle*; and the older *Llangibby Castle*, *Dunbar Castle*, *Llanstephan Castle*, *Llandovery Castle* and *Llandaff Castle*. Of these, three became war losses—*Dunvegan Castle*, *Dunbar Castle* and *Llandaff Castle*—and with the *Durban Castle* and *Pretoria Castle* (renamed *Warwick Castle*) both temporarily transferred to the Southampton service, the London fleet was indeed depleted.

Nevertheless, in May, 1947, the *Llandovery Castle*, the fourth Union-castle liner to be reconditioned, reinaugurated the service outwards via the west coast of Africa. She had accommodation for 215 First and 198 Tourist class passengers. The service was augmented by the *Llangibby Castle*, sailing on 24th July via Marseilles, Genoa, Port Said, Suez, Aden and on to East and South Africa. Two months later, on 12th September, after a refit occupying more than a year at the Fairfield yard at Glasgow, the *Llanstephan Castle* made her first post-war voyage in the London-based service. She sailed out via the west coast, returning via Suez. Remodelled accommodation was for 231 First and 198 Tourist passengers.

In mid-summer of 1947, an important year for Union-Castle, the first of the two liners of the war loss replacement programme being built at Harland & Wolff's yard at Belfast, known as Yard No. 1332, was christened *Pretoria Castle*. The day was 19th August, and the launching unique in shipping history, for it was performed at the word of Mrs J. C. Smuts, wife of Field Marshal Smuts, then Prime Minister of South Africa, speaking by radio telephone from her home at Irene, some twelve miles from Pretoria, the administrative capital of South Africa, and 6,000 miles from Belfast. At the press of a button a series of electric impulses travelled by land line to Cape Town, by radio to London and by land line again to Belfast, released the

A return to steam propulsion was made with the *Pretoria Castle* and her sistership *Edinburgh Castle* in 1948. Propulsion was by six steam turbines. *Skyfotos*

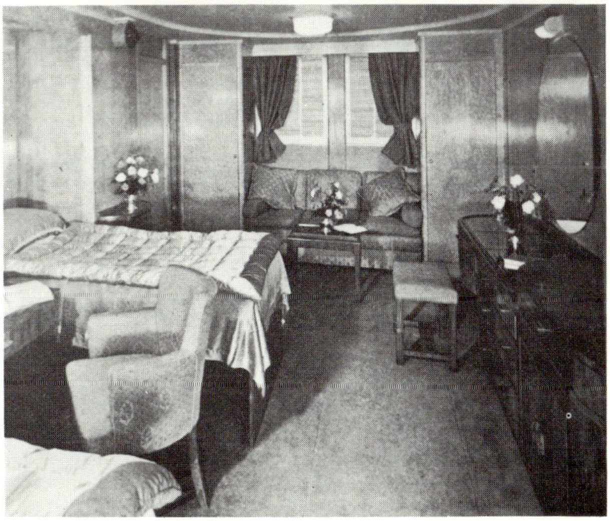

The First class dining saloon and a First class cabin-de-luxe of the *Pretoria Castle* of 1948.
*Union-Castle*

bottle of South African wine to break on the bow of the ship, and also started the vessel on her journey down the launching ways.

The *Pretoria Castle* was the largest merchant ship launched since war had ended. One very significant fact was that she and her sistership (Yard No. 1333) were of steam propulsion, marking the company's reversion to steam after twenty years of diesel-driven vessels; the last steamship to have been constructed being the *Llandaff Castle*, completed in December 1926.

Two months later, on 16th October, 1947, the sistership was launched as *Edinburgh Castle* by Princess Margaret. This was the third ship of this name in Union-Castle history. The first, of 2,672 gt., had been built in 1872 to the order of Donald Currie, founder of the Castle Mail Steam Packet Company,

The *Edinburgh Castle* of 1948 leaving Cape Town. Below is a drawing of the *Edinburgh Castle*, with an inset showing the original mast arrangement.

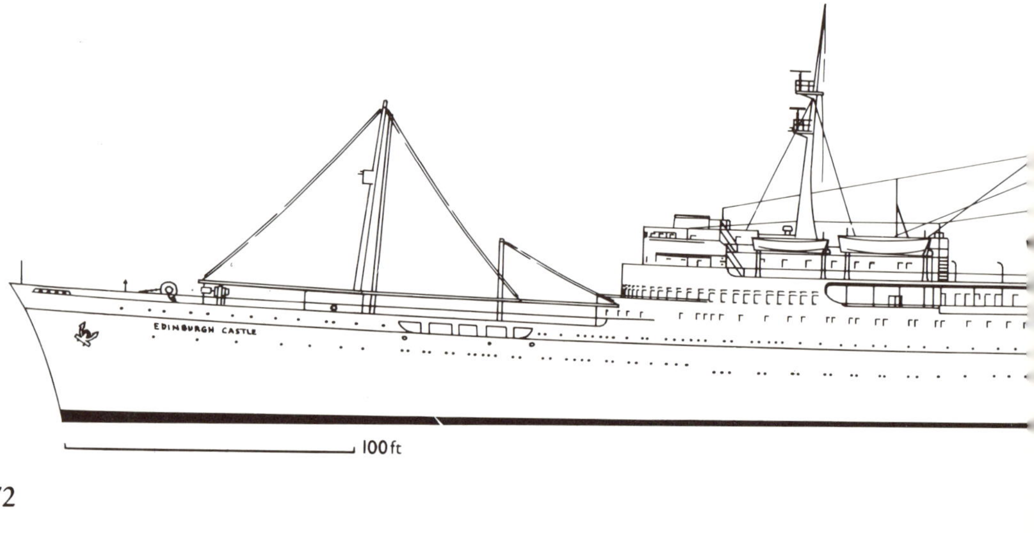

and had served first under charter in South American waters and later in the South African trade before being sold to Spain in 1880 and renamed *Espana*. She was scrapped in 1898. The second was the mailship of 13,330 gt. built in 1910 and withdrawn from service in 1938.

Both liners were completed in 1948, the largest vessels ever in the Union-Castle fleet. Details were:

| | | | |
|---|---|---|---|
| Length: | 747 feet 5 inches oa | Tonnages: | 28,705 gt |
| | 700 feet bp | | 15,800 tdw |
| Breadth: | 83 feet 6 inches | | |

Engines: six steam turbines, doubled reduction geared to twin shafts.

Each ship had a curved fashioned stem, cruiser stern, rounded forward superstructure and two masts.

Accommodation was provided for 227 First and 478 Cabin class passengers and the public rooms and cabins were spread over six decks. Much use of Commonwealth woods and veneers was made throughout the accommodation, and in the main lounge of the *Pretoria Castle* an inscription on one of

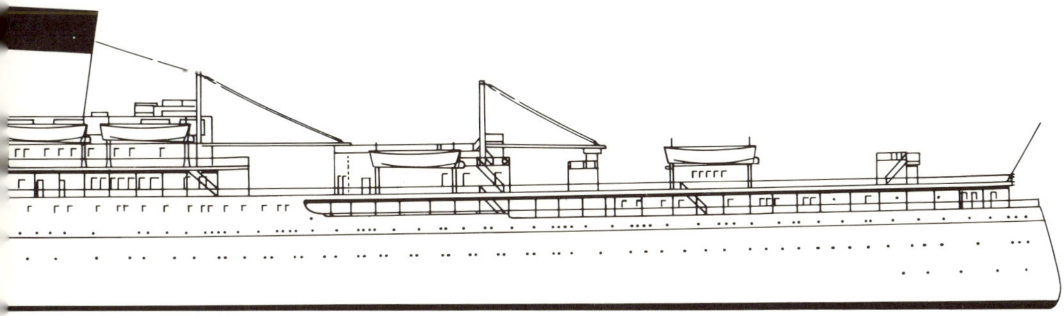

the panels commemorated her unique launching. For cargo there were seven holds with derricks of 3, 5, 10 and 30 tons lifting capacity. The *Pretoria Castle* left Southampton on her maiden voyage on 22nd July, 1948; the *Edinburgh Castle* on 9th December, 1948. Already another liner for Union-Castle, the *Bloemfontein Castle*, had been started by Harland & Wolff in June, for delivery in 1950.

Another cargo ship was purchased in 1948. Built under the name *Empire Duchess* in 1943 for the Ministry of War Transport, she was a war standard ship of B-type tramp design. Her builders were Short Bros., Sunderland; on measurements of 447 feet length oa, 431 feet length bp and a breadth of 56 feet, her gross tonnage was 7,067. Propulsion was by triple expansion engines. She was renamed *Braemar Castle*.

Wishing to have at its disposal extra tramp tonnage to supplement the liner tonnage in its fleet, the company acquired in November, 1948, the controlling interest of the King Line, completing the purchase in the following year (See Appendix D).

The *Winchester Castle* made her final voyage as an emigrant ship in the autumn of 1948 and arrived at Belfast on 13th November. She was quickly followed by the second of the temporary emigrant carriers, the *Carnarvon Castle*, which reached Belfast on 4th January, 1949.

Meanwhile in London the "Round Africa" service had received another ship; the *Dunnottar Castle*, after a ten-month refit at Belfast, sailed on her first postwar voyage to East Africa on 9th February, 1949. This gave the service four ships—the *Dunnottar Castle* and *Llangibby Castle* sailing via Suez and the east coast route to Cape Town, and the *Llandovery Castle* and *Llanstephan Castle* down the west coast. These last three ships, however, were ageing and replacement tonnage had to be considered.

The last emigrant voyage by the big mail ships was made from Southampton on 18th April, 1949, by the *Arundel Castle*. She was to have gone to Belfast for reconditioning on her return, but was sent for a spell of trooping service in the Mediterranean and did not go to her builders until 30th September. She was the last Union-Castle liner to be released from Government service.

Only a few days earlier, on 22nd September, the *Winchester Castle* had left Southampton on her first voyage after reconditioning, and the mail service was then back to eight ships, although two were on temporary transfer from the London service.

In 1949 the *Rovuma** was sold. She was a small cargo ship, built for the Union-Castle, based at Beira and used on a coastal feeder service. During her career she rose to fame, starring in the film "Sanders of the River", with

*The Rovuma River forms the southern boundary between Tanganyika and Mozambique, as the territories were then known.

Built in 1927, the twin-screw *Rovuma* was employed in the East African coastal service.
*Tom Rayner collection*

scenes depicting West Africa being actually taken on the South Africa Natal coast and at Maydon Wharf, Durban. The *Rovuma* was sold to Colonial Steamships Limited, of Mauritius, and was renamed *Floreal.* In 1954 she moved on to African Coasters Limited, Durban, and took the name *Boundary*, finally being sold for breaking up in 1962 after thirty-five years of service in East African waters. She was cut up in a Durban graving dock and her two boilers, found to be still in good condition, were sold for further service ashore.

Details: Built by Ardrossan Dockyard Co. Ltd., 1927,

Length: 211 feet 8 inches — Tonnage: 1289 g
Breadth: 35 feet — 1233 tdw

Engines: Triple expansion, driving twin screws. 9 knots.

On 25th August, 1949, the *Bloemfontein Castle* was launched at Harland & Wolff's yard at Belfast by Mrs Leif Egeland, wife of the High Commissioner for the Union of South Africa in London. The *Bloemfontein Castle* was the first intermediate liner to be built since the war had ended, and the institution of a single class—Tourist—was an innovation for Union-Castle. She was built to cater for an expected emigrant boom and to alleviate the still considerable pressure at the time for accommodation at lower range fares.

The main public rooms were on the promenade deck, a large lounge forward being extended the whole width of the ship so there were no passageways either side. Aft of this was a combined library and writing room, connected by a long gallery to a commodious smoking room. On the upper deck a dining room for 386 also extended the width of the ship. Accommodation for 739 passengers was spread through seven decks.

The *Bloemfontein Castle* was given the familiar Union-Castle profile of well-raked rounded stem, cruiser stern, a low streamlined funnel and a single mast abaft the bridge, giving a well-balanced appearance. There were two hatches forward and three aft, served by six 10-ton and four 5-ton capacity derricks. Cargo 'tweendeck spaces were insulated for the carriage of fruit, with certain compartments for chilled and frozen produce.

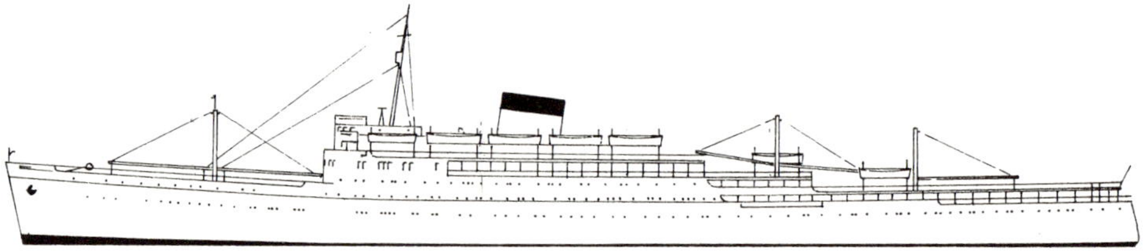

*Bloemfontein Castle* of 1950.

Details:

| | | | |
|---|---|---|---|
| Length: | 594 feet 6 inches oa | Tonnages: | 18,400 gt |
| | 570 feet 7 inches bp | | 10,750 tdw |
| Breadth: | 76 feet 4 inches | | (186,000 cubic feet refrigerated) |

Engines: two eight-cylinder oil engines driving twin screws. 18½ knots.

A shakedown cruise was made from London in late March, 1950, some 250 of the company's staff being invited. She left on her maiden voyage from London on 6th April, 1950, sailing around Africa outwards via the west coast, but she later sailed in a service via the west coast to Cape Town and Beira, turning there and sometimes calling at Southampton homewards in the busy fruit season. She took her name after the town of Bloemfontein, capital of the Orange Free State.

After a very lengthy refit at Belfast, the *Carnarvon Castle* returned to the mail service on 15th June, 1950. During reconditioning following her service as an emigrant ship, the accommodation was modified to conform to postwar requirements for 216 First and 401 Tourist class passengers, the old Second class having been remodelled to increase the Tourist class accommodation. Her return to service released the *Durban Castle*, which had been seconded to the mail service since her reconditioning from war service, and she returned to London for her place in the "Round Africa" service.

The return of the *Carnarvon Castle* left only one ship to complete the mail fleet in accordance with Union-Castle plans. This was the *Arundel Castle*, which eventually left Belfast on 9th September, 1950, and was back in service on 21st October, 1950, three days after the *Warwick Castle* arrived from her last mailship voyage on 18th October. The latter, too, quickly departed, to be phased into the London-based schedule.

From October, 1950, the mailship section of the fleet was complete and the Southampton-South Africa service was at last back to its weekly programme of sailings to Madeira, Cape Town, Port Elizabeth, East London and Durban, returning with occasional calls at Las Palmas. The sailing sequence of the ships was:

*Pretoria Castle*
*Arundel Castle*
*Athlone Castle*
*Carnarvon Castle*
*Edinburgh Castle*
*Winchester Castle*
*Capetown Castle*
*Stirling Castle*

From London, the intermediate service to Beira was maintained by *Bloemfontein Castle* and the "Round Africa" service by:

*Durban Castle*
*Dunnottar Castle*
*Llanstephan Castle*
*Warwick Castle*
*Llandovery Castle* and
*Llangibby Castle*

There was also a cargo ship movement in 1950 with the transfer of the *Braemar Castle* (ex *Empire Duchess*) to the associated King Line, the vessel being renamed *King James.* Also disposed of in 1950 was the 29-year old cargo ship *Sandown Castle.*

Constructed for the London-Beira run, the *Bloemfontein Castle* is here seen sailing from Cape Town. *A. Duncan*

*Sandown Castle* Built by Short Bros., Sunderland 1921
*Sandgate Castle* Built by Short Bros., Sunderland 1922

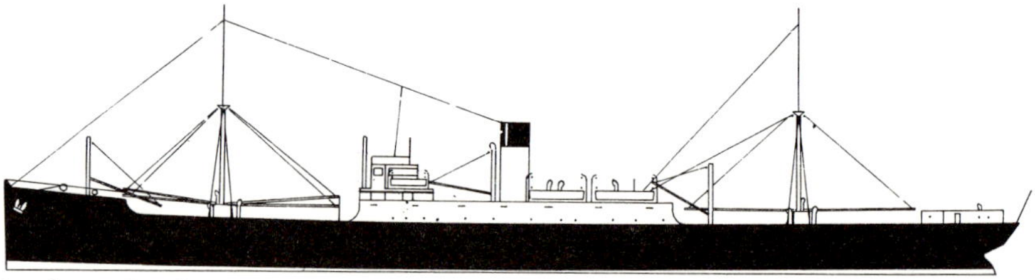

*Sandown Castle*

Measurements:

| Length: | 442 feet oa | Tonnages: | 7,607 and 7,634 gt |
|---|---|---|---|
| | 425 feet 5 inches bp | | 11,500 tdw |

Engines: Three steam turbines geared to a single shaft.

These ships aroused interest when they were built, for they were a type new to Union-Castle. They were the first geared turbine ships of the fleet, developing 3,200 shaft horsepower, giving a speed of 12 knots. They had two decks and a shelter deck on which was the bridge deck. The ships sailed regularly on the UK-South Africa route and at times on the US-South Africa run, but were laid up for a time in the depression of the 1920s. The *Sandown Castle*, recommissioned in 1923, delivered a shipment of 330 head of cattle at Birkenhead in the following year which caused some speculation about a rival trade to that of South America. The ship was chartered to a film company in the 1930s and was in "The Faithful Heart", based on a book which had its setting in the pre-1914 Southampton dockland.

After the war the *Sandown Castle* was given a French grey hull and did much service when shipping was so scarce. She sailed for twenty-nine years and was eventually sold to the British Iron & Steel Corporation in 1950 after a lay-up in the Tyne for a period. She was broken up by Clayton & Davie at their Dunston yard.

The *Sandgate Castle* was lost by fire a few days after leaving New York for South Africa in June, 1937.

**Sandown Castle* was named after a castle built in Kent by Henry VIII, long since lost in the sea by coast erosion. Sandgate Castle, also by Henry VIII, was a castle near Folkstone.

At the launching ceremony of the *Bloemfontein Castle* it had been announced that negotiations for new tonnage were taking place. Some ships of the "Round Africa" service were ageing and three more one-class vessels were ordered.

They were based on the design of the *Bloemfontein Castle*, but were slightly smaller and were given geared turbines. The number of passengers to be carried was considerably reduced, the first two ships built being given accommodation for 530, the third for 556. A large proportion of the cabins were within the Cabin class range of fares; some one and two-bedded rooms with bath/shower were at higher rates. The lowest grade came within Tourist class rates.

Details:

*Rhodesia Castle*
*Kenya Castle*
*Braemar Castle*

All built by Harland & Wolff Limited, Belfast.

Measurements:

| | | | |
|---|---|---|---|
| Length: | 576 feet 6 inches oa | Tonnages: | 17,041; 17,041; 17,029 gt |
| | 540 feet bp | | 10,690; 10,660; 10,834 tdw |
| Breadth: | 74 feet 5 inches | | |

Engines: Six steam turbines developing 12,000 shaft horsepower double reduction geared to twin shafts. Speed 17½ knots.

There were four complete decks, a lower deck forward and aft of the machinery space, promenade deck and boat deck. Nine watertight bulkheads, all extending to the upper deck, divided the hull. The air-conditioned dining saloon, seating 280 passengers, was on the upper deck and on the promenade

The *Rhodesia Castle* at Dar es Salaam on her maiden voyage in 1951.

deck were the lounge, smoke room and library. A clubroom was on the bridge deck. Other air-conditioned areas were the hairdressing shop and hospital. Two masts were fitted and there was a single short funnel, later extended in height. Two cargo holds were forward and three aft of the machinery space with six 10-ton, four 5-ton and one 30-ton capacity derricks.

The first of the trio, *Rhodesia Castle*, was launched on 5th April, 1951, and made her maiden voyage from London on 18th October. The *Kenya Castle* was launched on 21st June, 1951, and completed her trials in February, 1952. She arrived at Southampton on the 18th of that month and left there on 7th

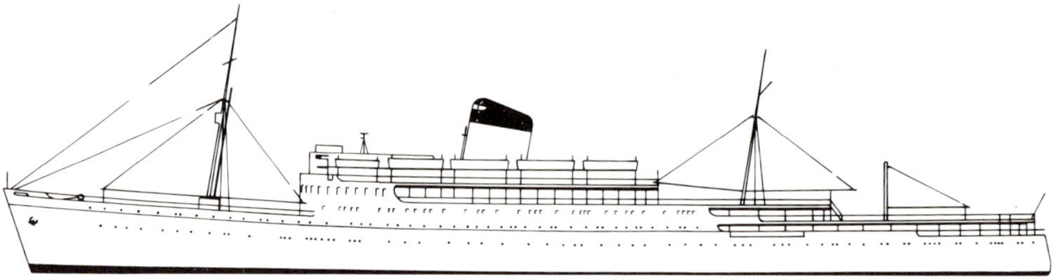

*Braemar Castle, Kenya Castle, Rhodesia Castle,* built 1951-52 and shown after addition of dome tops to the funnels in 1960-61.

March on a fourteen-day cruise to Lisbon, Las Palmas, Casablanca and Cadiz, proceeding back to London from where she sailed on her maiden "Round Africa" voyage on 31st March, via Suez to East and South Africa, returning via the Atlantic Isles.

The last of the trio, *Braemar Castle*, was launched on 24th April, 1952, by Mrs A. L. Geyer, wife of the High Commissioner in London for South Africa, and entered service on 20th November, 1952, sailing from London to South Africa via Las Palmas, Ascension and St Helena. The completion of this ship marked the completion of the Union-Castle's postwar building programme and the "Round Africa" service settled in, three ships circumnavigating Africa each way.

From London (via Suez) calling at Gibraltar, Marseilles, Genoa, Port Said, Port Sudan, Aden, Mombasa, Tanga, Zanzibar, Dar es Salaam, Beira, Lourenco Marques, Durban, East London, Port Elizabeth, Cape Town, St Helena, Ascension, and Las Palmas to London sailed the *Kenya Castle*, *Dunnottar Castle* and *Durban Castle*; and in the reverse direction (outwards via the west coast) sailed the *Rhodesia Castle*, *Braemar Castle* and *Warwick Castle*. Sailings from London were twice a month, one via the west coast and one via Suez.

The advent of these new ships caused surplus tonnage in the "Round Africa" service and in January, 1953, the *Llangibby Castle* joined the *Llandovery Castle* and *Bloemfontein Castle* in the intermediate run from London to Las Palmas, Cape Town, Port Elizabeth, East London, Durban, Lourenco Marques and Beira, where they turned southwards. The *Bloemfontein Castle* also included calls at Walvis Bay and Lobito.

But the *Llanstephan Castle*, built before the First World War, had now reached the end of her career, and in 1952 she was sold to the British Iron & Steel Corporation for breaking up.

*Llanstephan Castle*

Built by the Fairfield Shipbuilding & Engineering Company, Glasgow, 1914.

Measurements:

| | | | |
|---|---|---|---|
| Length: | 520 feet oa | Tonnages: | 11,346 gt |
| | 500 feet 6 inches bp | | 10,000 tdw |
| Breadth: | 63 feet 3 inches | | |

Engines: Quadruple expansion, twin screws. Speed 14 knots.

Launched on 29th August, 1913, the *Llanstephan Castle* made her maiden voyage shortly before the outbreak of the First World War. On her second homeward voyage from Durban just prior to the outbreak of hostilities she had reached the East African coast when information came that the German cruiser *Koenigsberg* was in those wasters. The *Llanstephan Castle* put in to Zanzibar and was then ordered back to Durban. From there she sailed via the west coast to the United Kingdom, replacing the *Kenilworth Castle*, which had been taken up as a troopship, on the mail service. She continued in this role until 1917 when she, too, was taken up under the liner requisition scheme, working as a transport until 1919.

With the end of the war she returned to the mail service, continuing in that service until the bigger ships were returned in 1920. From then on she was in the east coast service until 1925 when she joined the new *Llandovery Castle* on the "Round Africa" run which had been instituted in 1922. In 1938 she was converted to oil burning.

The *Llanstephan Castle* again became a troopship when the Second World War broke out, towards the end of the war being manned by the Royal Indian Navy and employed as a landing ship of the East Indies fleet. She returned unscathed to commercial service in 1947, carrying 220 First and 200 Tourist class passengers. She called at Southampton on 10th February, 1952, on her last homeward commercial voyage to London and then left London on 28th February, arriving at Cashmores, Newport, Mon., on 1st March for breaking up.

A sistership, *Llandovery Castle* was also built in 1914 by Barclay, Curle & Company, but she was torpedoed by submarine *U.86* on 27th June, 1918. These two ships were designed to meet the intense German competition on the intermediate service.

*Llanstephan, where Sir Owen Philipps was once Lord of the Manor, is in Wales. Llandovery Castle is in the market town of that name in Carmarthenshire.

When the *Kenya Castle* and *Braemar Castle* came into service some readjustment of the sailing schedules was necessary, and at the end of 1951 and beginning of 1952 two cruises were programmed for the *Warwick Castle*, the first cruises operated by Union-Castle for many years. The liner left London on the last day of the year for a fourteen-day cruise taking in Gibraltar, Casablanca, Las Palmas and Madeira, ending at Southampton on 14th January. The second had exactly the same itinerary, starting at Southampton on 16th January but returning to London.

Later in 1952 it was announced that the *Llandovery Castle*, second ship of that name and built in 1925, was to be withdrawn at the end of the year.

*Llandovery Castle*

Built by Barclay, Curle & Co. Ltd., Glasgow 1925.

Measurements:

| | | | |
|---|---|---|---|
| Length: | 487 feet oa | Tonnages: | 10,639 gt |
| | 471 feet bp | | 8,190 tdw |
| Breadth: | 61 feet 7 inches | | |

Engines: Quadruple expansion. Twin screws. Speed 14 knots.

Launched on 4th July, 1925, the *Llandovery Castle* was handed over on 25th September of the same year, the first ship completed after the 1914-18 war for the "Round Africa" service. She was designed to carry 221 First and 186 Third class passengers, but did not have the extra promenade deck of her namesake, lost in 1918.

During the Second World War she seems to have been a ship to attract enemy planes. Her first time as a target was on 23rd November, 1940, when she was at Southampton being converted to a hospital ship. During the blitz on the town she suffered serious damage which delayed conversion until the following March. She was then sent to the East African coast, ferrying sick and wounded from the East African campaign in Abyssinia and Eritrea to South Africa, and was again bombed at Suez in November, 1941, although not badly damaged. Moving to the Mediterranean, she was bombed three times on a voyage from Alexandria to Tobruk and again while at Tobruk. She was, indeed, the last hospital ship to leave Tobruk before it fell. In 1943 she took part in the Sicilian landings and the summer of 1944 saw her based at Southampton, ferrying wounded from Cherbourg and sometimes to Halifax, NS. She steamed some 250,000 miles as a hospital ship, carrying more than 38,000 sick and wounded.

The *Llandovery Castle* was released from Government service in September, 1946, and in May, 1947, re-inaugurated the "Round Africa" service. She arrived at London on 15th December, 1952, on her last voyage and was scrapped at Inverkeithing in 1953. A sistership, *Llandaff Castle*, was completed in 1926, but did not survive the war.

The *Braemar Castle* of 1952 outward bound in the English Channel. *Skyfotos*

In 1953 Britain celebrated the crowning of Her Majesty Queen Elizabeth II with magnificent pageantry. On 2nd June vast cheering crowds witnessed the colourful state processions to and from Westminster Abbey and millions more saw them through the medium of television. Throughout the land the people celebrated. Thirteen days later, on Monday, 15th June, hundreds of naval and merchant ships assembled in Spithead for the Royal Fleet Review and Union-Castle were proud to have their *Pretoria Castle* there as one of the largest representatives of the British Merchant Navy and carrying Government guests in what was to be the last Review which included a battleship, HMS *Vanguard.*

Coronation year, 1953, was also the centenary year for Union-Castle, the Southampton Steam Shipping Company, forerunner of the Union Steam Collier Company, having been formed in the summer of 1853.

As is so often the case, the beginnings were very small, but with gradual, sustained development the company had by 1953 grown to own a huge fleet of eight mail liners, eight liners on the London-based services, seven refrigerated fruit ships and three cargo ships—a total of twenty-six vessels aggregating some 411,000 gross tons, all employed in a magnificent service between the United Kingdom and South and East Africa. And two more cargo ships were building.

A double coincidence of the centenary year was that a Fleet Review had

The *Tantallon Castle* of 1954 working overside. Ahead of her is Houston Line's *Hesperia.*

also taken place in 1853, on 11th August, just as war with Russia was imminent. For the first time the Review, by Queen Victoria, included screw ships, although still built of wood. The Great Channel Fleet of six line-of-battle ships and seven frigates and corvettes, the flagship being the great four-deck, 131-gun, first rate line-of-battle ship *Duke of Wellington*, provided enormous interest.

The two new non-insulated cargo ships joined the fleet of Union-Castle in 1954. They were the first general cargo carriers to be built specially for the company for many years and were the first ships to be built for Union-Castle in their second century of trading. A shelter-deck type of vessel, the new type had a raked stem, rounded above the waterline, and cruiser stern. Eight watertight bulkheads divided the hull into nine watertight compartments. There were five main holds, three forward of the machinery space and two aft, all with corresponding 'tween decks. The holds were worked with one 80-ton, two 30, eight 10 and eight 5-ton tubular steel derricks.

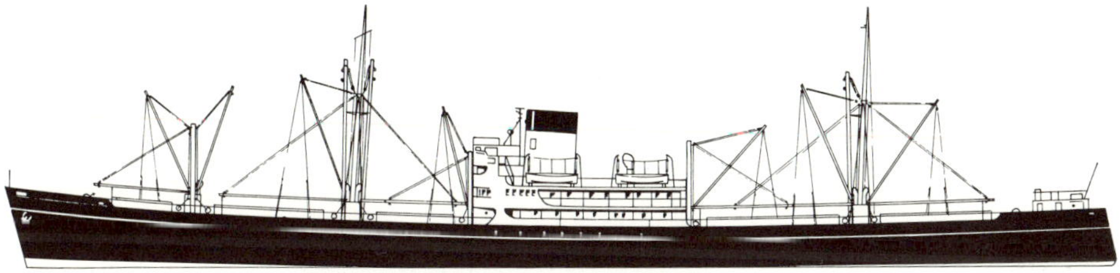

*Tantallon Castle* and *Tintagel Castle*.

Details:

*Tantallon Castle*
*Tintagel Castle*
Both by Harland & Wolff Limited, Belfast, 1954.

Measurements:

| | | | |
|---|---|---|---|
| Length: | 494 feet 7 inches oa | Tonnages: | /,448 gt |
| | 465 feet bp | | 10,840 tdw |
| Breadth: | 65 feet 10 inches | | |

Engines: Oil, single screw. Speed 16½ knots.

Accommodation was provided for twelve passengers in eight single and two double-berth cabins. A lounge was situated near the berths and a dining room on the shelter deck. A single deckhouse housed the passengers and crew.

The first to be launched was the *Tantallon Castle*,* on 22nd October, 1953, by Mrs S. Barr, wife of the company's General Manager; she was completed in March, 1954. She sailed on her maiden voyage on 11th March, 1954, loading at Continental ports and London, from where she sailed to South and East Africa on 2nd April, 1954.

The *Tintagel Castle*† was launched at the Victoria Yard of Harland & Wolff at Belfast on 4th February, 1954, by Mrs F. Keenlyside, wife of the General Manager designate of the Union-Castle Line. The ship was a landmark in the history of the yard in that the hull number was 1500, which represented the output of all the yards and associated companies of Harland & Wolff over ninety-six years. She left London on 11th June, 1954, on her maiden voyage.

At this time the company decided to adopt black hulls for their general cargo ships, as their pre-war cargo ships had been so painted, although the ships were now to have a white ribbon added, some two-thirds up from the boot-topping.

The motorship *Llangibby Castle*, employed for many years in the "Round Africa" service, leaving Cape Town.
*A. Duncan*

On 17th June, 1954, the *Llangibby Castle* called at Southampton on her last voyage to disembark passengers and discharge oranges and then sailed on to London to complete unloading before sailing to the breakers.

*This ship was the third *Tantallon Castle* in Union-Castle history. The first, a sailing ship, was built in 1865 for Donald Currie's Calcutta run, which she did outwards from London in 80 days and homewards in 78 as her best times. The first party of thirty-one Scottish emigrants was taken by this ship to Cape Colony in 1877. She was sold in 1883. The second ship of the name was a 5,636 gt. mail steamer, built in 1894, which in May, 1895, created a record in carrying 384 passengers to England, the largest number ever to travel in one ship on that route at that time. She was lost in May, 1901, when she ran aground on Robbin Island, off the Cape Peninsula. Tantallon Castle is near North Berwick, East Lothian, Scotland.

†The *Tintagel Castle* was the second ship of that name, the first being an intermediate steamer of 5,530 gt., built in 1896. She was sold to the Cie de Navigation Sud Atlantique in 1912 and was renamed *Liger*. Tintagel Castle, the reputed birthplace of King Arthur, was built on a ridge of rock connecting Tintagel Head with the mainland of Cornwall.

*Llangibby Castle*

Built by Harland & Wolff Limited, Glasgow, 1929.

Measurements:

| | | | |
|---|---|---|---|
| Length: | 507 feet oa | Tonnages: | 11,951 gt |
| | 485 feet 6 inches bp | | 12,039 gt (1947) |
| Breadth: | 66 feet 2 inches | | 8,465 tdw |

Engines: Oil. Twin screws. 15½ knots.

The *Llangibby Castle* was launched on 4th July, 1929, handed over on 21st November, 1929, and left London on her maiden voyage on 5th December, 1929, the first motorship in the "Round Africa" service. The choice of name of the Welsh castle Llangybi was made by Lord Kylsant. The ship's profile was hardly attractive, for her two squat motorship funnels were placed close together and well forward. She was designed to carry 250 First class passengers in midships accommodation and 200 Third class aft but, by public demand from passengers other than emigrants, the latter was reclassified Tourist in 1934.

The ship was quickly taken over as a troop transport when war broke out and 1940 saw her transporting South African troops to the war in East Africa. At the end of that year, on the night of 21st-22nd December, she suffered bomb damage in an air raid on Liverpool.

On 16th January, 1942, she was four days from the United Kingdom, loaded with troops for Singapore and in a heavy gale, when she was torpedoed by the submarine *U.402* in position 46.04N, 19.06W. Her stern, with aft gun and rudder, was blown away, but at a reduced speed of 9 knots she managed to reach Horta Bay in the Azores, after three days of being steered in erratic fashion by her propellers for some 700 miles.

She was allowed two weeks there, and although the submarines *U.402, U.572* and *U.581* were directed to her for the kill, she left on 2nd February and managed to reach Gibraltar in six days, after being towed part of the way. The submarine *U.581* was sunk on 2nd February by HMS *Westcott*. After an abortive wait of 57 days for a new rudder, she left for the United Kingdom, strengthened and strapped up aft and still steering erratically by her propellers. She reached her destination after six days, a voyage of some 3,400 miles behind her, without stern or rudder.

Back in service in 1942, the *Llangibby Castle* was in the North African campaign in the November and suffered some damage from gun batteries ashore. Then she became an assault ship for landings in Italy, was damaged in collision in Gibraltar, necessitating drydocking in the United Kingdom, and was fitted out as a landing ship, with eighteen landing craft, for D-day, when she landed Canadian troops on the beaches. Some seventy times she crossed the English Channel from and to Southampton with Allied servicemen and then went to the East, still as a troopship.

Some 300,000 miles of war service were behind her when she arrived at Harland & Wolff, Glasgow, in January, 1947. In July of that year she resumed the "Round Africa" service, on which she sailed for seven years. She left London on 28th June, 1954, for John Cashmore's yard at Newport, Mon., where she arrived early in July for breaking up.

## The fruit trade

South Africa's main trading ties lie with Great Britain. Imported from the United Kingdom are machines, vehicles, textiles, apparel, glassware, cement, drugs, chemicals, foodstuffs and all the other items that fall under the category of "general cargo". Exported from the Union are the many minerals and ores that are the riches of South Africa: and other major exports are wool, hides, wines and fruit. The latter can be classified as two types, deciduous fruits and the citrus type.

Most of the fruit exported to Britain has been discharged at Southampton, not only from the weekly mail ships but in the high fruit season from the London-based vessels, the R-class refrigerated motorships, Safmarine ships and Clan liners. Practically the whole of the deciduous fruits and two-thirds of the citrus fruits were received at the southern port.

There had not been much development in commercial fruitgrowing until the late 1880s, when a deputation of growers asked whether ships could be equipped with a cold chamber to take their products. The *Grantully Castle* of 1880 (3,454 gt.) was so equipped and left Cape Town for the United Kingdom with 320 boxes of grapes, but the trial was not a success and the idea was abandoned. Another attempt was made after experiments had been carried out as to the type of packing, temperature and storage needed and a small consignment of peaches was shipped in the *Drummond Castle* in special fruit chambers, arriving in fine condition in London in February, 1892. Slowly the trade developed and by 1907 some 10,000 cases of fruit were being exported annually.

The phenomenal growth of fruit exports to Britain can be gauged from the following figures:

| Deciduous fruit (packages) | 1910 | 1938 | 1953 | 1963 |
|---|---|---|---|---|
| Apples | 90 | 158,085 | 408,747 | 2,260,330 |
| Apricots | 3,383 | 98,136 | 114,490 | 21,108 |
| Grapes | 46,806 | 1,990,093 | 2,924,292 | 3,225,946 |
| Nectarines | 2,581 | 41,643 | 24,638 } | 307,536 |
| Peaches | 23,646 | 530,820 | 269,924 } | |
| Pears | 98,704 | 409,636 | 936,988 | 1,116,586 |
| Plums | 25,025 | 920,611 | 346,742 | 190,982 |
| **Citrus fruit (packages)** | | | | |
| Grapefruit | | 433,606 | 408,968 | 690,106 |
| Lemons | | 37,880 | 53,575 | 432,188 |
| Oranges | 10,387 | 2,717,231 | 3,639,376 | 2,860,943 |
| Tangerines | | 10,070 | 18,905 | 3,560 |

The refrigerated ship *Rochester Castle* of 1937 in the English Channel.

Deciduous fruits such as apples, apricots, grapes, peaches, nectarines, pears and plums arrived at Southampton from December to June, the South African season for these fruits being from November to May. The citrus fruit season lasts from May to October, the fruits being received up to Christmas.

Other fruits exported are fresh pineapples, melons and avocado pears and the dried fruit class of raisins, sultanas, currants, prunes, apricots and peaches.

In 1972 a total of 13 million packages of fruit were imported through Southampton from South Africa, representing 91% of all deciduous fruits and 54% of the citrus fruits shipped to the United Kingdom.

Another large export from South Africa is wool, the country being one of the five main producers of the world. It is exported to Europe, to Japan and to the United States, and most of that for the British market has been brought by Union-Castle ships through Southampton.

Records state that it was the Dutch East India Company which first imported sheep into South Africa in the mid-seventeenth century, for the indigenous animals there were of a non-wool type. Some small exports of wool were made at the turn of the century. The Merino breed was introduced to South Africa towards the end of the eighteenth century when a small flock was sent out from Holland, and other foundation stock came from Australia, France and Saxony to become the nucleus of some 40 million that were reckoned to be in the Union in the 1960s. The Merino breed of sheep, which originated in Spain, is noted for its long, fine, silky wool; the small flock which had been sent from Holland had itself been obtained from Spain.

In the 1960s, over 100,000 press-packed bales of wool were being discharged at Southampton from the Cape each year, each steel-banded bale weighing 215-300lb, the weight depending on whether the wool was in its natural state or had been "scoured" by having its natural lanoline grease content removed. The partly processed wool was known as "wool tops".

The wool was a regular shipment throughout the year, but heavier shipments were made during the shearing season. The heavier shipments, sometimes amounting to 8,000 bales, were received in England in the October-January period and were transported to London, to the West Country and to Bradford's woollen, worsted, rug and carpet industries. Some were transhipped to Antwerp, Rotterdam, Bordeaux and Germany in ships of the General Steam Navigation Company, while other shipments reached Dunkirk through the train ferry from Dover.

It is something of a paradox that only a short distance from the inward berth used by Union-Castle at Southampton stands a fourteenth-century woolhouse, now preserved and used as a shipping museum. Much English wool was actually exported through Southampton in the Middle Ages, and this trade was the basis of Southampton's early prosperity. At the woolhouse the wool was sampled, weighed and stored. The family of the Earls of Warwick held the hereditary rights to the custody of the weigh beam, which was farmed out to the highest bidder. Wool, once the largest export of the port, was eventually to become one of its largest imports.

The *Carnarvon Castle* leaving drydock at Southampton in April, 1954.

*Union-Castle*

CHAPTER FOUR

# British & Commonwealth

THE year 1955 undoubtedly ranks as the most important in Union-Castle history since the formation of the company in 1900. In the summer, the Government of South Africa renewed the mail contract for a further ten years, effective from 1st January, 1957.

The Union-Castle had ended their United States service in the early 1950s and on 4th October, 1955, a momentous announcement was made regarding a proposed merger of the Union-Castle Mail SS Company Limited and Clan Line Steamers Limited. The shareholdings in the two companies were to be acquired by a holding company, the British & Commonwealth Shipping Company Limited. The proposal had been a well-kept secret and had taken the London stock market completely by surprise. Indeed, only shortly before the announcement, rumours had been rife that the P & O SN Company were to acquire Union-Castle. After negotiations lasting several months the terms were finally agreed, effective on 31st January, 1956, and the two great companies were merged.

Comment was that both Boards had been far-seeing, for it was admitted that Union-Castle no longer dominated the African trade with which it had been linked for nearly a century and much would be gained from a combined fleet operating in other trade routes of the world. The merger would also give Union-Castle a link in the air, with Hunting & Son. There was also a ship replacement programme to be considered, for the three oldest liners, *Arundel*

*Castle*, *Carnarvon Castle* and *Winchester Castle*, were now thirty-four, twenty-nine and twenty-five years of age respectively.

The tonnage contribution to the merger was practically the same from each side. Taking in the Houston Line and Scottish Shire Line, the Clan contribution was fifty-seven ships of 428,000 gt. The Union-Castle Line, with Bullard, King and the King Line fleets, totalled forty-two ships.

The group could now be considered one of the giants of British shipping. The fleets at the end of 1955 were:

*Clan Line Steamers Limited.* (Managers: Cayzer, Irvine & Company Limited)

| Ships | |
|---|---|
| 48 | 48 Clan ships plus<br>*Clan Ross* (under construction) |
| | British & South American SN Company Limited (Houston Line (London) Limited) |
| | *Hesione*<br>*Hesperia*<br>*Hesperides*<br>*Hellenes*<br>*Herminius*<br>*Clan MacKinnon* |
| 6 | |
| | Turnbull, Martin & Company Limited (Scottish Shire Line Limited) |
| | *Perthshire*<br>*Lanarkshire*<br>*Stirlingshire* |
| 3 | |
| | *Argyllshire* (under construction) |
| — | |
| 57 | |
| — | |

*Union-Castle Mail SS Company Limited*

| Ships | |
|---|---|
| 27 | 27 Castle ships plus<br>*Pendennis Castle* (under construction) |
| | Bullard, King & Company Limited |
| | *Umtali*<br>*Umgeni*<br>*Umtata*<br>*Umzinto* |
| 4 | |
| | King Line Limited |
| 11 | 11 King ships |
| — | |
| 42 | |
| — | |

Note: The keel of the *Pendennis Castle*, Union-Castle's largest ever ship, ordered early in 1955, was laid down at Harland & Wolff's yard at Belfast on 28th November, 1955, for completion in 1958. The *Clan Ross* was launched on 17th January, 1956; the *Argyllshire* on 23rd May, 1956.

At Southampton, home terminal of the mail service, both inward and outward mail ships had used the berths at the southern point of the Old Docks (as they were then known, later in 1965 to be named Eastern Docks) since 1920. The inward ships berthed at Nos 35-36 Berths on the River Itchen quays and when discharged, moved round to Nos 38-39 Berths on the River Test quays to commence loading. The extreme berth at Dockhead, No. 37, was used for the feeder ships from Hamburg and Bremen until the war. In the middle of these berths, behind the respective sheds, were the Union-Castle dock offices and stores.

When the larger ships began to appear in the 1930s, these "Cape" berths, as they were known locally, reached saturation point and it was quite apparent that new accommodation would be needed. Tentative plans were made, only to be frustrated by the war, and when in 1948 even larger ships appeared and contracts were made to take the whole of South Africa's fruit trade for a number of years, new accommodation making possible quicker turn-round times to ensure a weekly service became imperative.

The obvious place was the New Docks (later Western Docks), and in 1953 a new building was started on the site of a former single storey shed at Berth No. 102, a shed which had been destroyed by bombs in 1940. In March, 1955, the outward sailing berth was transferred to Berth No. 104 and on 25th January, 1956, the new building at Berth No. 102, with waiting hall and buffet at its eastern end, was opened by His Excellency Mr G. P. Jooste, High Commissioner for the Union of South Africa, the first ship dealt with at the new terminal being the *Edinburgh Castle* on 10th February.

The first passenger liner to be ordered for the "Cape" run after the merger of Clan and Union-Castle, under the British & Commonwealth flag, was the *Windsor Castle*. Considerably larger than the *Pendennis Castle*, she was ordered in 1956 for completion in 1960, and at the time of announcing the order certain improvements were requested for the *Pendennis Castle*, building at Belfast. These included an increase in speed, to enable the voyage to Cape Town to be made in less than the thirteen and a half days then taken, and more space for both general and insulated cargo.

Two refrigerated ships, developments of the *Rustenburg Castle*, were also ordered in August, 1956, from the Greenock Dockyard Company, their allocated names being *Rotherwick Castle* and *Rothesay Castle*.

From January, 1957, it was decided that ships operating from Southampton were to have their masts painted white, and the first liner to wear this new colouring was the *Athlone Castle*.

In April, 1957, a unique record was set up by the *Arundel Castle* when she arrived at Southampton on the 12th at the end of her 200th voyage on the South African mail service. Her maiden voyage had taken place in April, 1921. In September, 1957, another unique occasion was celebrated. This was

Itchen Quays, Southampton, in June, 1950, showing from left to right *Durban Castle, Carnarvon Castle* and the Royal Mail liners *Alcantara* and *Andes*.

the centenary of Union-Castle associations with Southampton Docks in the South African trade, the first mail contract having been signed in September, 1857. The first sailing was made by the *Dane* on 15th September of that year.

But it was in December, 1957, that the more important event occurred. On the 9th of that month—and fittingly in the centenary year—the keel of the largest-ever Union-Castle liner, *Windsor Castle*, was laid. This time the company had placed the order with Cammell, Laird & Company Limited, of Birkenhead. The ship, the largest yet to be constructed on Merseyside, was to be ready in three years.

On the following day, arrangements had been made for the launching of the *Pendennis Castle* (see page 98).

There was a slogan at the time that every Thursday at 4 pm a Union-Castle vessel would sail from Southampton for South Africa, but in this particular year the regularity of sailings was broken during Christmas week, for as Boxing Day fell on a Thursday the sailing of the *Edinburgh Castle* was postponed until Friday, 27th December. For the first time for many years a Union-Castle liner arrived and another sailed on the same day.

## Boat trains

For many years boat trains to and from London and Southampton Docks had been titled at the top of each coach "Ocean liner express. Waterloo-Southampton Docks." As recognition of the ties between the shipping companies and the Port of Southampton these express trains began to be named in 1953, engine headboards being carried and in some instances adorned with an appropriate insignia, while carriage headboards were also given the name of the train. By the end of the year there were already "The

Cunarder", "Union-Castle Express", "South American" (Royal Mail Lines), "Statesman" (United States Lines), "Holland American" and, for the two British Rail cross-Channel services, "Normandy Express" and "Brittany Express". In 1957 it was decided to name all boat trains connecting with the Union-Castle mail service "The Springbok".

Early in 1958 it was announced that the *Dunnottar Castle* was to be withdrawn in August and offered for sale, having now become surplus to requirements in the "Round Africa" and intermediate services. She arrived at London on 5th August on her last voyage under the Union-Castle flag. Certain re-scheduling of London ships had necessarily to be made in mid-summer, and rather than have a liner tied lifeless to a London quay for two-three weeks, two ten-day cruises were arranged and quickly advertised at the start of the year. Indeed, good news coverage was given, for Union-Castle cruises were very rare. The *Rhodesia Castle*, the liner involved, left Tilbury in July for Gibraltar, Malaga, Casablanca and Lisbon, returning to Southampton, from where she sailed on the 28th on her second cruise to the same ports, returning to Tilbury on 7th August.

*Dunnottar Castle*

Built by Harland & Wolff Limited, Belfast, 1936.

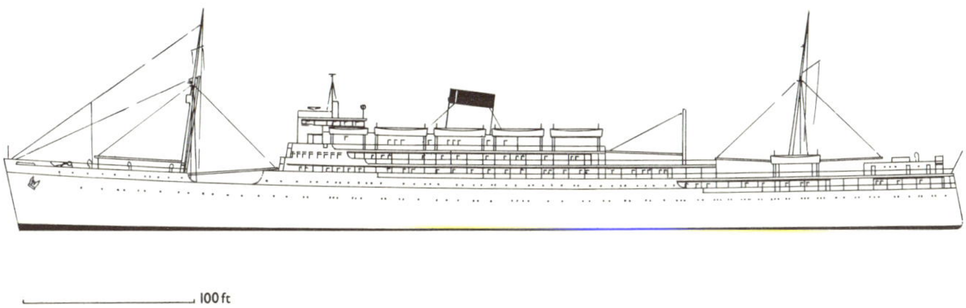


Measurements:

Length: 560 feet oa
540 feet bp

Breadth: 71 feet 10 inches

Tonnages: 15,004 gt
10,480 tdw

Engines: Oil. Twin screws. 18 knots.

The *Dunnottar Castle*,* launched on 25th January, 1936, was delivered in June, with a sistership, the *Dunvegan Castle*,† being delivered in the August. The two ships were larger than and of a different design from previous intermediate ships and could be classified as the forerunners of the intermediate ships that were to follow. The *Dunnottar Castle* was completed with accommodation for 260 First and 240 Tourist class passengers and had two open promenade decks. Her maiden voyage from London took place in July, 1936. Both vessels were motorships and speeds were comparable with the older Southampton mailships—Cape Town to Southampton within seventeen days. Indeed, they were used in that service when the large re-engining and modernisation programme was undertaken in the later 1930s.

The two ships returned to the London service just before the war and the *Dunnottar Castle*, loading in London, was requisitioned on 28th August and sent to Belfast for conversion to an armed merchant cruiser. She was given seven 6-inch and two 3-inch AA guns and commissioned on 14th October, 1939, as HMS *Dunnottar Castle* (Pennant F34), serving on escort duties in the South Atlantic in 1940. She was to have been converted to an escort carrier in 1942 but in June was altered to trooping, voyaging to Australia, India, North Africa and Sicily. These long voyages were interrupted after D-day when she became a cross-Channel transport from Southampton. By the time she was released from Government service in March, 1948, she had transported some 260,000 personnel and had sailed the same number of miles. After a refit, she emerged in February, 1949, with accommodation reduced to some 380 in two classes, making her first voyage on the 9th of that month. For nine years she circumnavigated Africa from London, outwards via Suez and home via the West coast.

In 1958 she was sold to Incres SS Company Limited, arriving in London in August on her last Union-Castle voyage. For a time the *Dunnottar Castle* was laid up in the South West India Dock and then, renamed *Victoria* and placed under the Liberian flag, she was towed from the Thames on 16th January, 1959, arriving two days later at Flushing, where some work was done on her. She went on to Dok-en-Werf Maatschappij Wilton-Fijenoord, Schiedam, where she arrived on 26th February, 1959, to begin a major conversion to a cruise liner. In conversion both masts, cargo handling gear, the bow and the stern were removed. New decks and a new bow and stern were built and her original Burmeister & Wain engines were replaced by two turbo-charged Fiat oil engines which gave her 18 knots. A large funnel, with mast attached, replaced the original and her accommodation was increased to 600 in one class. All this work was completed by 14th December, 1959, when she commenced cruising.

In October, 1964, she was transferred to the Victoria SS Company Limited, then owned by Einar A. Hansen, of Sweden, but she still flew the Liberian flag, with her cruises managed by the Incres Line. At the end of 1975 she was acquired at a U.S. Marshall's sale by the Phaidon Navigation Company (Chandris Inc), London, and in November was towed from New York to Piraeus by the tug *Heidi Moran*, arriving at the Greek port on 11th December. After refit she started cruising again on 6th June, 1976, under the Greek flag and the houseflag of the Victoria Shipping S.A. of Piraeus. In 1977 she moved again to Phaidon Navigation S.A. and was renamed *The Victoria*, under the Panamanian flag. Late in 1981 she moved to the Victoria Maritime Corp, and the Greek flag.

*Dunnottar Castle is just south of Stonehaven in Kincardineshire on the east coast of Scotland.
†Dunvegan Castle is on Dunvegan Bay, Isle of Skye.

The motorship *Dunnottar Castle* anchored in Dar es Salaam harbour.

The *Pendennis Castle* was handed over to Union-Castle on 14th November, 1958, and took on stores at Southampton preparatory to her maiden sailing on New Year's Day, 1959.

The liner's keel had been laid on 28th November, 1955, and she had been named by the Dowager Lady Rotherwick on 10th December, 1957, taking the water on the 24th of the same month, the delay being due to an industrial dispute.

The *Pendennis Castle* was the first of the Union-Castle ships to be fitted with Denny-Brown stabilizers, a late addition, for in order that this equipment could be fitted the ship had to be lengthened, although construction of the hull had already begun on the slipway. The original length of the ship was to have been 748 feet, but this was increased to 763 feet 3 inches. She was in fact quite a departure from the usual Union-Castle design, which dated back to the 1930s.

Another innovation was the bridge console, this being the first liner to be so fitted. Extending the width of the wheelhouse was the control panel, from which nearly all services of the ship could be controlled—steering gear, gyro compass, WT direction finder, lights, loud hailers, alarm bells to all parts of the ship, vent closure switches in case of fire, stabilizers, fourteen watertight doors and radio telephone. Also on the console were fitted smoke detection indicators, navigation light indicators, fault indicators for low voltage to engine room telegraphs and repeaters, and gyro-compass fault indicators.

*Pendennis Castle,* built 1958.

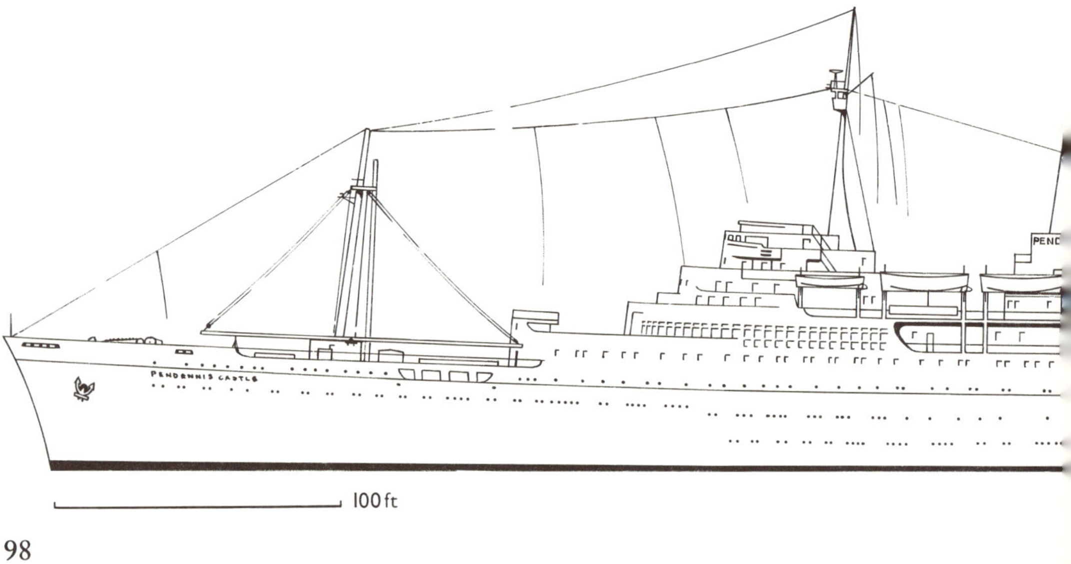

The liner's hull had a raked stem and cruiser stern, and amidships was a streamlined funnel and signal mast.

Accommodation on the *Pendennis Castle* was in two classes; for 167 First class passengers in single and two-berth cabins and for 475 passengers in two, three and four-berth cabins in Tourist class. Twenty-two interchangeable cabins could increase the First class number to 200 or Tourist to 541.

The First class dining saloon was built to seat 228, and on each side the floor was raised to accommodate a number of tables which offered a sense of spaciousness. The decor was of shades of pale grey, the upholstery of grey, green and pink. A portrait of Lord George Churchill, Admiral of the Blue, who commanded two successive seventeenth-century warships, the *Pendenis*, a 70-gun third rate built at Chatham in 1679, and the *Windsor Castle*, carrying 90 guns, a second rate, built at Woolwich in 1678, was hung on a main panel. A private dining room where small party functions could be held was built adjacent to the main room and was ornamented, furnished and hung with paintings all of Louis XV style. From the dining room, a wide staircase led to the First class main entrance hall where there were hairdressing salons, a shop and the bureau.

On the promenade deck were situated the First class lounge, a smoke room abaft the lounge and card/writing room and library. The lounge had a dance floor and was also used as a cinema. A feature of the lounge was a huge screen of "Filigrana" glass, specially made by Venetian craftsmen and set in a frame

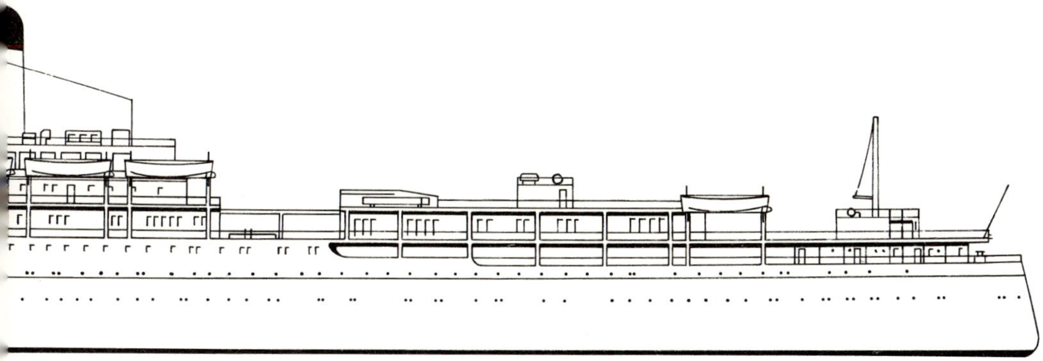

of polished brass. On each side were tall windows with mauve curtains harmonising with the coral pink, green and yellow upholstery and with the specially woven carpet in shades of soft green.

The smoke room was panelled in pine in the Georgian style and there was an antique fireplace and bar. The upholstery was in lacquer red and hunting green. A First class lido was abaft the principal deckhouse on the promenade deck and was arranged in a crescent around three sides of the swimming pool. On either side, the deck was raised to form terraces for chairs and tables. The lido bar, a wide room with folding glazed screens separating it from the swimming pool, was decorated with bamboo and split cane. The pool was equipped with a device to prevent excessive water movement and was lined with glass mosaic shaded from light blue to deep turquoise. The same colours were given to a glass mosaic forming the wide walkway surrounding the pool.

In the Tourist accommodation the dining room seated 277 and featured a mural painting of a Cape vineyard. The lounge on E deck was also used as a cinema. The lido was divided from the pool by screens which could be folded away in warmer weather. The pool was given tiles of blue, white and yellow, these colours also being selected to decorate the lido.

For the carrying of cargo, three holds were situated forward and four aft of the machinery space, with corresponding cargo 'tween decks to the underside of B deck. General cargo was allocated to Nos 1, 2, 5, 6 and 7 lower holds, the remaining holds and 'tween deck spaces being insulated for deciduous and

The rebuilt *Arundel Castle* of 1921 at Cape Town.

citrus fruits, with some compartments equipped for chilled and frozen produce.

Propelling machinery consisted of double reduction geared turbines driving twin screws. Speed was 22 knots.

Details:

Built by Harland & Wolff Limited, Belfast.

Measurements:

| | | | |
|---|---|---|---|
| Length: | 763 feet 3 inches oa | Tonnages: | 28,453 g |
| | 716 feet bp | | 15,976 dw |
| Breadth: | 83 feet 10 inches | | |

*Pendennis Castle, one of several castles built on the south coast by Henry VIII in 1543 for protection against attacks by the French, was provided for the defence of Falmouth Harbour.

The *Pendennis Castle* was a replacement for the *Arundel Castle*, the last liner afloat that had been built with four funnels, although for some twenty years of her life she had carried only two. Thirty-eight years old, she was withdrawn from service in December, 1958, at the same time as the *Pendennis Castle* arrived at Southampton to take her place in the mail service.

*Arundel Castle*

Built by Harland & Wolff Limited, Belfast, 1921.

Measurements:

| | | | |
|---|---|---|---|
| Length: | 630 feet 6 inches bp | Tonnages: | 18,980 gt |
| Breadth: | 72 feet 6 inches | | 19,118 gt (1937) |
| Length: | 686 feet oa (1937) | | |
| | 661 feet 3 inches bp (1937) | | |

Engines: Six steam turbines, single reduction geared to twin shafts. 20 knots.

The *Arundel Castle* was, at first, to have been named *Amroth Castle*. The hull was laid down at Belfast on 11th November, 1915, but with war construction taking precedence and indecision as to whether to complete the ship as a troop transport or an auxiliary cruiser, she was not launched until 11th September, 1919.

At that time four-funnelled ships were certainly not new, but the *Arundel Castle* was the first in the Union-Castle fleet and bore not the slightest resemblance to any previous Union-Castle vessels. Apart from the four tall, thin funnels, one of which was a dummy, she was given a straight stem, a cruiser stern and an arrangement of gantry davits abaft the fourth funnel for lifeboats which were stored inboard. She was also half as big again, in tonnage, as the previous flagship, *Balmoral Castle*. Accommodation was provided for 234 First, 362 Second and 274 Third class passengers, plus a number in open berths, if required.

For propulsion she was given geared turbines, being the first ship so equipped in the fleet. She burned coal, and her speed was no greater than that of pre-First World War ships. She was, however, the largest steamer sailing to the Cape from

Southampton. The *Arundel Castle* left Southampton on her maiden voyage at 4 pm on Friday, 22nd April, 1921, and arrived at Cape Town on 9th May, this sailing time having been introduced when the postwar service was resumed in October, 1919. The same 4 pm sailing time was fixed for departure from Cape Town, and this rigid schedule continued for many years. It was said that one's watch could be set by the departure of these ships.

In the following year the sistership *Windsor Castle* was delivered by John Brown & Company, Clydebank. Replacing the *Carisbrook Castle* (7,626 gt, 1898), temporarily in the mail service, and *Kinfauns Castle* (9,664 gt, 1899), which were broken up in 1922 and 1927 respectively, both she and the *Arundel Castle* settled down in the mail service. In the afternoon of 27th June, 1924, the *Arundel Castle* was the first ship to use the new 60,000-ton capacity floating dock at Southampton after its official opening in the morning by the Prince of Wales. Then nothing untoward happened until November, 1926, when the *Arundel Castle* collided with the small Cardiff-owned coastal collier *Maud Llewellyn* (1,454 gt, 1921) off Hook Buoy, Southampton Water. Both ships were outward bound, but there was no serious damage. The *Arundel Castle* was included in the huge modernisation programme undertaken by Union-Castle in the 1930s and was re-engined and lengthened to meet the requirements of the planned sixteen-and-a-half to fourteen days accelerated service. She left for Belfast in January, 1937, and emerged some nine months later with an entirely new profile; apart from lengthening, she had only two, widely spaced, funnels. The aft lifeboat davit gantry arrangement had also disappeared. A slightly curved stem enhanced her profile and she and her sistership, *Windsor Castle*, came to be regarded as the most handsome ships of the fleet. Four new watertube boilers replaced the single-ended versions and fed the new geared turbines which were connected to twin screws to achieve the necessary 20 knots.

The accommodation had been adjusted. The old Second and Third class accommodation had been combined, and an extra smoke room added on the boat deck for use of the new Tourist class passengers. The grouping was now 219 First, 167 Second and 194 Tourist class, although some cabins were interchangeable.

The *Arundel Castle* returned to the mail service in October, 1937, but when war broke out she was quickly taken over as a troopship, voyaging to North Africa and to the Sicilian landings and making some voyages under diplomatic immunity, repatriating Allied prisoners of war from Germany via Sweden and from Marseilles to Liverpool.

The last of the Union-Castle liners to be released by the Government, she did not return to the mail service until September, 1950, after a general overhaul by her builders, during which her accommodation was again adjusted to 164 First and 371 Tourist class.

On Friday, 5th December, 1958, she left Cape Town on her 211th and final voyage and some 10,000 people gathered at the Docks to see her go. Ships in port sounded their customary farewells and dipped ensigns, tugs formed an accompanying flotilla and aircraft dipped in salute. It has been a long, long tradition with the people of South Africa that liners sail festooned with streamers—but this was something different.

She arrived at Southampton on 19th December and left again on the 30th for Kowloon to be broken up after a career of thirty-seven and a half years, during which she had steamed 2,850,000 miles in peace and 625,565 as a troopship.

*Arundel Castle stands on a declivity of a hill overlooking the River Arun in Sussex.

There is hardly anything romantic about a shipbreaker's yard, where once-proud ships lie as rusting hulks awaiting the cutters' torches and where scrap pieces of all shapes and sizes, unrecognisable as featured parts of a ship, are strewn around in contribution to scenic defilement. But, as part of the record, it should be stated that at the time of her demolition, the *Arundel Castle* was the largest ship to have been scrapped in Hong Kong. The shipbreaking company that broke her up also owned a clock-making factory, and metal from the 19,000-ton ship undoubtedly went into the manufacture of alarm clocks!

On arrival at Hong Kong the entire contents of the ship, including paintings, were auctioned and the fittings removed. Then she was taken to Gin Drinkers Bay, picturesque in itself, a deep water graveyard where ships lie offshore, awaiting their turn to be cut down until only the hull remains, before being hauled on to the beach for final demolition.

Labour was by two-men gangs, working on piece-rates and together earning a fair daily wage, although the introduction of machinery was then becoming a factor in the number of working gangs.

Six months was regarded as sufficient time to strip a 6,000-ton ship. At the time there were ten rolling mills working in Hong Kong producing steel bars from scrapped ships, some going to thriving local industry and some going for export.

In mid-summer the war-built *Drakensburg Castle* was sold for breaking up at Hong Kong, where she arrived on 5th August. Just after that there came a surprise announcement that after only nine years of service the *Bloemfontein Castle* was to be sold to the Greek shipowners A. J. & D. J. Chandris, who were to place her with their newly-formed Grammi Ellados-Afstralias SA (National Greek Australian Line). The ship had been built for an expected expansion in emigrant traffic which did not materialise, and Union-Castle decided that she could no longer be usefully employed on the London, west coast of Africa and Beira route.

The ship came into the news early in 1953 when the Holland-Africa liner *Klipfontein* (10,555 gt, 1939) struck a submerged object two and a half miles off Zavora lighthouse, south of Cape Corrientes, on 8th January and sank, her complement of 116 passengers and 118 crew being rescued by the *Bloemfontein Castle*. On 9th November, 1959, the *Bloemfontein Castle* arrived at London on her final voyage under Union-Castle colours and was sent to North Shields for a quick refit to suit her for the new Mediterranean-Australian emigrant trade, in which she was to carry 1,400 passengers in inexpensive accommodation. Renamed *Patris* and flying the Greek flag, she made her inaugural sailing on 14th December, 1959, from Piraeus to Australia.

She was again in the news in February, 1975, when she was chartered by the Australian Federal Government for nine months as a floating hotel and became home for thousands of people made homeless by hurricane "Tracy", which had devastated most of Darwin's buildings on the previous Christmas Day. In 1976 she was converted to carry 260 cars in a service between Patris and Italy, and in 1980 was again sold, to the Karageorgis Company, renamed *Mediterranean Island* and, later, *Mediterranean Star*.

Two refrigerated ships were built in the last years of this decade, but they differed greatly from the other R-class ships in the fleet. Each had three decks, with midship deckhouse and fo'c's'le. There were five cargo holds, three forward and two aft of the machinery space, and ten 'tween deck compartments. Of the 469,000 cubic feet of cargo capacity, 450,000 cubic feet was insulated for the carriage of perishable cargo. To enable general cargo to be carried outwards there were larger hatch coamings and at Nos 2 and 4 holds there were 40-ton capacity derricks, with sixteen others between 5 and 10-ton capacity.

The first of the pair, *Rotherwick Castle*, was launched by Lady Rotherwick, wife of the Deputy Chairman of the British & Commonwealth Shipping Company, and the ship left Middlesbrough on her maiden voyage to Beira on 30th December, 1959. The *Rothesay Castle* was launched on the

The cargo ship *Rothesay Castle*, completed in 1960, outward bound in the English Channel.

same day that her sistership began her maiden voyage, 30th December, and left Hamburg on her maiden voyage to Cape Town on 31st July, 1960.

Details:

*Rotherwick Castle*
*Rothesay Castle*
Built by the Greenock Dockyard Company Limited.

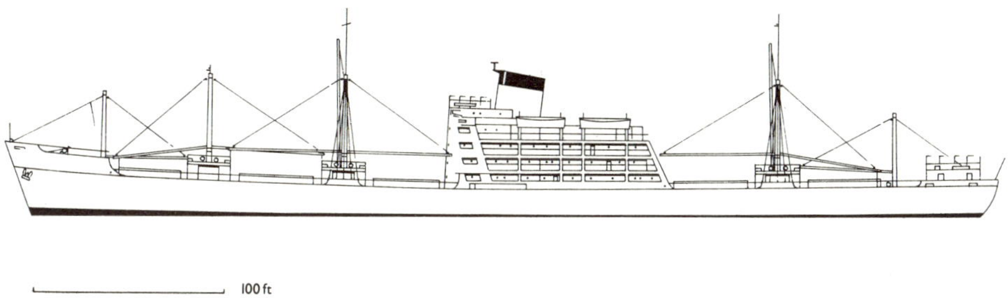

Measurements:

| | | | |
|---|---|---|---|
| Length: | 519 feet 10 inches oa | Tonnages: | 9,360 gt |
| | 480 feet bp | | 10,240 tdw |
| Breadth: | 66 feet | | |

Engines: Six cyl. 2-stroke single acting oil engine, 9,500 bhp. Speed 17 knots.

With the completion of these two vessels there were nine R-class (refrigerated) ships in the fleet. They could be split, roughly, into three types:

a) five built prior to 1946:

| | | | |
|---|---|---|---|
| *Roslin Castle* | 1935 | *Richmond Castle* | 1944 |
| *Rochester Castle* | 1937 | *Roxburgh Castle* | 1945 |
| *Rowallan Castle* | 1943 | | |

all of which could be recognised in profile with fo'c's'le and a split superstructure.

*Rochester Castle*, built 1937

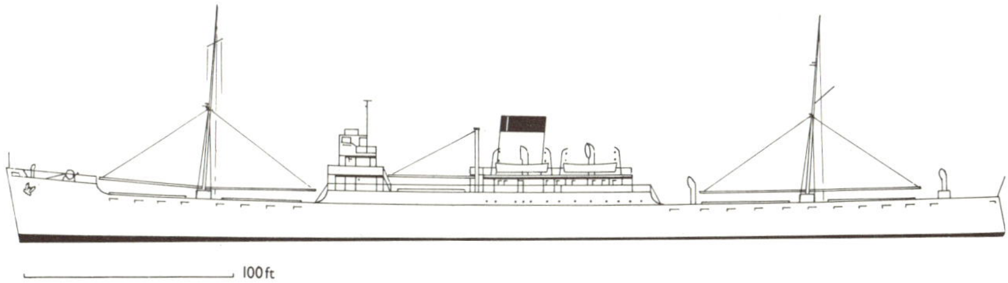

b) two constructed just after the war

*Rustenburg Castle* 1946 and *Riebeeck Castle* 1946

which were similar to (a), but had a composite structure on the bridge deck

*Riebeeck Castle* and *Rustenburg Castle*, built 1946.

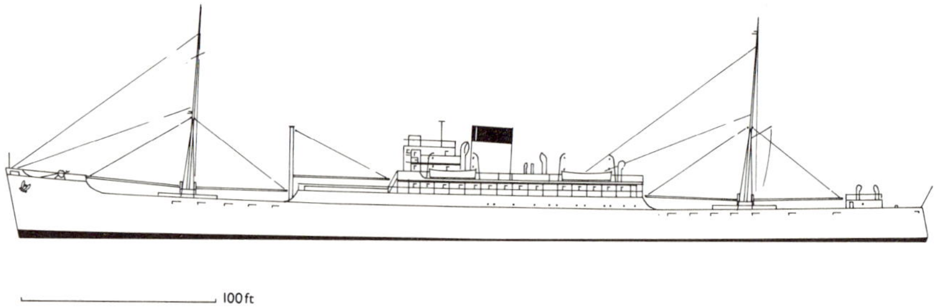


*Rotherwick Castle* and *Rothesay Castle*

c) which had a built-up superstructure, three holds forward and two aft of the machinery space, three sets of kingposts, two forward and one aft, and eighteen derricks ranging from 5 to 40 tons capacity. The *Rotherwick Castle* had a slightly shorter funnel.

Since 21st August, 1936, when the *Stirling Castle* had introduced the accelerated service, the time taken from Southampton to Cape Town had been thirteen and a half days. Now it was envisaged that the run would be cut by two days. To be enabled to do this the company, of course, required faster ships. Already the *Pendennis Castle* was in service and there were to be two more large passenger ships replacing the older motorships of the 1930s era. It was intended that seven ships would eventually replace the eight currently in service at the end of the 1950s.

The *Windsor Castle* was the second of the three liners planned. Her keel was laid down on 9th December, 1957, and on 23rd June, 1959, she was launched with a bottle of South African sparkling wine by Queen Elizabeth, the Queen Mother. The ship arrived at Southampton on 17th July, 1960, two days early, owing to the cancellation of an inaugural cruise due to a seamen's dispute. Her maiden voyage began on 18th August.

She was the first liner to be ordered for the mail run after the formation of the British & Commonwealth Shipping Company, and was the largest liner ever to be so employed. In fact she was the largest passenger vessel constructed in a British yard since Cunard's *Queen Elizabeth*. Passenger accommodation was provided for 191 First and 591 Tourist class passengers, although some cabins were interchangable.

With changing conditions and the upward trend in the standard of living since the war, more and more people were seeking travel abroad. It was expected by them that their holiday would begin at the gangway. In recognising this changing pattern, Union-Castle had the *Windsor Castle* designed for a high standard in both classes. An innovation was A deck which, apart from an area on the starboard side for First Class *de luxe* accommodation, was for Tourist class facilities from stem to stern.

The lounge, on two levels, was forward of the bridge, overlooking the sun deck. Then, on the port side, were the library and a suite of three rooms in a row—the writing room, Rotunda Room and the bar. The Tourist class covered promenade and dance deck extended the width of the ship, and then there came the lido with its cafe, which surrounded the swimming pool. The First class public rooms were on the Promenade Deck, with the lounge forward. Here was a raised dais, and placed behind the orchestra stage was a beautiful glass aviary, designed by Lin Tissot. Surrounding a dance floor in the lounge were four sets of three columns in Graeco-Roman fluted style. On the starboard side were drawing room, card room and library and then aft, the First class Verandah Cafe, overlooking the swimming pool and games deck. Deck B was an accommodation deck, C deck was part accommodation but also had shops, hospital and hairdressing salons. The cinema, seating 300, was also on this deck. Both dining rooms were situated on D deck, the First

When delivered in 1960 the *Windsor Castle* became flagship of the Union-Castle fleet.

class with a small annexe for parties up to twelve persons being placed forward and the Tourist dining room aft, with the galley in between.

All cabins, both passenger and crew, were air-conditioned, as were the dining rooms and cinema. A flying staircase curved downwards to the First class dining room, entered through a cherry-red carpeted lobby and wide glass doors. At the end of the room were large murals, the centre one of Windsor Castle by daylight being flanked by others of St George's Chapel and the River Thames, near Windsor, by moonlight.

For the carrying of cargo a refrigerated capacity of 352,000 cubic feet was provided for fruit and other perishable goods and a further 271,000 cubic feet for general cargo. There was also garage space for twenty-six cars. A deck crane of 2-tons lift capacity, placed well forward, and two derricks, each of 10-ton capacity, aft comprised the cargo handling gear. Power-operated hatch covers with push button control were fitted to the seven holds.

Two new devices designed to protect the hull from fouling and corrosion were fitted. The hull was surrounded by holed plastic piping through which compressed air and bubbles of poisonous liquid were discharged, the hull then becoming thinly coated with the poisonous mixture, harmless to fish but destroying the organisms which cause fouling. To fight corrosion, small dome-like shapes of cast magnesium were studded about the hull to attract

*Windsor Castle*, built 1960.

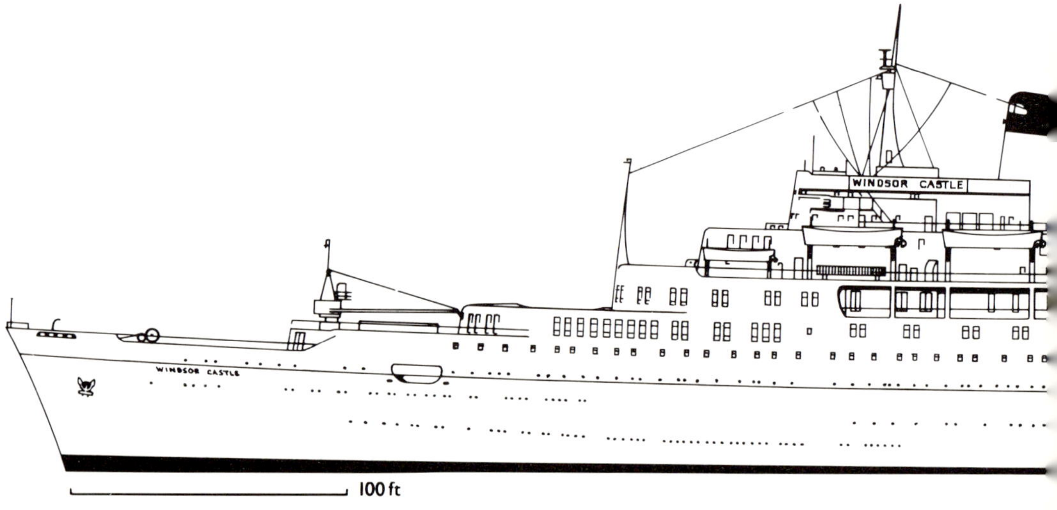

the particles in the sea water which cause corrosion. As the domes waste away a protective electrostatic field is set up, protecting the steel.

For propulsion the *Windsor Castle* was given high-pressure steam turbines developing 45,000 shp, geared to twin screws and giving 23 knots.

Details:

Built by Cammell, Laird & Company (Shipbuilders & Engineers) Limited, Birkenhead.

Measurements:

| | | | |
|---|---|---|---|
| Length: | 783 feet 1 inch oa | Tonnages: | 36,123 gt |
| | 730 feet bp | | 16,252 tdw |
| Breadth: | 92 feet 6 inches | | |

*She was the third *Windsor Castle*. The first, built in 1872, was for Donald Currie's Indian trade, but she sailed in the Cape run from the following year until wrecked on a reef near Dassen Island, some 30 miles NNW of Cape Town, on 19th October, 1876. The second *Windsor Castle* (18,967 gt), built in 1922, was torpedoed and sunk by aircraft off Cape Tenes on 23rd March, 1943.

The *Windsor Castle* replaced the *Winchester Castle*. The last voyage of the motorship began from Southampton on 11th August, 1960, and on her return on 23rd September she was withdrawn and sold to Japanese breakers, arriving at Mihara on 5th November, 1960.

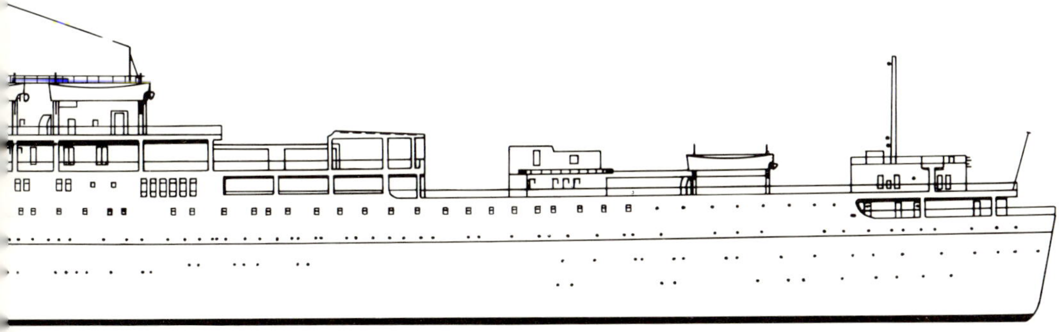

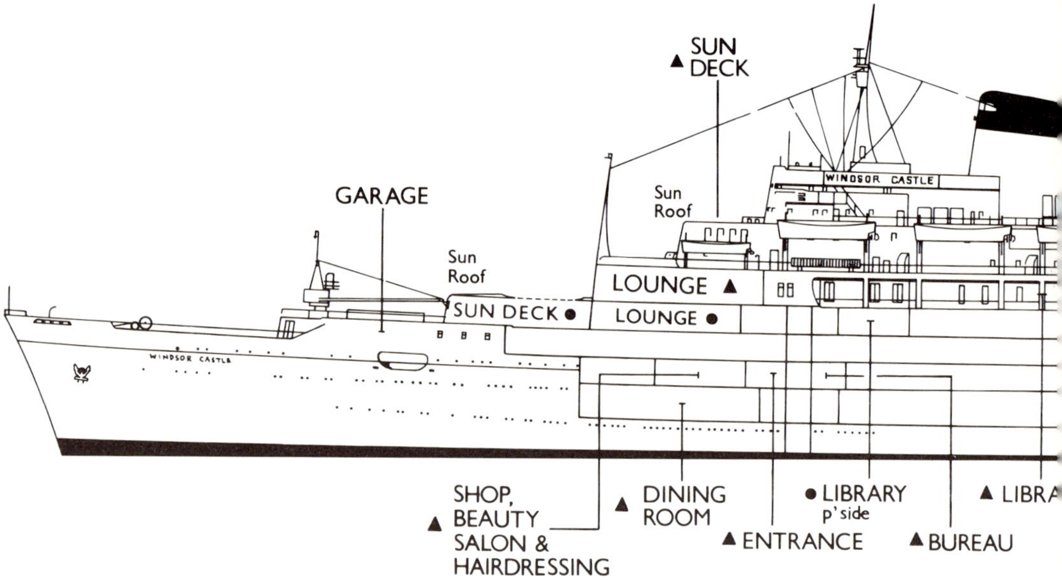


WINDSOR CASTLE

*Winchester Castle*

Built by Harland & Wolff Limited, Belfast.

Measurements:

| | | | |
|---|---|---|---|
| Length: | 657 feet 5 inches oa | Tonnages: | 20,109 gt (as built) |
| | 631 feet 6 inches bp | | 20,001 gt (1938) |
| Breadth: | 75 feet 6 inches | | 12,425 tdw (1938) |

Engines: Two ten-cylinder oil engines (1938) 20 knots.

The second motorship in the fleet, the *Winchester Castle* was launched on 19th November, 1929, and was delivered in October, 1930, sailing on her maiden voyage on the 24th of that month. Her initial accommodation was for 260 First, 241 Second and 250 Third class passengers. At the start she was given two rather squat funnels, but after new engines of 26,000 bhp were installed in 1938, giving her a speed of 20 knots, she returned with only one funnel with a far more graceful rake. She and her sistership *Warwick Castle* were not lengthened, and she retained her original straight stem after being re-engined.

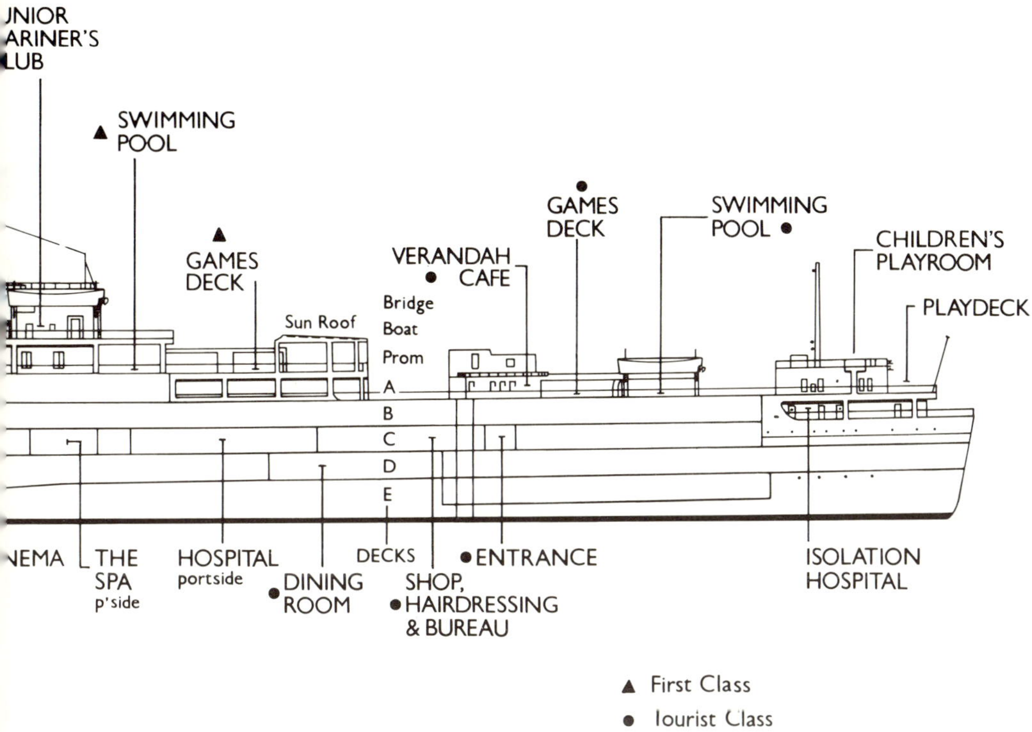


Early in the war the *Winchester Castle* was requisitioned as a troopship, and then in 1941-42 served as a training ship for assault troops in Loch Fyne. In May, 1942, she took part in the Madagascar landings as a Landing Ship (Infantry) and two months later, on 22nd July, rescued the crew of the American cargo ship *Honolulan* (7,493, 1921) of the American Hawaiian SS Company, which had been sunk by enemy action in the North Atlantic. She took part in the North African landings in November, 1942, and landed troops in the south of France in August, 1944.

After the war the *Winchester Castle* was released by the Government in 1946 and worked as an emigrant ship, carrying some 1,300 emigrants each voyage, and did not go to her builders for refitting until 1948. She was then given a substantial refit, many alterations being made to the accommodation, the original Second class being rebuilt and enlarged for Tourist passengers. A feature which was much admired was a replica of King Arthur's table placed in the First class smoke room. After her refit she had accommodation for 186 First and 400 Tourist class passengers.

Her first voyage after reconditioning began on 22nd September, 1949, and she continued in service until September, 1960, when she was sold to Japanese shipbreakers.

At the end of 1960 the fleet consisted of

Mailships (in sailing sequence)

| | Built | | Built |
|---|---|---|---|
| *Edinburgh Castle* | 1948 | *Pretoria Castle* | 1948 |
| *Carnarvon Castle* | 1926 | *Capetown Castle* | 1938 |
| *Windsor Castle* | 1960 | *Pendennis Castle* | 1958 |
| *Stirling Castle* | 1936 | *Athlone Castle* | 1936 |

"Round Africa" ships

| | | | |
|---|---|---|---|
| *Durban Castle* | 1938 | *Rhodesia Castle* | 1951 |
| *Warwick Castle* | 1939 | *Braemar Castle* | 1952 |
| | | *Kenya Castle* | 1952 |

Refrigerated ships

| | | | |
|---|---|---|---|
| *Roslin Castle* | 1935 | *Riebeeck Castle* | 1946 |
| *Rochester Castle* | 1937 | *Rustenburg Castle* | 1946 |
| *Rowallan Castle* | 1943 | *Rotherwick Castle* | 1959 |
| *Richmond Castle* | 1944 | *Rothesay Castle* | 1960 |
| *Roxburgh Castle* | 1945 | | |

Cargo ships

| | | | |
|---|---|---|---|
| *Kenilworth Castle* | 1944 | *Tantallon Castle* | 1954 |
| | | *Tintagel Castle* | 1954 |

On the east coast and in Central Africa the political wind of change which had started as a gentle breeze in the late 1950s was beginning to blow much stronger at the turn of the decade. On 1st July, 1960, the Belgian Congo became an independent state. The great change had begun, and gradually a programme evolved for the self government of each colony. On the west coast Ghana became a republic on 1st July, 1960, and in the same month France handed over the Ivory Coast and other West African colonies; on 1st July, 1960, the Somali Republic came into being and on 9th December, 1961, Tanganyika became an independent state within the Commonwealth, becoming a republic a year later. Aden acceded to the Federation of Saudi Arabia in January, 1963, and on 1st February that year Nyasaland became a self-governing Protectorate, achieving independence as the State of Malawi eighteen months later, on 6th July, 1964. Both Kenya and Zanzibar became self-governed in June, 1963, both becoming independent within the Commonwealth in the following December; and Northern Rhodesia became the independent republic of Zambia in October, 1964.

Over many years the British colonies had been administered by Colonial Officers, many of whom were from Britain. Their terms of service included

The balcony of the First class lounge on the motorship *Winchester Castle*. *Union Castle*

periods of home leave every two or three years, and it was these officers and their families who helped to fill the passenger accommodation of the Union-Castle "Round Africa" ships. But all this was now to be altered. Many were packing their bags for the last time, and those who continued to serve had to agree to new conditions of service, with shorter tours of service and shorter home leave. Use of the aeroplane was encouraged. And the airlines also carried the tourist and holidaymaker at competitive fares, an ever-increasing number booking package tours. The downward trend in sea travel had begun. The passenger-carrying ship was the victim.

In 1961 the "Round Africa" service was maintained by the *Warwick*

*Castle*, *Kenya Castle* and *Rhodesia Castle*, sailing via the Suez Canal and the east coast, returning to the United Kingdom via the west coast; and by the *Durban Castle* and *Braemar Castle*, sailing in the reverse direction. Of these ships, the *Durban Castle* and *Warwick Castle* carried passengers in First and Tourist classes, the others being Cabin-class vessels only.

The *Braemar Castle* made a fifteen-day Easter Mediterranean cruise beginning on 25th March, 1961, and this was repeated on 21st October. Just after this it was announced that the two older ships, *Durban Castle* and *Warwick Castle*, were to be withdrawn in the following year, the first-named in April, the *Warwick Castle* in June. This was the end of the "Round Africa" service, and from April, 1962, when the *Kenya Castle* sailed from London, the route was advertised as the intermediate East Coast service. Ports of call from London were Gibraltar, Genoa, Port Said, Suez, Aden, Mombasa, Zanzibar, Dar es Salaam, Beira (with passengers only) and Durban—there to turn north again with additional calls at Lourenco Marques (alternate ships), Tanga, Naples and Marseilles, the last two ports being with alternate ships. The round voyage was scheduled for thirty-three days.

Once a year, leaving London in January, a ship made a complete voyage round Africa, outwards via Suez. Apart from this, however, it was still possible to circumnavigate Africa on Union-Castle ships, for the intermediate liners were scheduled to arrive at Durban on Tuesdays, sailing northwards again on Thursdays, while the mail ship also arrived on Tuesdays and sailed southwards again on Thursdays, allowing passengers to tranship without having to spend a night ashore.

The cessation of the "Round Africa" service meant that the London-based ships would no longer be able to call at St Helena and Ascension, but arrangements were made for the mailships *Edinburgh Castle* and *Pretoria Castle* to call at the islands, both northbound and southbound on some voyages, with cargo ships calling in between so that a six-weeks service could be maintained.

The *Durban Castle* and *Warwick Castle* (originally named *Pretoria Castle*), ordered in January, 1937, and completed just before the outbreak of war, were to be the last motorships constructed for the London service. They were very similar to the *Dunnottar Castle* and *Dunvegan Castle* of 1936, but were a little longer and wider, each having three holds forward of the machinery space and two aft. The 'tween decks had insulated space for 178,000 cubic feet. In the *Dunnottar Castle* and *Dunvegan Castle* there were two open promenade decks, but in the later ships the lower promenade deck was abolished, the plating thus being one deck higher and the cabin accommodation on that deck built out to the full width of the ship. Accommodation, when built, was for 220 First and 330 Tourist class passengers.

*Durban Castle*

Built by Harland & Wolff Limited, Belfast.

Measurements:

| | | | |
|---|---|---|---|
| Length: | 594 feet 7 inches oa | Tonnages: | 17,382 gt |
| | 560 feet bp | | 10,802 tdw |
| Breadth: | 76 feet 5 inches | | |

Engines: Two eight-cylinder Diesels. Twin screws. 18 knots

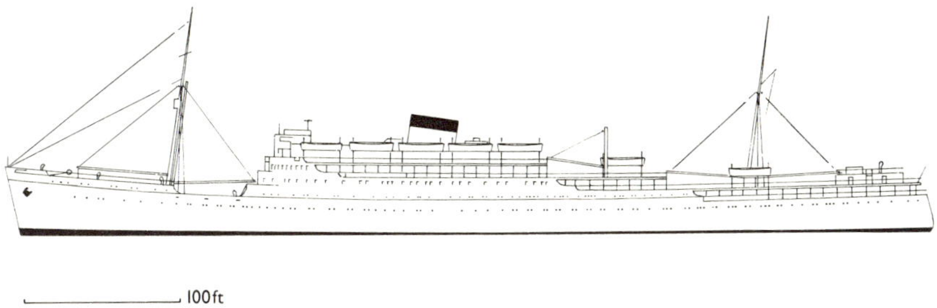


The first of two motorships, the *Durban Castle* was launched on 14th June, 1938, and left London on her maiden voyage on 31st December. When war broke out she was quickly requisitioned as a troopship and in 1941 brought HM the King of Greece and members of the Greek Royal family to the United Kingdom from Durban, where they had taken refuge (via Egypt) when Greece was overrun.

The *Durban Castle* made a number of trooping voyages and was then fitted out as a Landing Ship (Infantry), taking part in the North Africa and South of France landings in 1942 and 1944 respectively, before returning to the role of a troopship.

Released in 1946, she went to Belfast for refitting to a passenger ship for 180 First and 350 Tourist passengers and was then sent to Southampton, working in the mail service until 1950 when she returned to the London service for which she had been designed. She continued in the "Round Africa" run until her last arrival in London on 28th March, 1962. She was quickly sold to the German Eisen und Metall KG, Hamburg for breaking up.

*Warwick Castle*

Built by Harland & Wolff Limited, Belfast
Measurements:

| | | | |
|---|---|---|---|
| Length: | 594 feet 7 inches oa | Tonnages: | 17,387 gt |
| | 560 feet bp | | 10,590 tdw |
| Breadth: | 76 feet 5 inches | | |

Engines: Two eight-cylinder Diesels. Twin screws. 18 knots.

The motorship *Pretoria Castle* was launched by Mrs Charles te Water, wife of the then High Commissioner of the Union of South Africa, on 12th October, 1938, and was completed in April, 1939. Her maiden voyage from London began on the 20th of that month.

She managed to complete two round voyages before war broke out, being requisitioned on 2nd October, 1939, to become an armed merchant cruiser. As HMS *Pretoria Castle* (Pennant No. F.61) she was fitted with eight 6-inch and two 12-pdr AA guns and in November, 1939, was deployed in the South Atlantic.

On 16th July, 1942, she was purchased outright by the Admiralty for conversion to an escort carrier and to be used for training purposes. She was sent to the Swan, Hunter & Wigham Richardson yard where her superstructure was cut away to provide a flight deck; she emerged on 18th March, 1943, armed with four 4-inch, sixteen 2-pounder and twenty 20 mm AA guns, and a capability for fifteen aircraft and one catapult. She was actually the largest escort carrier to fly the British flag, although never used operationally.

In January, 1946, she was released from Government service and was repurchased by Union-Castle, being refitted by her builders to her original build. However, she now bore the name *Warwick Castle* (the mail ship of that name having been sunk during the war), the name of *Pretoria Castle*, from the administrative capital of the Union, being reserved for one of the two mailships which was to be launched by radio from South Africa by Mrs Smuts.

The *Warwick Castle* was then sent to Southampton to join the mail service, in a temporary capacity, while other mailships were reconverting from war service, and made her first postwar sailing in March, 1947. Her accommodation was for 180 First and 359 Tourist passengers as against her pre-war capacity for 220 First and 335 Tourist class passengers.

The *Warwick Castle* continued using Southampton until 1950 when she was transferred to London and the "Round Africa" service in which she continued until her last arrival at London on 1st June, 1962. Sold to Spanish shipbreakers, she arrived at Barcelona on 26th July, 1962, for demolition.

The third of the big three passenger liners arrived at Southampton on 19th December, 1961, the fifth new passenger ship to enter the mail service since the war. And she was to be the last.

The *Transvaal Castle* was built at Clydebank by John Brown & Company and was launched on 17th January, 1961, by Lady Cayzer, wife of Sir Nicholas Cayzer, Chairman of the British & Commonwealth Shipping Company. With this new ship Union-Castle dropped the old-established practice of carrying two or more classes of passengers and a new term was introduced—she was an "Hotel-class" ship. In this new conception the luxury of personal accommodation was regulated by price, for there were eleven types of cabin from which to choose, ranging from the standard three-four berth to the de-luxe suite. All cabins and public rooms were air-conditioned, the public rooms and all amenities being freely available to every passenger. There was accommodation for 728 passengers. Another innovation was the employment of waitresses, or stewardettes, as they were called, the *Transvaal Castle* being the first British liner to employ women in this role.

Most public rooms were on the promenade deck. Forward of the entrance lobby was the assembly room, decorated in pastel shades. The centrepiece was a large mural of *Venice en fête* by Sidney Smith. Adjoining the assembly room was a smaller, more intimate meeting place on the starboard side named the Orangery Bar, and forward of this was a large smoke room, divided into three by big screens, and this looked out to the recreation deck. Going aft from the entrance on the promenade deck was the verandah cafe, the games deck and swimming pool.

On the observation deck, above the promenade deck, was the Cellar Bar and Vineyard—one of the highest places in the ship! The A deck was entirely cabin accommodation, while shops and the cinema were placed on B deck. The large dining room on C deck was extended to the full width of the ship

The *Transvaal Castle* on trials in 1961. *Union-Castle*

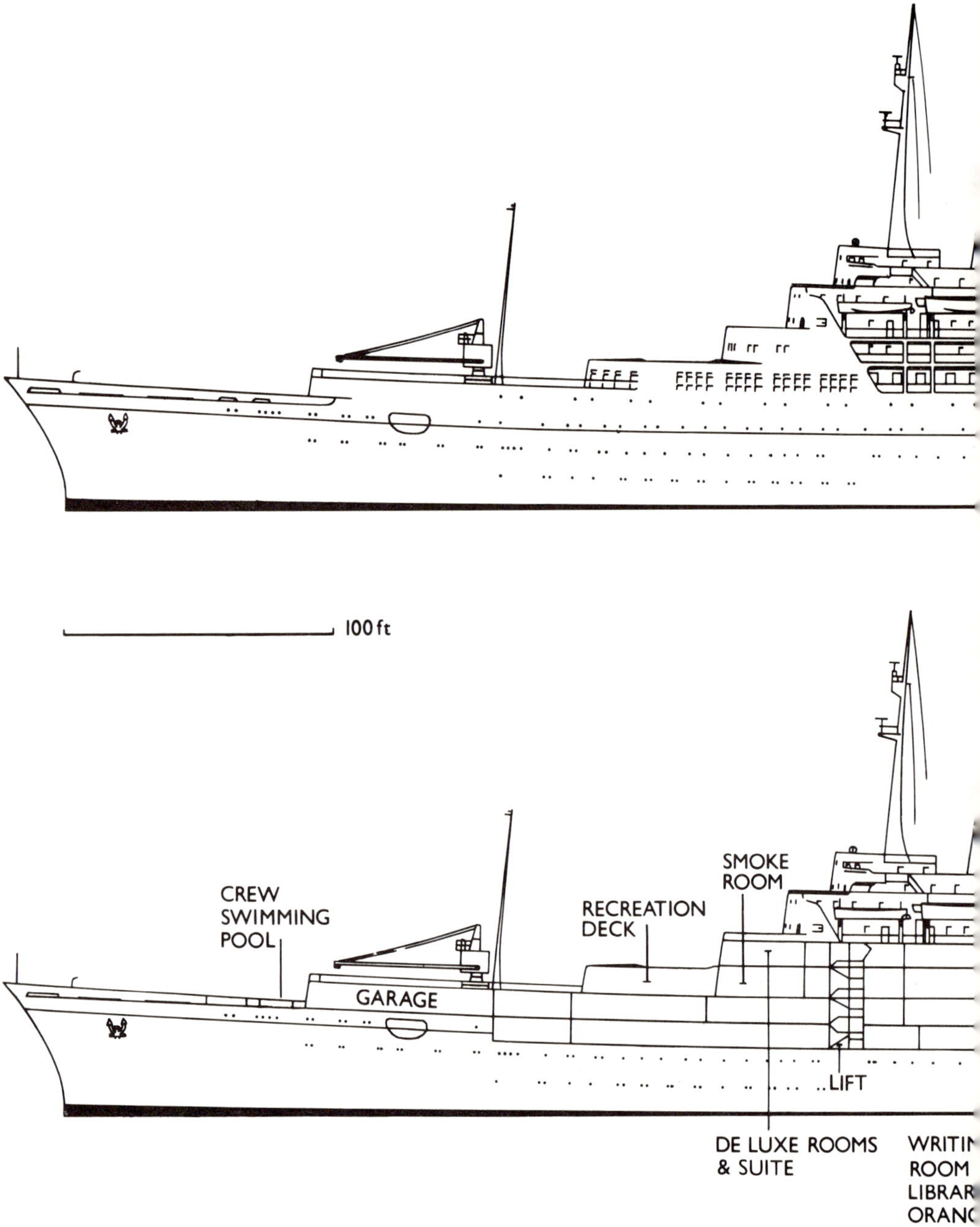


TRANSVAAL CASTLE

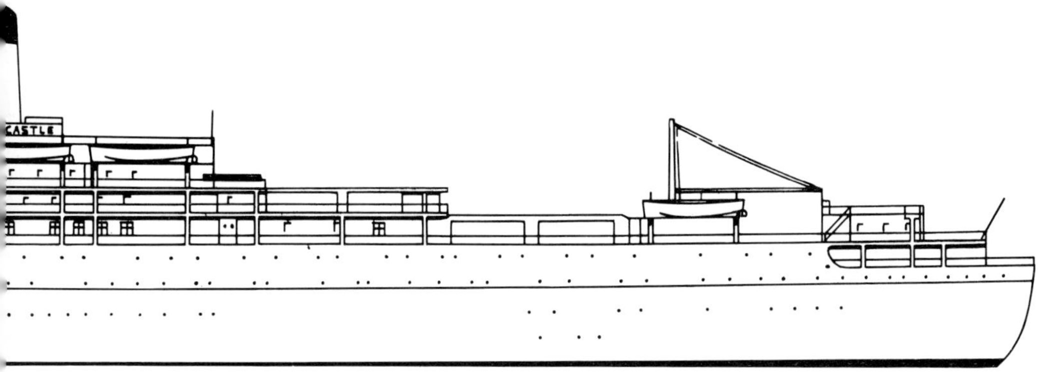

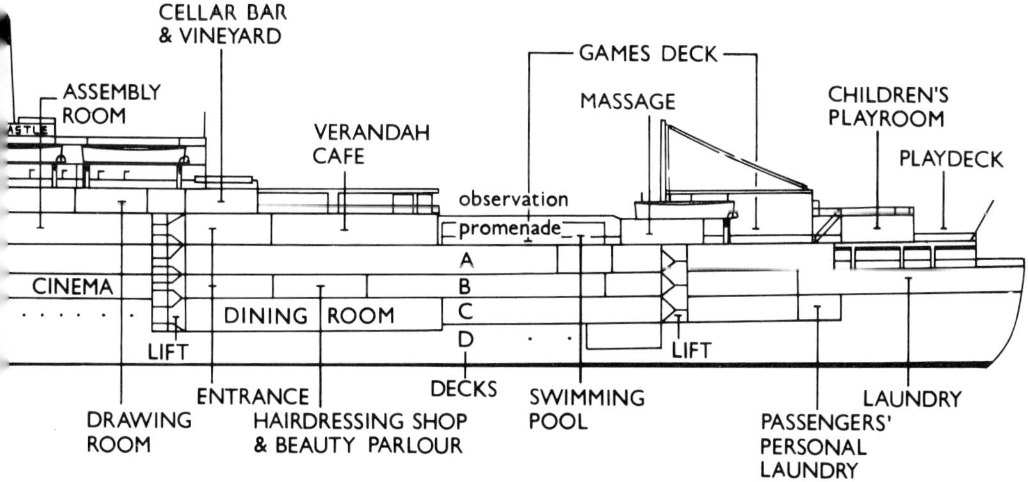
CELLAR BAR
& VINEYARD
ASSEMBLY
ROOM
VERANDAH
CAFE
GAMES DECK
MASSAGE
CHILDREN'S
PLAYROOM
PLAYDECK
observation
promenade
A
B
C
D
CINEMA
DINING ROOM
LIFT
LIFT
DECKS
ENTRANCE
DRAWING
ROOM
HAIRDRESSING SHOP
& BEAUTY PARLOUR
SWIMMING
POOL
PASSENGERS'
PERSONAL
LAUNDRY
LAUNDRY

*Transvaal Castle's* public rooms.

and could seat 400. Large murals by Felix Kelly depicted a South African homestead and the dining area was as a garden surrounding the house.

Total cargo capacity was 643,000 cubic feet, of which 361,000 cubic feet was refrigerated for the carriage of perishable cargo. A garage was placed forward. There were seven holds and cargo handling equipment comprised a 2-ton electrically operated traversing deck crane forward serving Nos 2 and 3 holds and two 10-ton capacity derricks aft.

For propulsion the *Transvaal Castle* was given four steam turbines geared to twin shafts and developing 44,000 shp. The speed was 23½ knots. She was the first Union-Castle ship to be given a bulbous bow.

On 18th January, 1962, one year and one day after launching, she commenced her maiden voyage from Southampton to South Africa.

Details:

Measurements:

| | | | |
|---|---|---|---|
| Length: | 760 feet 2 inches oa | Tonnages: | 30,212 gt |
| | 700 feet bp | | 16,342 tdw |
| Breadth: | 90 feet | | |

Following the entry of the *Transvaal Castle* into service the two mailships *Pretoria Castle* and *Edinburgh Castle* were withdrawn for about ten weeks each, the *Pretoria Castle* from 5th January to 8th March, 1962, the *Edinburgh*

*Castle* from 30th March to 8th June, for extensive overhaul by Harland & Wolff Limited at Southampton. At the same time air-conditioning was installed in the ships.

In order to allow this work to be done the *Carnarvon Castle*, scheduled to be withdrawn on the advent of the *Transvaal Castle*, continued in service until her arrival at Southampton on 1st June.

## *Carnarvon Castle*

Built by Harland & Wolff Limited, Belfast

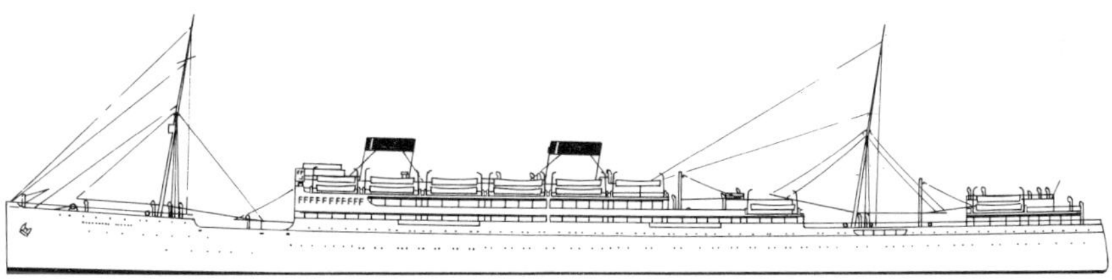

Measurements:

| | | | |
|---|---|---|---|
| Length: | 656 feet oa (1926) | Tonnages: | 20,050 gt (1926) |
| | 630 feet 7 inches bp | | 20,123 gt (1939) |
| | | | 20,141 gt (1949) |
| | 686 feet oa (1938) | | |
| | 661 feet bp | | 15,800 tdw |
| Breadth: | 73 feet 6 inches | | |

After thirty-six years of service, the *Carnarvon Castle* arrived at Southampton on 1st June, 1962, flying a paying-off pennant 108 feet long—three feet for each of thirty-six years.

She was the first of the Union-Castle motorships, and was the first mail ship for the South African service to exceed 20,000 gross tons. Launched on 14th January, 1926, she was completed in June and entered the mail service on 16th July the same year. Her hull was straight-stemmed and she was given a cruiser stern. She had two squat, horizontally-topped funnels, the first of this shape in the fleet. The forward one was a dummy. Her diesel engines gave her a speed of 16½ knots. Accommodation was provided in three classes, 311 in First, 276 in Second and 266 in Third class.

In 1934 HRH Prince George travelled to Cape Town in her and then in 1937 she was one of the five ships sent to Belfast for higher-powered diesel engines to be fitted, to give her the required speed necessary to get her from Southampton to Cape

Town in 13½ days—a requirement of the new mail contract. The *Carnarvon Castle* returned to Southampton in the summer of 1938 with a new look. Gone were the two squat funnels, in their place being one of low, streamlined shape. A new, raked bow took the place of her vertical stem and she was longer by 30 feet. She was now also

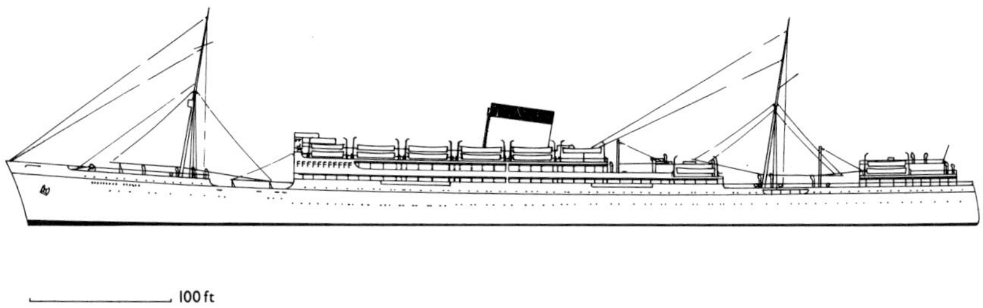


capable of 20 knots. The accommodation had also been altered to 226 in First and 245 in Second, while Third class was renamed Tourist class, with space for 188 passengers. On 8th July, 1938, she re-entered service and two months later set a new record of 12 days 13 hours 38 minutes from the United Kingdom (Nab Tower) to Cape Town. This remained until beaten in January, 1954, by the *Edinburgh Castle* which, after having been delayed for five days at Plymouth due to engine trouble, completed the passage from England to Cape Town in 11 days 21½ hours.

When war broke out the *Carnarvon Castle* was in South African waters and was sent to Simonstown to become an armed merchant cruiser. During this conversion her masts were replaced by a tripod, stepped by the funnel, and this arrangement she carried for the next ten years. Armed with eight 6-inch and two 3-inch AA guns, HMS *Carnarvon Castle* (Pennant No. F.25) was commissioned on 9th October, 1939, and was deployed on escort duty in the South Atlantic.

Sent in search of the German raider *Thor*, she met up with her on 5th December, 1940. In the action that followed both ships were repeatedly hit, the electrical gear of the *Carnarvon Castle* being quickly shot away. The *Thor* made off in a smoke-screen and the *Carnarvon Castle* made for Montevideo, where plates from the sunken *Admiral Graf Spee* were used to make temporary repairs before she returned to Table Bay for more permanent repairs to be made. She was to have become an escort carrier in 1942 but at the end of 1943 was sent to New York for conversion to a troopship, and continued as such until March, 1947, when she was released by the Government and altered to carry 1,300 emigrants on the Southampton-Cape Town run. She continued in the emigrant service until 1949 when, after an extensive rebuild at Harland & Wolff lasting seventeen months, she returned to the mail service, this time with accommodation for 216 First and 401 Tourist class passengers. She re-entered service on 15th June, 1950.

On 1st June, 1962, the *Carnarvon Castle*, then thirty-six years old, arrived at Southampton on her last mail voyage, sailing on the 27th of the same month for lay-up at Portland. She was soon sold for breaking up, arriving at Mihara, Japan, on 8th September for demolition.

Two Clan Line ships were renamed for the Union-Castle cargo section of the fleet in 1962 to assist in carrying cargo that was offering on the East African coast, the demand being brought about through the withdrawal of the "Round Africa" passenger liners *Durban Castle* and *Warwick Castle*. The *Clan Stewart*, which had been transferred to the South African Marine Corporation in 1961 as the *South African Sculptor*, was renamed *Kinpurnie*

The final sailing of the motorship *Carnarvon Castle* from Cape Town in May, 1962. *Vic Young*

*Castle* and the *Clan Ross*, which had also seen service from 1961 in the South African Marine as *South African Scientist*, became *Kinnaird Castle*.

Details:

*Kinpurnie Castle*

Completed by the Greenock Dockyard Company Limited, February, 1954, as *Clan Stewart*

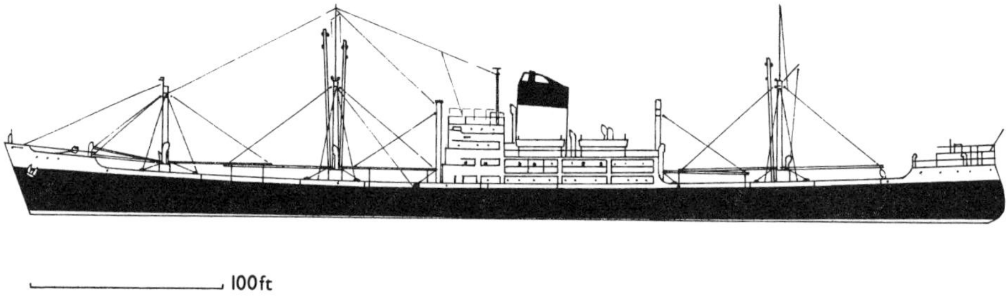


Measurements:

| | | | |
|---|---|---|---|
| Length: | 512 feet 7 inches oa | Tonnages: | 8,163 gt |
| | 477 feet bp | | 11,070 tdw |
| Breadth: | 66 feet 4 inches | | |

Engines: Three steam turbines to single shaft. 16¾ knots.

*Kinnaird Castle*

Completed by the Greenock Dockyard Company Limited, April, 1956, as *Clan Ross*

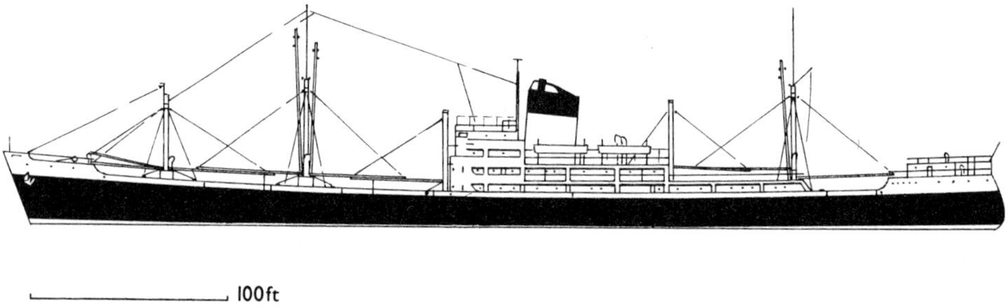


Measurements:

| | | | |
|---|---|---|---|
| Length: | 502 feet 9 inches oa | Tonnages: | 7,698 gt |
| | 465 feet bp | | 10,100 tdw |
| Breadth: | 65 feet 9 inches | | |

Engines: Three steam turbines to single shaft. 16¾ knots.

In May, 1963, a new contract was negotiated with the South African Government for a further accelerated service from Southampton to Cape Town. The operational date of this contract was to be 1st January 1966, and it was to run for a period of eleven years—to 31st December, 1976. The time of a single voyage was to be cut from thirteen and a half days to eleven and a half.

At the time, the mail fleet comprised three new liners, two of seventeen yeas of age, *Pretoria Castle* and *Edinburgh Castle*, and three pre-war ships, *Capetown Castle*, *Stirling Castle* and *Athlone Castle*. In order to fulfil the conditions of the contract it was necessary to build faster ships to replace the ageing pre-war liners and in 1963 tenders were invited for the construction of two 10,000 ton cargo liners, two-thirds of the 600,000 cubic feet of cargo space being refrigerated. However, these vessels were to be much more powerful than the conventional cargo ship, for in order to take their place in the new, faster service they were to have a service speed of 22½ knots, which required the provision of very high-powered machinery. The contracts were awarded to Swan, Hunter & Wigham Richardson Limited, Wallsend, the delivery dates to be April and July, 1965. On their completion the three older liners were to be withdrawn, leaving seven ships to maintain the mail service.

And in July, 1963, another move took place, this time ashore, when a new three-storey office on a one-and-a-half-acre site was acquired in the Western Docks at Southampton, very close to both inward and outward Union-Castle berths. Named Currie House, it accommodated the administrative personnel, while the old office in Canute Road continued passenger bookings.

The Travel Savings Association, a scheme designed for those people who enjoyed travelling as a holiday, was launched in January, 1963. The basic idea was for people to make planned payments towards their holiday, earning bank interest and enjoying discounts on a large range of goods and services. Full pages were taken up for advertising the scheme in the national press.

Early in the year the Canadian Pacific liner *Empress of Britain* was taken up on a five-year charter to cruise from British ports, commencing in September, 1963, and the *Empress of England* was chartered for some cruises from South African ports in February, 1964. At about the same time, Canadian Pacific acquired a 51% controlling interest in the newly-formed Travel Savings Limited, and in March, 1963, the Union-Castle Company entered as a third partner, taking a third interest. By this time some 9,000 berths had been booked. The Royal Mail Lines also acquired 25% of the equity capital of Travel Savings in the autumn of 1963.

In the spring of 1963, with a fall-off in the South American passenger trade, the Pacific Steam Navigation Company's *Reina del Mar* was chartered by Travel Savings Limited to make seven transatlantic crossings in the May-September period of 1964, the passengers to use the ship as an hotel during their stopover in either New York or Montreal.

The *Reina del Mar*, which from the summer of 1964 wore Union-Castle colours, was the only passenger liner in the Union-Castle fleet in post-war years that was not built specifically for the company.

Ordered for the Pacific Steam Navigation Company's service from Liverpool to the west coast of South America, she was launched on 7th June, 1955, at Harland & Wolff, Belfast. Leaving Belfast for sea trials on 21st March, 1956, she commenced her maiden voyage on 3rd May from Liverpool to Valparaiso; for a running partner she had the *Reina del Pacifico* (17,872 g, 1931). The *Reina del Mar* was a handsome ship, and with a slightly curved, rounded stem, cruiser stern, foremast and streamlined funnel, she presented a nicely balanced profile. Accommodation was provided in three classes, 207 First, 216 Cabin and 343 Tourist. Measurements were 600 feet 9 inches length overall, 560 feet (bp) and a breadth of 78 feet, giving a gross tonnage of

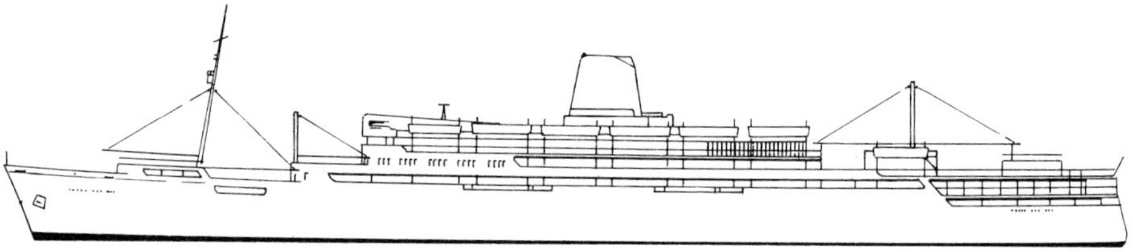

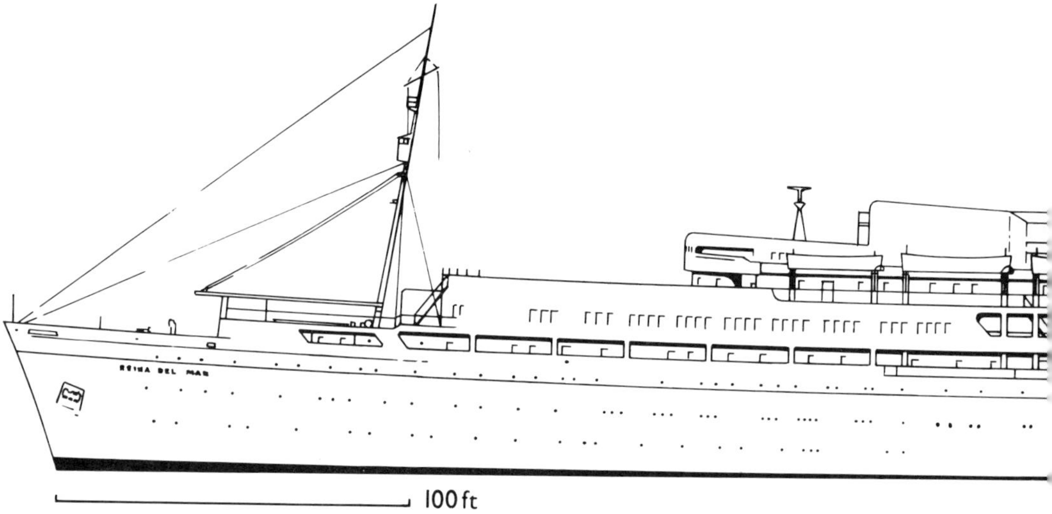

20,255. The propelling machinery consisted of six steam turbines, geared to twin shafts, developing 18,700 shp and giving 18 knots.

But she was to become yet another victim of the increasing competition of air travel and in 1963, after only seven years' service, it was announced by the Pacific Steam Navigation Company that she was to be withdrawn in March, 1964. Arriving at Liverpool on 5th March, 1964, on her last voyage from South America, she was quickly sent to Harland & Wolff at Belfast and arrived there on 10th March to begin conversion to a cruise ship. Her cargo spaces were turned into extra accommodation and public rooms, to take a total of 1,047 passengers. The forward lounge on the promenade deck was lengthened and extended to the side of the ship and the forward restaurant enlarged to accommodate 412 instead of 200 passengers. A permanent cinema was installed and the boat deck was extended aft to meet the deck over the after lounge. Accommodation was either for First and Tourist or "one class".

*Reina del Mar,* built 1956, shown as a cruising ship. **Inset:** As built for the South America service of the Pacific S.N. Company.

By summer she had been converted and was remeasured at 20,750 gt. On 10th June, 1964, she left Liverpool for New York on her first voyage as a cruise liner. The programme was for seven eighteen-day cruises, five to New York and two to Montreal, giving three days and two nights in either port, during which time the ship could be used as an hotel.

On 24th August she arrived at Southampton for the first time and at the end of the summer was repainted at Southampton in Union-Castle colours. Up to then she had retained the yellow funnel of the Pacific Steam Navigation Company, but with initials TSA in blue inside a blue circle added. In the December she sailed for South Africa for cruising, returning to the United Kingdom in March, 1965, from where fifteen cruises were made in the period up to mid-September.

Following the announcement of the chartering of the *Reina del Mar*, in the summer of 1963 a further charter was made for the P & O liner *Stratheden* to make four cruises in the forthcoming winter, three of them replacing the *Empress of Britain*'s sailings, as the latter vessel was sent to South Africa to join the *Empress of England*. The last of these four cruises, a thirty-three-day West Indies journey, left Southampton on 4th January, 1964, and then, on return to Southampton, the *Stratheden* was sold to Greek shipowner John S. Latsis.

Block bookings were also made in four Union-Castle liners for the 1964 season. Towards the end of 1963 it was reported that Travel Savings had purchased the *Reina del Mar* outright and that when handed over from the Pacific Steam Navigation Company in March, 1964, she would be registered under a Travel Savings subsidiary company, which was to be formed. Later it was reported that A. J. Chandris was to purchase the *Reina del Mar*, have her reconstructed and renamed, and sail her with a Greek crew. The Travel Savings announcement stated that it had been "decided to sell the ship to a Greek company which will be associated with the Chandris group. The TSA is not a shipping company, but primarily a sales organisation and its efforts should be directed towards the promotion of popular cruises." Chandris had a 20% share option, equal with Royal Mail Lines, Canadian Pacific, British & Commonwealth and Max Wilson, progenitor of the idea. In the event it was decided not to sell and the option was not taken up, the ship remaining under the British flag and being placed under Union-Castle management.

Although the original charter of the *Empress of Britain* was fixed for five years, a cancellation clause was added when companies other than Canadian Pacific acquired an interest in the TSA, allowing the TSA option to terminate the charter at certain stages. Early in 1964 TSA exercised this option, seeking withdrawal as from 5th January, 1965. In February, 1964, Canadian Pacific offered her for sale and by the end of the month she was sold to the Greek Line for the Haifa, Piraeus, Naples, Lisbon and New York service, for delivery in January, 1965.

Used solely for cruising, the *Reina del Mar* was purchased by Union-Castle in 1973.
*Skyfotos*

Then, in the spring of 1964, it was announced that Travel Savings were to abandon their "Savings scheme" after that year. The projected cruise of the *Reina del Mar* to South Africa and to Tokio for the 1964 Olympic Games was cancelled and she was re-scheduled to take over the cruise programme of the *Empress of Britain*, except the Christmas cruise commencing 21st December, which was cancelled. The *Reina del Mar* sailed in December, 1964, to cruise from South Africa, returning in March, 1965.

Meanwhile, on 16th October, 1964, all Travel Savings shares were acquired by Union-Castle (25% had been held by Max Wilson, Canadian Pacific, Royal Mail and Union-Castle) and a further four-year charter at the expiry of the current charter on 30th September, 1965, was made, with option to extend for a further five years from 1st October, 1969.

The re-scheduling of the cruise itineraries had the effect of releasing the *Empress of Britain* earlier than first arranged and she was handed over to the Greek Line at Liverpool on 16th November, 1964, leaving the Mersey two days later for conversion at Genoa. She was renamed *Queen Anna Maria.*

So, after only a short period, the "Savings scheme" which had started in such a blaze of publicity was run down, members of the Association not purchasing cruises in 1964 being asked to withdraw their deposits. It had been hoped that the small interest obtained on savings would amount to something useful as the fund began to grow, but the scheme had proved too difficult and expensive to operate. The initial advertising and promotional expenses were very high and, although there was a great deal of enthusiasm in South Africa for the scheme, the populous British end did not fulfil the original expectations.

Fruit shipments to Southampton had been increasing yearly, and between February and April, 1964, no fewer than twenty-one ships, most under the British & Commonwealth flag, but including one or two on charters, called to discharge deciduous fruit. These were in addition to the normal weekly mail ship arrivals.

The extent of the valuable cargo trade can, perhaps, be exemplified in the arrival of the *Capetown Castle* on Friday, 26th June, 1964. Docking early in the morning, she disembarked 700 passengers and commenced discharge of 10,000 tons of cargo, which was completed the following Wednesday. The cargo included 1,387 bales of wool, skins and hides, 2,145 bags of mail,

The cargo ship *Southampton Castle,* built in 1965, was one of the fastest diesel-powered cargo liners of her time. *Vic Young*

160,000 packages of citrus fruits, 474 cases of pineapples, 1,000 quarters of chilled beef, 3,205 cartons of frozen beef and 2,162 trays of avocado pears.

At the end of the year plans were announced for what was to be the final accelerated service. For years, the sailing time from Southampton had been 4 pm Thursday, the inward ship arriving at 6 am the next day, Friday. At Cape Town the arrival of the mail ship was at 6 am Thursday, the homeward-bound ship sailing at 4 pm the following day, Friday. The absolute regularity was a fact of which Union-Castle were proud and led to an oft-repeated phrase that one could set one's watch by these sailings.

But this was to change, for the thirteen and a half days service was now to be reduced to eleven-and-a-half, and seven ships were to be used instead of eight. Furthermore, two were to be cargo liners, the first cargo-only ships built for the mail service, but powerfully engined to enable them to maintain their places in the schedule. Timings were changed, the outward ship now to leave Southampton at 1 pm on Friday, the homeward ship arriving at 6 am on Monday. The arrival time at Cape Town was to be 6 am on Wednesday and the homeward ship would leave the same day at 4 pm.

The first of the two new cargo liners was launched on 20th October, 1964, by Princess Alexandra and took the name *Southampton Castle*. The second, *Good Hope Castle*, was launched four months later, on 16th February, 1965, by Mrs De Wet, wife of the South African Ambassador in London.

These two vessels were the fastest diesel-powered cargo liners afloat, designed for a service speed of 22½ knots but probably capable of 25 knots, to enable them to keep up with the mail liners. For propulsion there were two eight-cylinder Wallsend-Sulzer diesel engines, geared to twin shafts, designed to give a continuous output of 34,720 bhp at 119 rpm.

The hull form incorporated a cruiser stern and raked stem, with bulbous bow to reduce resistance and save power. In an extremely large funnel, which seemed to overwhelm the superstructure, were installed two waste heat boilers used to supply steam for a turbo-alternator providing electric power. When in port, or as a relief, diesel generators were used.

The deadweight capacity was 11,200 tons and large capacities for deciduous and citrus fruits were provided. With a temperature control, a wide range of chilled or frozen products could also be carried. Four holds were placed forward and three aft of the machinery space. There were six 15-ton derricks, and a 40-ton swinging derrick was fitted to work No. 3 hold and deck containers, which could be stowed on the hatch. Containers could also be carried on Nos 4, 5 and 6 hatches. Another special cargo carried was wine, thirteen permanent tanks and their piping being fitted for the carriage of 60,000 gallons in bulk.

Early in May, 1965, the *Southampton Castle* arrived at Southampton, beginning her maiden voyage on the 27th of that month and arriving at Cape

Town on 10th June. The delivery of the *Good Hope Castle*, due to enter service on 20th August, was delayed by labour shortage at the building yard and when she was eventually ready for trials a 60 mph south-easterly gale further delayed her. After trials, when she had worked up to 25 knots at about two-thirds power, she was handed over on 9th December, 1965, nearly four months behind schedule.

Details:

*Southampton Castle*
*Good Hope Castle*
Built by Swan, Hunter & Wigham Richardson Limited, Wallsend.

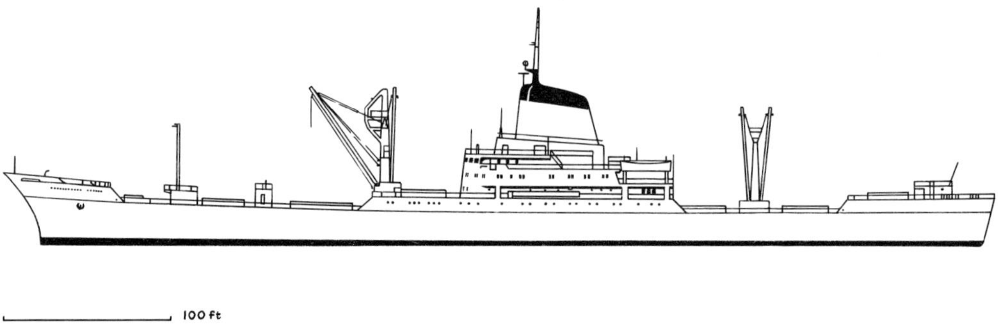


Measurements:

| | | | |
|---|---|---|---|
| Length: | 592 feet 9 inches oa | Tonnages: | 13,152 gt |
| | 545 feet bp | | 11,200 tdw |
| Breadth: | 77 feet 5 inches | | |

*The *Southampton Castle* was named after a medieval castle at Southampton which once stood within the old walled town. Southampton Corporation presented the ship with a replica of the Corporation seal, which has been in use since medieval times, and a drawing of the City coat-of-arms in colour.

CHAPTER FIVE

# The Final Service

WHEN the *Edinburgh Castle* and *Pretoria Castle* were built the mail voyage was thirteen-and-a-half days to Cape Town, but these two ships were designed to make a faster voyage and were able to fit in to the new eleven-and-a-half days schedule introduced in July, 1965. However, before the introduction of the new service both ships were withdrawn for some modernisation of their accommodation, each missing one complete round voyage. More cabins were given private facilities and the carrying capacity was adjusted to 155 First and 491 Tourist class passengers. At the same time, on each ship the foremast was considerably shortened to aid radar reflection and was thereafter used as a kingpost for derricks. The mainmast was removed and a new structure incorporating a mast was placed aft of the bridge.

The final sailing in the old service was taken by the *Stirling Castle* on Thursday, 8th July, 1965—the end of an era of the "4 o'clock sailing", a feature since the resumption of the mail service after the war.

The inaugural sailing in the new accelerated service was by the *Windsor Castle* on Friday, 16th July, 1965, with Cape Town eleven-and-a-half days, Port Elizabeth thirteen-and-a-half days, East London fifteen-and-a-half days and Durban sixteen-and-a-half days away. But there was a slight hitch, for the *Good Hope Castle* was not delivered until the end of the year. Her maiden voyage began on 14th January, 1966, and only then did the accelerated service become fully operational.

The *Capetown Castle* was slotted in to take the sailings of the uncompleted *Good Hope Castle*. When the new ship finally joined the service, the *Capetown Castle* was given a refit and then continued in a "one-class" extra service with a sixteen days run to Cape Town via Madeira, calling sometimes at Ascension, St Helena and Walvis Bay.

In sailing sequence, ships in the mail service were:

*Windsor Castle*
*Southampton Castle*
*Edinburgh Castle*
*S.A. Vaal* (ex *Transvaal Castle*)
*Pendennis Castle*
*Good Hope Castle*
and
*S.A. Oranje* (ex *Pretoria Castle*)

The two name changes were occasioned by the transfer of two ships to Safmarine in late 1965. These transfers came about from negotiations between

Safmarine and its two major shareholders, the Industrial Development Corporation of South Africa and the British & Commonwealth Shipping Company. The effective date of the sale was 1st January, 1966. The *Transvaal Castle* was renamed *S.A. Vaal* at Cape Town on 12th January, 1966, by Mrs Swart, the wife of the then State President; the *Pretoria Castle* was renamed *S.A. Oranje* by Mrs Verwoerd, wife of the Prime Minister of South Africa, at Cape Town on 2nd February, although the vessel had actually been repainted at Southampton during her cargo discharge between 10th and 22nd January. This was the first step towards Safmarine becoming responsible for providing and operating three of the seven weekly mailships; Safmarine were to provide the next mail ship replacement. However, it was agreed that, for the time being at least, Union-Castle would continue to man and operate the vessels on a bareboat charter arrangement.

With a further rundown of passenger traffic between London and East Africa the *Braemar Castle* was withdrawn at the end of 1965. This left the *Kenya Castle* and *Rhodesia Castle* in the service, and a working arrangement was made with the British India S.N. Company to operate their passenger/cargo liners *Kenya* and *Uganda* in schedule with the two Union-Castle liners to give a passenger ship sailing from London to East Africa, via the Suez Canal, every three weeks. It was at first thought that the *Braemar Castle* could be employed cruising, but the cost of the refit necessary to fit her for that trade was too high and she was sold for breaking up, leaving London on 3rd January, 1966, for Faslane, where she arrived on the 6th. This indeed was clear evidence of the fast changing scene in Africa; she was only thirteen years old.

* * *

Two news items appeared in 1965. Since Union-Castle had become incorporated in the British & Commonwealth group, their ships had flown the British & Commonwealth burgee as well as the Union-Castle flag from the mainmast. The first news item was an announcement that it had been decided that the Union-Castle houseflag was to be flown from the jackstaff, leaving the British & Commonwealth burgee on its own on the mainmast.

The second item, later in the year, was of far-reaching importance; it was the announcement of the formation of Overseas Containers Limited. This company was to amalgamate container interests and develop container traffic, its sponsors being four of Britain's largest shipping groups—P & O, Ocean Transport & Trading, Furness Withy, and the British & Commonwealth Shipping Company. It was to play a significant part in the forthcoming container revolution.

Between early 1965 and early 1966 the British & Commonwealth Shipping

*Transvaal Castle*

Company took delivery of four motorships. Ordered in 1962, three were placed under nominal ownership of the Union-Castle Company and one, the *Clan Ross*, with the Houston Line, another subsidiary company of the group. All ships were given Clan Line livery.

| | | |
|---|---|---|
| *Clan Ramsay* | Completed | 3.1965 |
| *Clan Ranald* | Completed | 6.1965 |
| *Clan Robertson* | Completed | 11.1965 |
| *Clan Ross* | Completed | 3.1966 |

Details:

All built by the Greenock Dockyard Company Limited.

Measurements:

| | | | |
|---|---|---|---|
| Length: | 529 feet 4 inches oa | Tonnages: | 10,541 gt |
| | 485 feet 4 inches bp | | 11,730 tdw |
| Breadth: | 68 feet 6 inches | | |

Engines: Seven-cylinder 10,350 bhp oil engines to a single screw.
Speed 17 knots.

The hull was fitted with seven main watertight bulkheads, three decks below upper deck in the fore part of the ship and two decks below upper deck aft providing, together with the forecastle 'tween deck in way of No. 1 hold, five main cargo holds and fifteen 'tween deck spaces. All except the forecastle 'tween deck were refrigerated, with a minimum temperature of 28°F, suitable for citrus and deciduous fruits. Deep frozen cargo was provided for under No. 5 hatch, where the temperature could be reduced. Cargo capacity was 28,706 cubic feet (bale) of general and 506,864 cubic feet insulated. An interesting feature of the deck machinery was the fitting of electrically-operated accommodation ladders, the operation controlled by one man.

In 1966 no fewer than thirty-four ships, in addition to the mail fleet, brought South African fruit into Southampton between early March and June, including the three Union-Castle "Clans", and in early June, 1967, the *Clan Ramsay* carried a record cargo of South African fruit comprising 335,968 cases of apples, grapes, pears, oranges, grapefruit and lemons.

The introduction of the two new fast cargo liners and the start of the accelerated service meant that three mail liners, the *Stirling Castle*, *Athlone Castle* and *Capetown Castle*, would be surplus to requirements. The *Athlone Castle* was very quickly sold for breaking up, but the *Stirling Castle* made one or two voyages to South Africa and short cruises before she, too, was sent to the shipbreakers.

Last of the pre-war liners, the *Capetown Castle* filled in for the sailings of the *Good Hope Castle*, which was delayed in the builder's yard, and then made a number of one-class voyages from Southampton to Cape Town, calling at the Atlantic Isles. From Southampton, she also called at Flushing before sailing on southwards. She was eventually withdrawn in September, 1967, and put up for sale.

*Stirling Castle* and *Athlone Castle*

Built by Harland & Wolff Limited, Belfast.

Measurements:

| | | | |
|---|---|---|---|
| Length: | 725 feet oa | Tonnages: | 25,554 gt |
| | 696 feet bp | | 15,421 tdw (*Stirling Castle*) |
| Breadth: | 82 feet 6 inches | | |
| | | | 25,567 gt |
| | | | 15,138 tdw (*Athlone Castle*) |

Engines: Two ten-cylinder oil engines. Speed 20 knots.

Very handsome, powerful-looking ships, these two liners came out in the 1930s. A large, raked funnel, 32 feet high and 50 feet wide, blended beautifully with the streamlined superstructure which, with the fo'c'sle joined to the bridge deck, was continuous to the curved, raked stern. Of the three decks, two were open amidships. The ships were ordered in 1934, just after the signing of a new ten-year Freight Agreement, and although the then existing mail service was regarded as satisfactory, the two ships were designed with sufficient speed to make the Southampton-Cape Town voyage in under fourteen days. The foresight was justified, for in early 1936 a new ten-year mail contract was made, to begin from 1st January, 1937, under which from the end of 1938 the existing 16 days 15 hours journey should be accelerated to take not more than fourteen days.

The *Stirling Castle*, first of the new fast liners with accommodation for 300 First and 500 Cabin-class passengers, was launched on 15th July, 1935, by Mrs Robertson Gibb, wife of the Chairman of the company, and left on her maiden voyage from Southampton on 7th February, 1936. Sailing from Southampton on 21st August of that same year, she completed the voyage to Cape Town on 4th September in 13 days 9 hours, beating the record voyage of the Union Line's *Scot*, which had left Southampton forty-three years earlier on Sunday, 19th March, 1893, arriving in Table Bay 14 days 19 hours later.

From 1940 the *Stirling Castle* served as a troopship, coming through the war unscathed after steaming 505,000 miles and carrying 128,000 personnel. From 1943 she sailed in the trooping service from the United States, and in one eastbound run from New York carried over 6,000 men. She returned to the mail service in 1947 after reconditioning, with accommodation for 243 First and 540 Tourist class passengers. She continued on the Cape run until the new accelerated service came in 1965, but for this she was too slow and was withdrawn. The *Stirling Castle* arrived at Southampton on her last voyage from South Africa on 30th November, 1965, cruised for a few weeks, and her sale was then negotiated to Formosan shipbreakers. The sale, however, was cancelled as the buyers failed to obtain the necessary licences, and she finally left Southampton on 1st February, 1966, for Mihara, Japan, where she arrived on 3rd March to be broken up.

*The *Stirling Castle* was named after the castle in Stirling, Scotland, one-time residence of Scottish kings, and was the second ship to bear the name. The first was Donald Currie's iron sailing ship, built in 1863 for the East India trade.

* * *

Her sistership, *Athlone Castle*, was launched on 28th November, 1935, by Princess Alice, Countess of Athlone. The Earl of Athlone had been Governor-General of South Africa from 1923 to 1931, and it was from this association and the popularity they had both achieved in South Africa that the ship was so named. Her maiden voyage began from Southampton on 22nd May, 1936, and she later commenced the accelerated service, leaving Southampton on 22nd December, 1938. War was less than a year ahead, and in this she, too, served as a troopship, coming through unscathed and returning to service in May, 1947, after refitting by her builders. Instead of having accommodation for 242 First and 487 Cabin class, she was now able to accommodate 250 First and 530 Tourist.

Her last voyage from Cape Town began on 23rd July, 1965, and she arrived at Southampton on 6th August at the end of her 141st round voyage to South Africa. She was quickly sold and left again on 16th August, bound for the shipbreakers' yard at Kaohsiung, Taiwan, where she arrived on 13th September.

* * *

These two ships were the first of the fast liners for the accelerated service of the late 1930s and with the first two R-class ships, *Roslin Castle* and *Rothesay Castle*, which were ordered at the same time and completed in 1935, were the first ships built for Union-Castle after the fall in 1931 of the Royal Mail Steam Packet empire, by whom the company had been controlled since 1912. With these new liners, a new class of accommodation was also introduced, second and tourist classes being withdrawn for a cabin class.

The disposal of ships continued throughout 1967, no fewer than six units of the fleet being sold during that year. This was the beginning of the rundown of the Union-Castle fleet.

Early in the year the two remaining liners of the East Africa intermediate service made their last voyages. After discharging in London, the *Kenya Castle* arrived in the River Blackwater on 22nd April to lay up and was quickly followed by the *Rhodesia Castle* on 4th May. This was the demise of the Union-Castle passenger trade to the East Africa coast, for not only had practically all colonies of the British Empire now reached independence, with the consequent rundown of their colonial officers, administrators and civil servants who had helped to fill the passenger lists, but those that remained were using the ever expanding air services.

The *Rhodesia Castle* was the first to be sold; after only sixteen years of service she arrived at Kaohsiung on 26th October, 1967, for demolition.

Her sistership *Kenya Castle* was more fortunate, for she was sold to the National Hellenic Mediterranean Line S.A., a member of the Chandris group, and under her new name *Amerikanis* (American lady), left the Blackwater on 2nd August, 1967, arriving at Piraeus on 12th August for conversion to her new role. She was to sail in a service from Haifa, Greece and Italy to Canada and New York, also (mainly) cruising from New York to the West Indies. After conversion she sailed from Piraeus on 8th August, 1968, and arrived New York on 21st August.

So ended the East Africa intermediate passenger service.

Meanwhile the war standard cargo ship *Kenilworth Castle* was withdrawn, and she arrived at Hong Kong on 4th June for demolition.

The *Capetown Castle*, last of the pre-war liners, was the fourth ship to be withdrawn in 1967. Too slow for the accelerated service of 1965, she had been sailing in an "extra" service, a sixteen day run to Cape Town with some outward voyages including a call at Flushing, and there was also a ten-day cruise to Gibraltar, Palma, and Lisbon in September, 1966. On 3rd August, 1967, she left Southampton on her last voyage to the Cape, arriving back on 9th September. She was quickly away again on the 19th of the same month and arrived at Spezia on 26th September for demolition, with twenty-nine years of service and 180 voyages behind her.

The withdrawal of the *Capetown Castle* caused the cessation of the "extra" service which had provided a link between the United Kingdom and the islands of Ascension and St Helena, and between those islands and South Africa. To maintain this communication it was arranged that the cargo liners *Southampton Castle* and *Good Hope Castle* would call at the islands, making two calls in each direction over seven weeks.

This new service was inaugurated at the request of the Commonwealth Office. It was arranged that the two ships would be altered so that each had cabin accommodation for twelve passengers, allocation of the accommodation being vested in the Government of St Helena. The work was done by Cammell, Laird & Company, Birkenhead, *Good Hope Castle* being altered first to enable her to take the mailship sailing on 3rd November, 1967, calling at Ascension and St Helena on the return leg and inaugurating the service; the *Southampton Castle* took the mail sailing on 1st December.

*Kenya Castle*

## *Capetown Castle*

Built by Harland & Wolff Limited, Belfast.

Measurements:

| | | | |
|---|---|---|---|
| Length: | 734 feet oa | Tonnages: | 27,002 gt |
| | 703 feet bp | | 14,925 tdw |
| Breadth: | 82 feet 6 inches | | |

Engines: Two ten-cylinder oil engines. Twin screws. Speed 20 knots.

The *Capetown Castle* was similar to the earlier pair of ships, *Stirling Castle* and *Athlone Castle*. A raked stem and cruiser stern gave her the Union-Castle appearance of the day and she had a rounded superstructure forward. She was, however, slightly larger, and had the base of her superstructure plated in. The largest Union-Castle motor-driven liner, she was also the longest motor liner in the world—a record that she held to the end.

The *Capetown Castle* was launched on 23rd September, 1937, by Mrs J. D. Low, the Mayoress of Cape Town, and left Southampton on her maiden voyage on 29th April, 1938. Accommodation at that time was for 290 First and 500 Cabin class passengers. At the start of the war she was taken up as a troopship, sailed some 500,000 miles and came through unscathed, though narrowly escaping damage when bombs dropped very near to her stern when off Northern Ireland early in the war. Quickly released from Government service when war ended, she was refitted and her accommodation altered to carry 250 First and 550 Tourist class. Her first postwar sailing to South Africa was on 9th January, 1947.

Until 1965 she continued in the mail service, hitting the national newspaper headlines twice. The first occasion was on 17th October, 1960, when she suffered an engine room explosion in the starting system when off Las Palmas, causing some fatalities. Her place was taken by the *Braemar Castle* for one voyage. The second was when, in early 1965, twenty gold ingots worth £100,000 were stolen from a temporary strongroom in the ship. It was not until she arrived at Durban on her next voyage that police who had flown out from England to meet her found the bullion cemented into the bottoms of sand lockers on the decks and in a gap between two cargo holds.

From 1965 the *Capetown Castle* continued in an "extra" service for another two years. There was little alteration to accommodation to note, except that the Tourist lounge was turned into a cinema.

When the ship was being prepared for the breakers a discovery was made on the underside of a First class cabin drawer. It read "1941. Summer world cruise at the Government's expense. Wishing all who sail in *Capetown Castle* all that we have had ourselves. God speed. Bon voyage". The Churchill "V" sign was followed by signatures of five British Army NCOs who had shared the cabin. The panel was kept by the company as a memento, and later by the Missions to Seamen.

*The *Capetown Castle* was the first Union-Castle liner to bear a name other than that of an ancient British stronghold, being named after the most important historic building in South Africa, Cape Town Castle, of which the first stone was laid in 1666 and which took many years to complete, severely taxing Government funds. A painting of The Castle, Cape Town, was presented to the ship by the Corporation of Cape Town.

The fifth ship to be withdrawn in 1967 was the *Kinpurnie Castle* which, although registered in the ownership of the Clan Line, wore Union-Castle livery. She arrived in London on 9th October on the last Union-Castle voyage from Beira and was sold to the Greek flag and renamed *Hellenic Med.*

In November one of the early R-class (refrigerated) ships, *Roslin Castle**, was withdrawn. She was one of a pair ordered early in 1934 and was completed in May, 1935, these two being the first refrigerated cargo motorships in the Union-Castle fleet designed for the South African fruit trade to the United Kingdom. The *Roslin Castle* came through the war unscathed, although her sistership *Rothesay Castle* was lost off the west coast of Scotland in January, 1940.

Wine has been one of the most constant and increasing imports from South Africa into Britain, the bulk of it being brought in Union-Castle ships.

It is recorded that the first vines at the Cape were planted by Dutch settlers as long ago as 1655, the first wine being pressed four years later. In 1688 there arrived at the Cape some 200 Huguenot settlers, refugees from religious troubles in France, bringing with them many skills, not the least of which was an expertise in vine-growing, which they taught to the Dutch farmers. By the mid-nineteenth century a flourishing wine trade had been built up with Britain, but the withdrawal of preferential duty rates that had initially boosted imports caused a gradual reduction in shipments, and the trade languished for many years.

At the turn of the century the trade was virtually in the doldrums, local consumption being unable to take all the wine that was produced. But in 1917-18 the Cape wine growers banded together and, pooling resources, formed a co-operative with the intention of organising their wine production, not only for local consumption but for selling it to world markets. The society was named Ko-operative Wijnbouwers Vereniging van Zuid-Afrika Beperkf—trading initials KWV—the Afrikaansche title for Co-operative Wine Growers Association of South Africa Limited, with its main offices at Paarl, some forty miles north-east of Cape Town. Steadily the society organised its resources, improving quality, fixing economic prices and planning a marketing strategy for overseas sales.

A marketing organisation, known as the South African Wine Farmers Association (London) Limited, was set up in Britain in 1931. At that time imports into Britain were about half a million gallons yearly but, helped by lower duties on Empire wines, the figure rose to a million and a half by the

*There were three ships named *Roslin Castle*. The first was an East Indian sailing ship in the Currie fleet from 1863-1883. The second was completed in 1883 by Barclay, Curle & Company. After lengthening in 1888 (4,487 gt.) she became the fastest vessel in the mail service. She was sold to the German flag in 1905. Roslin is a village in Midlothian, standing on the North Esk River, some six miles south of Edinburgh.

time war broke out. Thereafter, duty increases almost cancelled the effectiveness of the preference, only 700,000 gallons being imported in 1955, but in 1958 and again in 1959 duty reductions greatly helped the trade. By this time many more of the world's markets were buying South African wines, outlets encouraged by South Africa as a hedge against the fluctuating British fiscal policy.

In 1964 SAWFA built a new depot for its imported wines in West Bay Road, in Southampton's Western Docks, the traditional "topping out" ceremony taking place in the December. Until then the SAWFA depot had been at the London rail depot of Nine Elms but with an increase in imports—from one million gallons in 1960 to nearly two millions in 1964—increased capacity for storage was obviously required. The 2½-acre

The *S.A. Vaal*, seen here at Southampton, was equipped with wine tanks to carry bulk imports of South African sherry.

site, with storage for 424,000 gallons, was quite near to the inward "Cape" berth and wine in bulk was pumped ashore from ship to road tanker for conveyance to the store.

The two new fast cargo liners joining the mail service at the time, the *Southampton Castle* and *Good Hope Castle*, had been equipped with special glass-lined tanks capable of taking 60,000 gallons and the first bulk shipment to arrive was in the *Southampton Castle* on 9th July, 1965. In 1967 yet another store was opened, doubling the storage capacity. By 1968 imports into Britain reached two and a half million gallons and both the *S.A. Vaal* and *Windsor Castle* had been equipped with wine tanks. The latter ship was fitted in September, 1968, the total tankage capacity being 81,000 gallons, with the largest tank taking 27,000 gallons. The seven tanks could be emptied at a rate of 12,000 gallons per hour. The first bulk wine to be carried in the liners arrived in the *Windsor Castle* on 30th December, 1968.

The KWV has grown tremendously over its sixty years and is one of the largest wine-producing organisations in the world. It has lavishly equipped laboratories in the main wine area of the Cape, with millions of gallons of old matured wines in stock. A great discovery was made in 1933 when it was found that strains of "flor"—wine yeast used in the production of sherries—could be isolated from South African wine, and selected strains were used in the production of more delicate sherries. The second phase was the mastering of the maturation system, and from then on South Africa produced fine sherries.

Most wines come from the south-western districts of Paarl, Stellenbosch, Worcester, Tulbagh and Robertson in Cape Province. All are within 150 miles radius of Cape Town and are in two main areas, a coastal strip which stretches inland to the first mountain range, and an inland area inward from the mountains, this being drier and higher.

The fleet at the end of 1968 could be divided into three sections: the mail service from Southampton, the refrigerated ship section and the cargo ships. Seven mail ships were based at the southern port, two of them Safmarine vessels. The sailing sequence was *Windsor Castle*, *Good Hope Castle*, *Edinburgh Castle*, *S.A. Vaal*, *Pendennis Castle*, *Southampton Castle* and *S.A. Oranje*. Full South African control of the Safmarine liners was taken early in 1969 and from then on the South African flag was worn.

The refrigerated fleet still included the 1937-built *Rochester Castle*, the wartime *Rowallan Castle*, *Richmond Castle* and *Roxburgh Castle*, and the two ships built just after the close of hostilities, *Riebeeck Castle* and *Rustenburg Castle*. There were also the larger *Rotherwick Castle* and *Rothesay Castle* and the three "Clan"-class refrigerated ships under nominal ownership of Union-Castle.

The two remaining cargo ships were the *Tantallon Castle* and *Tintagel Castle*. There was also one other cargo ship, the *Kinnaird Castle*, which, under King Line management, was running in Union-Castle service. The *Kinpurnie Castle* (originally *Clan Stewart*) had been disposed of during 1968 to Greek owners.

But this situation was not to last for long, for the fleet was cut by one-third in the number of ships during 1970-71 when six of the R-class refrigerated ships, which had been laid up for some time, were sold. The first to go was the *Rochester Castle*, the sole survivor of the six pre-war refrigerated ships, and she was sold in 1970 to the Cypriot flag under the name *Glenda*. However, she was very soon sold for demolition in China and arrived at Whampoa on 13th November, 1970.

*The R-class ships*

Details:

All built by Harland & Wolff Limited, Belfast.

| | | |
|---|---|---|
| *Roslin Castle* | 7,016 gt | Completed 5.1935 |
| *Rothesay Castle* | 7,016 gt | 5.1935 |

Measurements:

Length: 443 feet 6 inches oa
426 feet 6 inches bp

Breadth: 61 feet

Engines: Eight-cylinder oil. Single screw. 16 knots.

| | | |
|---|---|---|
| *Rochester Castle* | 7,795 gt | Completed 5.1937 |
| *Roxburgh Castle* | 7,801 | 6.1937 |
| *Richmond Castle* | 7,798 | 2.1939 |
| *Rowallan Castle* | 7,798 | 3.1939 |
| *Rowallan Castle* | 7,950 | 4.1943 |
| *Richmond Castle* | 7,971 | 9.1944 |
| *Roxburgh Castle* | 8,003 | 2.1945 |
| *Riebeeck Castle* | 8,322 | 3.1946 |
| *Rustenburg Castle* | 8,322 | 6.1946 |

Measurements:

Length: 474 feet 3 inches oa 457 feet bp

Breadth: 63 feet

Engines: Eight-cylinder oil. Single screw. 16 knots.

The first of these ships was the *Roslin Castle*, which entered service in May, 1935, quickly followed by the *Rothesay Castle*. The *Rothesay Castle*, however, was short-lived, for on 4th January, 1940, she went ashore at Sanaig Point, Isle of Islay, in position 55.53N 6.21W while on a voyage from New York to the Clyde with a cargo of chilled meat, ham and bacon.

A repeat order for two slightly larger ships was placed in 1936 and these were named *Rochester Castle* and *Roxburgh Castle*, entering service in 1937. The *Roxburgh Castle* was particulary unfortunate during hostilities. On the night of 20th-21st December, 1940, she was bombed and damaged while at Liverpool and four months later, on 4th May, 1941, was again bombed and damaged at the same port. Finally, she fell victim to a submarine's (*U.107*) torpedo off Ferraria Point light, 38.12N 26.22W, in the Azores on 22nd February, 1943.

It may be said that the *Rochester Castle* was luckier. In August, 1942, she was one of a fleet of fourteen fast Allied cargo ships which, with a mighty covering force—a total of some sixty ships—formed a convoy bound for the island fortress of Malta. Operation "Pedestal" was the codename given to the convoy. Ship after ship succumbed to air and sea attack; the *Rochester Castle* was hit in No. 3 hold by two E-boat torpedoes in the early hours of 13th August, but at 5.30 am managed to rejoin the convoy. Only five ships of the battered convoy reached Malta, including the

*Rochester Castle*, which arrived at 18.00 hours on the 13th with a gaping hole 20 feet × 18 feet and some 200 smaller fragment holes in her hull. She remained at Malta, suffering many air raids without further damage, until December, 1942, when she sailed for Cape Town and on to New York for more permanent repairs, arriving back in the Mersey in the following June with chilled meat from Buenos Aires. She continued in service until 1970 and was finally broken up as *Seng Kung* in 1981 at Kaohsiung.

The next pair, again of slightly larger tonnage, came out in 1939 and were named *Richmond Castle* and *Rowallan Castle*. Both were lost. The *Rowallan Castle* was in convoy MW 9B, westbound from Alexandria in February, 1942, when she was hit by bombs on the 14th in position 34.54N 19.40E and had to be sunk by British naval gunfire. Six months later, on 4th August, the *Richmond Castle* was sunk by submarine torpedo in position 50.25N 35.05W.

Midway through the war the company took delivery of the *Rowallan Castle*, the *Richmond Castle* in 1944 and the *Roxburgh Castle* in 1945, all three ships perpetuating the names of Union-Castle vessels lost in the war. They were sisterships and all survived, being finally disposed of in 1971. The *Rowallan Castle* arrived at Kaohsiung for demolition in September, the *Richmond Castle* and *Roxburgh Castle* at Shanghai in August and July respectively.

The last two refrigerated ships were built in 1946, taking the names *Riebeeck Castle* and *Rustenburg Castle*. Both lasted until 1971 before arriving in September at Kaohsiung and Shanghai respectively for demolition.

The four "Clan" reefers, together with Safmarine tonnage, were now supplementing the mail service. During the 1970-71 season 8,126,082 boxes of deciduous fruit—apples, apricots, grapes, peaches, pears and plums—were imported in the United Kingdom, of which 95.4%—7,766,904 boxes—were discharged at Southampton. So were 3,289,620 boxes of citrus fruits—grapefruit, lemons, oranges and tangerines—52% of the United Kingdom imports of this type of fruit.

An alteration in the sailing time of the mailships from Cape Town was made in 1971 with the sailing of the *Edinburgh Castle* on 2nd June. Instead of departing at 4 pm each Wednesday, the timing was brought forward to Noon so as to give better arrival times at Las Palmas and Madeira.

Meanwhile, at the other end of the line, Union-Castle were transferring most of the work concerned with booking and shipment of cargo from London to new premises in Herbert Walker Avenue in Southampton's Western Docks, adjacent to the import and export berths, the change becoming effective from 1st November, 1971.

From the South Atlantic island of St Helena on 1st July, 1973, came a message that the *Good Hope Castle*, which should have arrived there the previous evening, had been in radio silence since leaving Ascension Island in the afternoon of 29th June. Neither could her sistership *Southampton Castle*, which was in the vicinity, raise her on radio telephone, and anxiety increased as the *Good Hope Castle* became more and more overdue. Fears were confirmed in a later message from Ascension that the ship was ablaze and had been abandoned, burning and listing, but that everyone aboard was safe.

The fire had broken out on 29th June when the ship was only thirty-five miles from Ascension and bound for Cape Town. A broken lubricating oil pipe to the starboard main engine turbo-blower sprayed oil on to an exhaust manifold, and before the resulting fire could be extinguished it spread through the engine room casing into the accommodation. The eighty-two passengers and crew took to the boats, spending some thirty-six hours in them before being taken on board the Liberian steam tanker *George F. Getty* and landed at Ascension, where the passengers were accommodated in Georgetown and the crew quartered at the United States air base.

On the night of 1st-2nd July, the *Good Hope Castle* was sighted by the *Southampton Castle*, some twenty-four miles off Portland Point, Ascension, with a 30° starboard list, but no signs of fire or smoke and with the port propeller visible in the swell. Two days later, on 4th July, the motorship *Clan Malcolm*, on a voyage to India, arrived at the scene with intentions of picking up part of the crew and putting them back on board the *Good Hope Castle*, the remainder to be repatriated to Britain in the *Southampton Castle*. At dusk that evening the *Clan Malcolm* circled the *Good Hope Castle*, reporting evidence of further severe fires, with No. 6 hatch covers glowing red, Nos 5 and 6 hatch deck cargo alight, flames on the port side of the accommodation and in the vicinity of No. 4 hatch, and with the bridge front collapsed. Next day the *Good Hope Castle* was drifting in a near-gale some 100 miles WNW

The *Good Hope Castle*, which returned to service after a fire drama in the South Atlantic.
*Lloyds List*

of Ascension, still on fire. An after-deck cargo of drums had exploded, mail in Nos 5 and 6 hatches was burning, the midship accommodation was gutted, but the hull beneath the weather-deck was seemingly still intact and in good condition.

At this time the West German ocean salvage tug *Albatros* (871 gt, 1965) was called on for assistance and on 7th July a Union-Castle superintendent, who had flown to Ascension to join the *Clan Malcolm*, was able to board the *Good Hope Castle*, albeit briefly, and report that there were no flames or smoke but that the deck was severely buckled and hot, with the bridge and accommodation completely gutted.

Two days later the tug was alongside, able to put pumps aboard and prepare a towing connection. The tug later reported further pockets of fire causing concern, for by then the prevailing weather and heavy swell prevented her from putting a fire-fighting party aboard. Nevertheless, the ship was taken in tow for Dakar, with arrival estimated as 23rd July.

The *Good Hope Castle* was boarded at times when the weather permitted, various reports indicating that the fire-ravaged areas were cooling down and the list reduced to 5-7°. An average towing speed of some 5 knots was maintained, although on 20th July the *Albatros* had to stop and uncouple the tow while she replaced a fractured exhaust valve in her own main engine. The tow continued but by-passed Dakar and headed for Las Palmas. Permission to put into port there was refused, but stores were taken and two men were placed on board the *Good Hope Castle*, housed in the boatswain's store in the forward masthouse. The decision was then made to continue the tow directly to Antwerp. By 6th August the vessels were some 200 miles SW of Cape St Vincent and on 18th August they arrived safely in Antwerp.

Inspection there revealed that the fire had destroyed the entire midships structure, including the bridge deck and navigating bridge, with only the funnel and its internal uptakes remaining undamaged. The weather deck and poop were buckled and cracked and hatch covers, deck machinery, masts and derricks and their housings were fire-damaged. There was also distortion to the shell plating in the way of the engine room and 'tween decks. Generally, the machinery space was found to be undamaged and a subsequent drydocking showed no twisting, hogging or sagging of the hull structure.

Tenders for repair were invited, 1,000 tons of steel renewals being estimated as necessary. On 28th September, 1973, the *Good Hope Castle* left Antwerp in tow of another Bugsier tug, *Heros* (479 gt, 1964), bound for Bilbao and the ship repair yard of Astilleros Espanoles, S.A., where she arrived on 9th October. After extensive repairs she left Bilbao on 19th May, 1974, and arrived at Southampton on the following day, taking up service again on the last day of that same month.

In 1973 the voyage time was again altered, although this time for a reason other than acceleration of service. World oil prices had increased enormously and, in the interests of economy and to lower the consumption of oil, one more day was added to the voyage.

At the end of 1973, after nine years of charter and having achieved great popularity as a cruise liner, the *Reina del Mar* was purchased outright by Union-Castle from Royal Mail Lines, the Pacific Steam Navigation Company's parent company. She had been in the registered ownership of Royal Mail Lines since 1969, but there was no change of name.

It caused some surprise, therefore, when after only a few months of ownership Union-Castle announced in June, 1974, that owing to the greatly increased costs of oil, which the ship burned at 135 tons per day, plus crew wages, maintenance costs, etc., the ship was no longer a viable undertaking and would be withdrawn in April, 1975. Her last cruise from Southampton began on 26th October, 1974, and after a series of three cruises from Cape Town to South America, she arrived back at her home port of Southampton in late March. The *Reina del Mar* was withdrawn from service from 1st April, and was quickly sold for breaking up, leaving Southampton on 28th May for Kaohsiung, Taiwan, where she arrived on 30th July, 1975.

In May, 1975, there came the inevitable announcement that Union-Castle and Safmarine were to phase out two ships of the mail service, the *Edinburgh Castle* and the *S.A. Oranje*, each vessel having recorded twenty-seven years of service. This announcement heralded the start of the final rundown of the mail service and the disappearance of the grandeur of luxury liner travel on the Cape Run.

The first ship withdrawn was the *S.A. Oranje*, formerly the *Pretoria Castle*, a name she had held from her launching in 1947 until 1966 when the Union-Castle and Safmarine decided to share the tonnage of the mail service. Her last arrival at Southampton from the Cape was on 8th September, 1975; after destoring, she loaded cargo only for Durban, and sailed from Southampton for the last time on 19th September, arriving at the South African port on 6th October. After discharge she sailed on, arriving at Kaohsiung, Taiwan, where so many other fine ships have been broken up, on 2nd November.

Her sistership, *Edinburgh Castle*, lasted only a few more months. Her last round trip commenced on 5th March and she arrived back at Southampton on 12th April, 1976. After destoring, she left Southampton to an accompanying lament from two pipers bound for Durban, where she arrived on 10th May. Again, only cargo had to be discharged and she, too, left for Kaohsiung, where she arrived on 3rd June for demolition.

Other withdrawals of cargo ships were being made, the *Kinnaird Castle* being sold at Durban in October, 1975. She had made news in the previous May when she completed an eight months voyage that was originally

The mail ship *S.A. Oranje,* formerly *Pretoria Castle,* withdrawn from service in 1975.
*R. Sherlock*

scheduled for three, having been delayed in congested African ports. No less than 120 days were spent anchored at Lobito, Angola, awaiting a berth. Her new owners were Dasonab Compania Naviera S.A. of Panama, who renamed her *Nazeer.*

Both the *Rothesay Castle* and the *Rotherwick Castle* were also disposed of at the end of 1975. The *Rothesay Castle*, second ship of that name in the Union-Castle fleet, was sold to Lloyd Uruguayo and was renamed *Laura*, while her sistership became the *Sea Fortune* of the Sea Fortune Shipping Company of Monrovia, a one-ship company owned by Trans Globe Maritime Limited, Hong Hong.

The passenger booking office in the Union-Castle building in Southampton's Canute Road finally closed down in April, 1976, the reservations organisation being vested in a travel office.

The building was on a site that was once the Gloucester Baths, backing on to the River Test, and was within the boundary of the land acquired by the Southampton Dock Company in 1836. The Baths buildings were taken over and converted to the first Dock House, headquarters of the Southampton Dock Company, but shortly after the opening of the Outer Dock (now Princess Alexandra Dock) in 1842, the old structure was demolished and a new building was erected in 1847 as the Customs House. It continued as such until 1892, but the then Commisioners of Customs refused to renew their lease, removing their offices to the old P & O offices in Canute Road.

The building, of flat facade, was taken over in 1895 by the Union Steamship Company, whose offices had been at No. 2 Canute Road, later occupied by the Free Labour Association. It was to remain the Southampton headquarters of the Union Line and then Union-Castle Mail SS Company for the next eighty-three years. In 1910 it was given a facelift, with new pillared entrance, while inside the walls of small-roomed offices were removed to give an open-plan arrangement.

The melancholy withdrawals continued, the next major ship to leave the fleet being the *Pendennis Castle*. Her last voyage in the mail service began from Durban on 27th May, 1976, with arrival at Southampton on 14th June.

Only seventeen years old, she did not immediately go the way of other liners, and was sold to Ocean Queen Navigation Corporation with registration at Panama and ownership in the Philippine Islands. Her role was to be that of a cruising liner; she was given the name *Ocean Queen*, her hull was painted white and her funnel was painted a golden brown. She sailed from Southampton on 6th July, 1976, and arrived at Hong Kong on 9th August, but instead of beginning her new work she was laid up. During her mail service she had been a popular ship and had returned a very fast time in February, 1968, steaming from Cape Town to Southampton in 10 days 15 hours 12 minutes, even though rough weather prevailed in the Bay of Biscay. This fast voyage was necessitated by a fifteen hours delay in loading at Cape Town. Towards the end of 1977 she was sold again, to the Kinvarra Bay

The *Pendennis Castle*, here seen in Table Bay, was withdrawn from service in 1976 and was broken up four years later. *Union-Castle*

Shipping Company Limited, being renamed *Sindbad*, still under the Panamanian registry. Later the same year she became *Sindbad I*. But she never traded under these names and arrived at Kaohsiung in April, 1980, for breaking up.

To fill the gaps in the sailing schedules left by the withdrawal of the mail ships, chartered vessels began to appear in the sailing lists: *Benlawers* of the Ben Line, Danish ships of the Ove Skou fleet and, on long time charter, the Blue Star Line's *Andalucia Star*, which joined the service on 25th June, 1976, and was repainted in Union-Castle livery.

Towards the end of 1976 the four Clan R-class were renamed in "Castle" nomenclature and were repainted in Union-Castle colouring. The *Clan Ramsey* became *Winchester Castle*; the *Clan Ranald* became *Dover Castle*

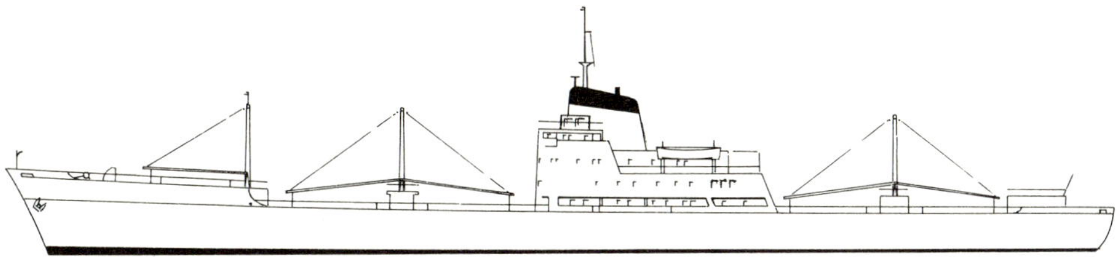

The Clan R-class ships after renaming.

and the *Clan Robertson* was renamed *Balmoral Castle*. The Houston Line vessel *Clan Ross* became *Kinpurnie Castle*. All these were revivals of previous Union-Castle names*.

In January, 1977, the London booking offices of the company in Old Bond Street closed. The end of an era was near.

*The previous *Winchester Castle* was the motor vessel built in 1930 and broken up in 1960. Winchester, in Hampshire, was the capital of England in Anglo-Saxon times.

Two earlier ships bore the name *Dover Castle*. In 1872 the first of Currie's steamships was built, but was chartered out for South American service. On her maiden voyage from Callao to Liverpool she caught fire and was scuttled on 26th August, 1872, off the Chilean coast. The second *Dover Castle* was an intermediate steamer built in 1904. She was sunk by submarine (*UC.67*) torpedo off Bona on 26th May, 1917, while serving as a hospital ship. Dover Castle stands on a cliff.

There were also two earlier ships named *Balmoral Castle*; a 3,000 ton steamer for the mail service built in 1877 and sold to Spain in 1882, and the 13,300 ton mail steamer built in 1910. She was withdrawn in 1938 and scrapped in 1939. Balmoral Castle is a Royal residence in Aberdeenshire.

One previous ship named *Kinpurnie Castle* was a "Clan" ship, built in 1954 and renamed in 1962.

At the end of 1976 the last mail service sailing lists appeared. They were short, only ten outward and nine homeward voyages arranged for the two remaining passenger vessels. Both ships were to make final arrivals on 19th September, 1977, the *S.A. Vaal* at Durban and the *Windsor Castle* at Southampton. This, however, was subsequently altered so that the *S.A. Vaal* should sail from Durban on 21st September and arrive at Southampton on 10th October.

This change was undoubtedly due to the tentative sale of the ship, for in the spring came an announcement that she had been sold to a cruising company, Festivale Maritime Corporation of Panama (formed by the American International Travel Service Inc., who already operated two ex-British liners under Carnival Cruise Lines Inc.), and was to be renamed *Festivale.* She was to be extensively modified and rebuilt to carry 1,200 passengers and fitted with recreational facilities to a high-class standard for cruising from Miami to the Caribbean.

In July the sale of the *Windsor Castle* was also announced, with delivery to her new owner, John S. Latsis of Athens, after she returned to Southampton on 15th September.

On Friday, 12th August the *Windsor Castle* left Southampton at 2 pm—one hour later than normal, due to a signal fault delaying the Waterloo-Southampton Docks boat train—with some 800 passengers, many on a sentimental journey, mails and cargo. The departure signalled the end of the mail service, for it was the last outward sailing by a British liner, and with it went a way of life for those whose links were with Britain and South Africa. As the brochure said "The 6,000 mile journey to or from South Africa could be a refreshing holiday in itself. You sailed, in the main, through warm sunlit seas and it was relaxation and enjoyment all the way, backed up, of course, by the traditional, friendly Union-Castle service".

The *Windsor Castle*'s last departure from Cape Town, her 124th in her seventeen years, on Tuesday, 6th September merited a very special send-off. As always paper tape was strewn from ship to shore, but now two military bands also played; there was an Air Force flypast, and escorting the liner was a South African naval frigate. From the frigate sailors boarded the liner in mock pirate attack and made a presentation to the Captain. Then the passengers settled to the homeward voyage—many to wallow in nostalgia.

Souvenir hunters abounded, ashtrays, towels, clocks, pictures, plaques and other movable objects being earmarked for mantlepiece trophies. One poignant presentation was made on arrival at Southampton, when the bottom rung of the ship's rope ladder, suitably inscribed, was presented to the Company's "choice" pilot—a ladder which he had so often climbed. The company also had struck a medallion—just 1,000 in number—commemorating the 120 years of the mail service.

Meanwhile, the *S.A. Vaal* had sailed from Southampton, fully booked, on Friday, 2nd September on her last round trip. She was dressed overall, as were her tugs; passengers and dockers waved, laughed and exchanged fond farewells; but underneath the gestures lay a tinge of sadness. The weather was dull and wet, the streamers hung heavily, and when the ship's siren gave farewell blasts many eyes were misty, for this departure marked the end of a service of which the port was so proud.

The *Windsor Castle* left the port for the last time on Monday, 3rd October, 1977, with a new look. Renamed *Margarita L* and wearing the Greek flag and the deep-yellow, black-topped funnel of her new owner, John S. Latsis, she left Southampton amid farewell blasts from her siren and from other ships in

A look back to the seamen's strike of June, 1966, with Union-Castle vessels in the Western Docks at Southampton. In the foreground, left to right, are the *Good Hope Castle, Reina del Mar* and *Edinburgh Castle* at 101 Berth. Astern on 102 berth is *Pendennis Castle* and at berth 104 is *S.A. Vaal.*

port. Bound for Piraeus, she was sailing into strange waters, for all her years had been spent on the Cape run.

It was purely coincidental that over the weekend before she sailed, no fewer than six of the world's ever-decreasing number of liners were gathered at the port. The *Queen Elizabeth 2* had arrived from New York and the P & O giants *Canberra* and *Oriana*, between cruises, completed with the *Windsor Castle* the gathering of the four largest operational liners in the world. The P & O *Uganda* was also there, and there were two visiting cruising ships, the Greek *Calypso* and the 30,567 gt. *Eugenio C* of the Italian-flag Costa Line.

So she sailed, and those that saw her realised sadly that a long, long chapter in the shipping history of the port was now drawing to a close, affecting the lives of many hundreds of crew members, shore staff and the staff of many ancillary undertakings connected with one of the oldest, largest and most regular of the world's shipping services.

One week later, on Monday, 10th October, the *S.A. Vaal* entered the port for the last time, ending the 120-year-old passenger/cargo liner service. The last bag of mail shipped from the Cape was handed to the Head Postmaster of Southampton who then handed a letter from the Mayor of Cape Town to Southampton's Mayor.

After discharging at 102 Berth the ship lay at her usual outward (No. 104) berth in the Western Docks until Saturday, 29th October, when, with the funnel repainted grey, with black top, she cleared the port for the last time, sailing for Japan where Kawasaki Heavy Industries were to convert her for a new life as a cruising liner.

The last two arrivals were cargo ships. The sailing and arrival schedule at Southampton for the last three months of service was:

| Sailed: | | Arrived: | |
|---|---|---|---|
| 22nd July | *Andalucia Star* | 30th August | (returned to Blue Star Line after one year time charter) |
| 29th July | *Southampton Castle* | 5th September | |
| 5th August | *Tzaneen* | — | |
| 12th August | *Windsor Castle* | 19th September | |
| 19th August | *Good Hope Castle* | 26th September | |
| 26th August | *Zebediela* | — | |
| 2nd September | *S.A. Vaal* | 10th October | |
| 8th September (Thursday) | *Kinpurnie Castle* | 18th October (Tuesday) | |
| 16th September | *Southampton Castle* | 24th October | |

The last sailing was exactly 120 years and one day from the first sailing of the *Dane* in 1857. Officially the Southampton—South Africa mail service ended with the arrival of the *Southampton Castle* on 24th October, 1977. It was a service which at one time could boast of eight large passenger liners and one in reserve off Netley in Southampton Water—all employed on the Cape run.

For several months the two fast cargo liners of the mail service lay, double-banked, at 101 Berth in the Western Docks; then they were sold to the Costa Armatori SpA of Genoa. The *Good Hope Castle* sailed under her new name of *Paola C* on 16th February, 1978, and the *Southampton Castle* on 24th February under the name *Franca C*, both to trade under the Italian flag.

The remaining fleet comprised four refrigerated fruit ships, the *Balmoral Castle*, *Dover Castle*, *Kinpurnie Castle* and *Winchester Castle*, and also within the British & Commonwealth group the Clan Line owned fifteen cargo ships, with six bulk carriers under the flag of the King Line Limited.

In 1979 the four refrigerated ships lost their "Castle" nomenclature, which was replaced by the suffix "Universal". This tag originated from the Union-Castle/Safmarine's Universal Reefer Consortium, formed to market

The *Windsor Castle*, which made the last outward sailing to the Cape by a British liner on 12th August, 1977. *Skyfotos*

their reefer ships. Next year *Winchester Universal* (ex *Winchester Castle*) was sold to the Greek flag, but in 1981 three more refrigerated cargo ships were acquired from foreign owners and placed under Union-Castle control as *Caribbean Universal*, *Edinburgh Universal* and *Stirling Universal*. Later in the same year *Caribbean Universal* was transferred to the Safmarine fleet.

By the third quarter of 1983, the Clan Line and all its ships had faded from the scene, with the British & Commonwealth fleet consisting of two Union-Castle reefers, one "King"-named bulk carrier, two "Scottish" tankers and the Hong Kong-registered bulk carrier *Bridgeworth* (35,750 grt.), which was added to the fleet during 1983.

Yet, although the Union-Castle and Safmarine liners finished their service from the United Kingdom to South Africa in 1977, a tiny link was to be maintained by a small ship. In 1977 Curnow Shipping Limited, of Porthleven, Cornwall, formed the St Helena Shipping Company Limited, jointly owned by Curnow and the Government of St Helena, and in 1978 the Canadian-built *Northland Prince* (1963, 3,192 grt.) was leased to the Government of St Helena and refitted to carry some eighty passengers.

Renamed *St Helena* and managed by Curnow, the ship commenced a service from Avonmouth to the lonely Atlantic islands of Ascension and St Helena and then on to Cape Town.

In 1982 the ship was requisitioned for service during the Falkland Islands crisis, being replaced by the 698-ton, twelve-passenger *Aragonite*. Later in the year the 188-passenger/cargo liner *Centaur* (1963, 7,990 grt.) was chartered and placed on the route, but was withdrawn within a few months.

In the summer of 1983 Curnow Shipping announced the formation of the new Cape Albion Line in conjunction with TFC Tours and with it the revival of the luxury liner service between the United Kingdom and South Africa. To operate the service the 8,665-ton cruise liner *World Renaissance* was chartered, her first voyage, southbound, being scheduled for 25th November, the run to Cape Town to take seventeen days. Built in France in 1966 and later reconstructed, the ship has modern accommodation for 516 passengers.

Meanwhile, Curnow Shipping continued to run the *St Helena* on the passenger, cargo and mail service between Avonmouth and Cape Town, following the return of the vessel from fourteen months' naval service in the Falklands as a minesweeper support ship.

But when Safmarine announced in November, 1983, that their new passenger service from Southampton to Cape Town was to begin in April, 1984, Curnow Shipping declared, only a few days before their first sailing of *World Renaissance* from Plymouth, that they would be withdrawing from the route. The charter of *World Renaissance* expired in April, 1984.

*Balmoral Castle* of 1910.

# UNION LINE, CASTLE LINE and UNION-CASTLE LINE

Chronological Order

Original service:
M = Mail
I = Intermediate
Co = Coaster
T = Tender
Tg = Tug
E = Extra
C = Cargo

| Date acquired: Union Line | Date acquired: Castle Line | Name: | Grt | Original service | History: |
|---|---|---|---|---|---|
| 1854 | | *Union* | 336 | — | First vessel built for Union Steam Collier Co., registered 16th June, 1854. 1857: Sold to P & O for mail service between Mauritius and Reunion. 1858: Lengthened; later used on Bombay-China service. 1863: Resold to Hong Kong buyers. |
| 1854 | | *Briton* | 407 | — | 1857: Foundered in Bay of Biscay while on voyage to Seville. |
| 1854 | | *Norman* | 530 | M | 1863: Used on South African coastal service. 1864: Returned to U.K. and taken over by shipbuilders Lungley in part-payment for new tonnage. 1867: Sold British (same name). 1881: Lost by stranding. |
| 1854 | | *Saxon* | 493 | — | Not used on South African service. 1858: Sold to London buyers. 1898: *Garryowen* (British). 1923: Scrapped. |
| 1855 | | *Celt* | 514 | M | ex *Gothenburg* 1855. 1862: Taken over by shipbuilders Lungley in part-payment for new tonnage. 1870: *Possidon* (Greece). 1910: *Poseidon* (Turkey). 1933: Name deleted from ship registers. |
| 1855 | | *Dane* | 530 | M | 1864: Transferred to Mauritius service. 1865: Chartered to H.M. Government to carry supplies to Zanzibar for forces engaged in suppression of slave trade. 28.11.1865: Sailed Simonstown but ran ashore and wrecked approaching Port Elizabeth. |

| Date acquired: Union Line | Date acquired: Castle Line | Name | Grt | Original service | History: |
|---|---|---|---|---|---|
| 1857 | | *Phoebe* | 613 | M | Built 1851 for P. P. Brenan & Co., Liverpool. Sold to Preston & Co., Liverpool. 1861: Sold to New Zealand Steam Shipping Co. 1876: Absorbed into Union S.S. Co. of New Zealand. 1878: Sold to Newcastle, N.S.W., buyers. 1901: Hulked. 1904: Scrapped Sydney. |
| 1858 | | *Athens* | 739 | M | 5.1865: Wrecked during storm in Table Bay. |
| 1860 | | *Cambrian* | 1,055 | M | 1872: Sold to French buyers. |
| 1861 | | *Briton* | 1,160 | M | 1873: *Dromedary* (H.M. transport). 1884: Scrapped London. |
| | 1863 | *Pembroke Castle* (sailing vessel) | 1,171 | — | Traded in Indian service. 1883: Sold to Dundee & Calcutta Line of Clippers (Barrie Shipping Co.), renamed *Glasgow*; converted from ship to barque rig. 25.12.1893: Dismasted and abandoned off Scilly Isles. |
| | 1863 | *Roslin Castle* (sailing vessel) | 1,174 | — | Traded in Indian service. 1883: Sold to Dundee & Calcutta Line of Clippers (Barrie Shipping Co.), renamed *London*; converted from ship to barque rig. 29.12.1892: Wrecked at Key West, Florida. |
| | 1863 | *Stirling Castle* (sailing vessel) | 1,165 | — | The first of Currie's "Castle" traders for Indian service. 1874: Sold. |
| | 1863 | *Warwick Castle* (sailing vessel) | 1,158 | — | Traded in Indian service. 1870: Sold British (same name). 1890: *Cimbria* (Denmark). 1905: *Cimbria* (Italy). 1911: Scrapped. |
| 1863 | | *Roman* | 1,282 | M | Later used on Intermediate service. 1888: Used on feeder service between Southampton and Hamburg. 1889: *Adana* (Turkey). 1912: Name deleted from ship registers. |
| 1863 | | *Saxon* | 1,142 | M | 1876: Sold to Hull buyers. |
| 1864 | | *Anglian* | 661 | — | Inter-Colonial service. 1869: Sold to Palgrave Murphy, Dublin. 1882: *City of Lisbon* (British). 1903: Sunk in collision with Isle of Man steamer *Douglas* off New Brighton. |

| Date acquired: Union Line | Date acquired: Castle Line | Name | Grt | Original service | History: |
|---|---|---|---|---|---|
| | 1864 | *Arundel Castle* (sailing vessel) | 1,042 | — | Traded in Indian service. 1883: Sold to Dundee & Calcutta Line of Clippers (Barrie Shipping Co.). Renamed *Chittagong*; converted from ship to barque rig. 1896: *Imperator* (Norway). 1901: Sold (same name) to Mitchell Cotts & Co.; used as a hulk at East London. 1918: Rerigged as a barque, renamed *Chittagong* (Mitchell Cotts & Co.). 1920: *Annitsa Zalocosta* (Greece). 1922: Scrapped. |
| | 1864 | *Kenilworth Castle* (sailing vessel) | 1,062 | — | Traded in Indian service. 1871: Wrecked. |
| 1865 | | *Mauritius* | 587 | — | Inter-colonial service. 1869: Sold British (same name). 1901: *Industria* (Spain). 12.1910: Sunk in collision. |
| 1865 | | *Natal* | 618 | Co | 1883: Sold to Trinder, Anderson & Co. for Australia/Singapore service, (same name). 1887: (same name, Siam). 1890: *Srie Bandjor* (Siam). 1899: *Alava* (Philippines). 26.9.1905: Ashore at Cavite, Philippines. Total loss. |
| | 1865 | *Tantallon Castle* (sailing vessel) | 1,057 | — | 1883: Sold to Dundee & Calcutta Line of Clippers (Barrie Shipping Co.). Renamed *Dacca*; converted from ship to barque rig. 1898: *Macca* (Norway). 1912: Scrapped Holland. |
| 1866 | | *Celt* | 1,439 | M | 1874: Lengthened; tonnage increased to 2,112 gt. 2.1875: Wrecked near Ratel River, between Cape Agulhas and Danger Point. |
| 1866 | | *Dane* | 788 | — | Inter-colonial service, mostly South Africa—Ceylon. 1871: *Atlantico* (Spain). 1878: Lost at sea. |
| 1866 | | *Norseman* | 1,386 | M | 1873: Sold to West Indies & Brazil Telegraph Co., used as a cable ship. 1892: Damaged in a storm and 1898. Scrapped Holland. |
| | 1867 | *Carnarvon Castle* (sailing vessel) | 1,200 | — | Traded in Indian service. 1887: Sold British (same name). 1897: *Nurnberg* (Germany). 1905: *Nurnberg* (Norway). 1.1910: Abandoned at sea. |
| | 1868 | *Carisbrooke Castle* (sailing vessel) | 1,315 | — | Traded in Indian service. 1889: Sold to Dundee & Calcutta Line of Clippers (Barrie Shipping Co.). Renamed *Errol*. 1900: To Norway (same name). 18.6.1909: Wrecked on Middleton Reef, S. Pacific. |

| Date acquired: Union Line | Date acquired: Castle Line | Name | Grt | Original service | History: |
|---|---|---|---|---|---|
| 1869 | | *Northam* | 1,330 | M | Built 1858 for P & O. 1876: Sold to Liverpool buyers, renamed *Stars and Stripes*; converted to sailing ship. 21.12.1878: Caught fire and abandoned at sea. |
| 1871 | | *Danube* | 2,039 | M | Built 1866 for R.M.S.P. Co. 1888: Scrapped. |
| 1871 | | *Syria* | 1,959 | M | Built 1863 for P & O as a paddle steamer. 1871: converted to a screw steamer. 1878: Acquired by shipbuilders Laing in part-payment for new steamer *Durban* (built 1877) 4.4.1880: Foundered while bound to Liverpool from New Orleans. |
| 1872 | | *European* | 2,272 | M | Built 1869 as *Europe*. 12.1877: Wrecked off Ushant. |
| 1872 | | *Zulu* | 944 | Co | Name originally intended to be *Zanzibar*; for coastal service from Zanzibar. 1877: Sold locally. |
| 1872 | | *Asiatic* | 2,066 | M | Purchased in anticipation of a new mail contract. Later used on Intermediate service. 1888: Sold to Glasgow buyers (same name). 1891: *Jaffar* (British). 1895: Scrapped. |
| | 1872 | *Courland* | 1,241 | M | Built for Leith, Hull & Hamburg S.P. Co. Chartered to D. Currie, then 1875: Sold to D. Currie. Put on African coastal service. 1895: Sold to Dada Abdoola & Co., Durban. 1901: Sold to Bombay S.N. Co. 1925: Scrapped Bombay. |
| | 1872 | *Dover Castle* | 2,341 | E | See text. |
| | 1872 | *Edinburgh Castle* | 2,678 | M | See text. |
| | 1872 | *Elizabeth Martin* | 1,246 | M | Named after Donald Currie's mother. 1877: South African coastal service. 1882: *Athens* (Greece). 1891: *Samos* (Greece). War loss, First World War. |
| | 1872 | *Gothland* | 1,482 | M | Built 1871 for Leith, Hull & Hamburg Line. Used on Cape mail service. 1876: Transferred to Liverpool & Hamburg Line. 1915: Sold to Admiralty as a blockship but not used. 1919: Sold British (same name). 1922: *Trude Bremer* (Germany). 1924: Scrapped Germany. |

| Date acquired: Union Line | Date acquired: Castle Line | Name | Grt | Original service | History: |
|---|---|---|---|---|---|
| | 1872 | *Iceland* | 1,474 | M | Built 1871 for Leith, Hull & Hamburg Line. Used on Cape mail service. 1873: Transferred to Liverpool & Hamburg Line, used on U.K.-Continent service. 18.12.1876: Stranded on Texel Island, off Dutch coast. |
| | 1872 | *Lapland* | 1,269 | M | Built for Leith, Hull & Hamburg S.P. Co. Chartered to D. Currie then 1875: Sold to D. Currie. Later used on South African coastal service. 1882: Reverted to U.K.—Continent service. 1902: *Shuna* (British). 1906: *Sofia M* (Greece). 1911: *Scutari* (Turkey). 1912: *Varvara* (Greece). 19.7.1917: Sunk by submarine torpedo in Mediterranean. |
| | 1872 | *Walmer Castle* | 2,446 | M | Later used on Extra and Intermediate services. 1880: *Valencia* (Spain). 1889: Sunk in collision in North Sea. |
| | 1872 | *Westmoreland* | 1,372 | M | Built 1870 for Liverpool & Hamburg Line. 1872: Used on Cape mail service (one voyage only). 1912: *Mogador* (France). 4.11.1917: Sunk by submarine torpedo in Mediterranean. |
| | 1872 | *Windsor Castle* | 2,670 | M | See text. |
| 1873 | | *African* | 2,019 | M | 1881: Used on South African coastal service. 1885: Sold British (same name). 15.2.1887: Wrecked at Abu Madaff, Red Sea. |
| 1873 | | *American* | 2,126 | M | 23.4.1880: Foundered at sea after losing propeller off Las Palmas. |
| 1873 | | *Anglian* | 2,026 | M | 1886: Used on South African coastal service. 1894: Sold to Huddart, Parker Ltd., Australia; (same name). 1913: Converted to a hulk at Adelaide. 1933: Scuttled off Sydney Heads. |
| 1873 | | *Basuto* | 1,034 | Co | 1876: Sold French (same name). 11.10.1876: Foundered in heavy weather off La Coruna on first voyage for new owners. |
| 1873 | | *Kafir* | 982 | Co | 2.1878: Wrecked near Cape Point. |
| 1873 | | *Namaqua* | 352 | Co | Used on Port Nolloth—Cape Town coastal service, mainly for carriage of copper ore. 3.1876: Wrecked off Port Nolloth. |

| Date acquired: Union Line | Date acquired: Castle Line | Name | Grt | Original service | History: |
|---|---|---|---|---|---|
| 1873 | | *Teuton* | 1,741 | M | Built 1869 as *Glenartney*. 1875: Lengthened and tonnage increased to 2,313 gt. Later used on Intermediate service. 8.1881: Wrecked off Quoin Point, Cape Colony. |
| | 1873 | *Florence* | 616 | Co | Built 1865 for Leith, Hull & Hamburg S.P. Co. 1873: Chartered by D. Currie and after alterations used on South African coastal service. 1889: *Kriti* (Turkey). 1900: *Crete* (Greece). 1912: *Guirrit* (Turkey). 1919: Scrapped. |
| 1874 | | *Nyanza* | 2,082 | M | Built 1864 for P & O as a two-funnelled paddle steamer. 1874: Converted to screw steamer and altered to brig rig, with one funnel. 1880: Transferred to Cape Town—Zanzibar service. Was so much admired by Sultan of Zanzibar that he purchased her (after only one voyage) for use as a private yacht. When not in use as a yacht was used in passenger/mail/cargo service to Bombay. Eventually laid up at Zanzibar and 1904: Sold for scrapping. |
| | 1875 | *Koodoo* | 53 | Tg | Used in service at Port Elizabeth. circa 1924: Withdrawn. |
| | 1876 | *Dunrobin Castle* | 2,820 | M | 1883: Transferred to Intermediate service. 1893: *Notre Dame de Salut* (France). Later *Etoile* (France). 1914: Scrapped Genoa. |
| 1876 | | *Nubian* | 3,088 | M | Bought while still building on stocks. 1891: Re-engined, the two original funnels being replaced by one. Placed in Intermediate service. 12.1892: Wrecked in River Tagus, near Lisbon. |
| | 1876 | *Stettin* | 876 | M | Built 1864 for Leith, Hull & Hamburg S.P. Co. 1876: Placed in South African mail service as a replacement vessel for *Windsor Castle* (1872) when that ship was wrecked in October, 1876. Later used on South African coastal service. 1878: Returned to North Sea trade. 1933: Scrapped Bo'ness. |
| | 1877 | *Balmoral Castle* | 2,948 | M | See text. |
| | 1877 | *Dublin Castle* | 2,911 | M | 1882: *Santo Domingo* (Spain). 7.1898: Wrecked off Cuba. |

| Date acquired: Union Line | Date acquired: Castle Line | Name | Grt | Original service | History: |
|---|---|---|---|---|---|
| | 1877 | *Melrose* | 840 | Co | Originally intended to be named *Maritzburg*. Operated in South African coastal service, advertised as a "Royal Colonial Mail" steamer. 1890: First vessel to use South African coal as fuel. 1894: *Annie Hough* (British). 1901: *Emyrne* (France). 5.1911: Wrecked. |
| | 1877 | *Taymouth Castle* | 2,069 | E | 1878: Used on Intermediate service. 1891: *Ocamo* (British). 1915: *Ocamo* (Canadian). 1922: Scrapped. |
| | 1877 | *Warwick Castle* | 3,056 | M | 1891: Re-engined and rebuilt (3,956 gt.), transferred to Intermediate service. 1897: *Jerome* (Booth Line). 1911: *Kerasounde* (Turkey). 1921: Scrapped. |
| 1877 | | *Durban* | 2,875 | M | Later used in Intermediate service and afterward as a cargo ship. 6.1893: Wrecked near Santa Cruz, Teneriffe. |
| 1877 | | *German* | 3,028 | M | 1889: Transferred to Intermediate service. 1896: *Sempione* (Italy). 10.1902: Hulked. |
| 1878 | | *Pretoria* | 3,199 | M | Later used on Intermediate service. 1897: Sold Canada (same name). 1907: *Saidieh* (British). 1.6.1915: Sunk by submarine torpedo six miles N.E. from Elbow buoy. |
| 1878 (circa) | | *Seagull* | 24 | Tg | Used in service at Southampton. 1898: Sold. |
| 1878 | | *Union* | 110 | Tg | Used in service at Durban. 9.1894: Foundered on Chinde Bar. |
| | 1878 | *Conway Castle* | 2,966 | M | 1883: Transferred to Intermediate service. 10.5.1893: Grounded and wrecked 50 miles from Tamatave, Madagascar, en route to Durban. |
| | 1878 | *Dunkeld* | 1,158 | Co | 1890: *Alcira* (Spain). 7.9.1914: Sunk in collision off Cape de Gata. |
| | 1878 | *Venice* | 511 | Co | 1898: *Lusitano* (Portugal—Lourenco Marques). 1902: Hulked. |
| | 1879 | *Duart Castle* | 1,839 | E | Built 1878 as *Adjutant*. 1891: *Oruro* (British). 1923: *Oruro* (Indian). 1925: Scrapped. |
| 1879 | | *Arab* | 3,192 | M | 1891: Transferred to Intermediate service. 1900: Scrapped. |

| Date acquired: Union Line | Date acquired: Castle Line | Name | Grt | Original service | History: |
|---|---|---|---|---|---|
| 1880 | | *Trojan* | 3,650 | M | 1889: Transferred to Intermediate service. Used during Boer War as hospital ship. 1900: Scrapped. |
| | 1880 | *Grantully Castle* | 3,454 | M | 1896: *Augustine* (Booth Line). 1912: Scrapped Falmouth. |
| | 1880 | *Kinfauns Castle* | 3,507 | M | 1883: Sold to Russian Volunteer Fleet, renamed *Moskva.* 1895: Sold to Russian Navy for use as a training ship, renamed *Prut.* 1909: Fitted out as a minelayer. 29.10.1914: Sunk by gunfire of German battle cruiser *Göben* 10 miles south of Cape Fiolen, Black Sea. |
| | 1881 | *Drummond Castle* | 3,663 | M | 1894: Transferred to Intermediate service. 17.6.1896: Wrecked off Ushant. |
| | 1881 | *Garth Castle* | 3,704 | M | 1892: Transferred to Intermediate service. 1901: Sold to Elder Dempster Line but promptly resold to Khedivial Mail Line, renamed *Ismailia.* 1921: *Brunette* (Italy). 1923: Scrapped. |
| 1881 | | *Spartan* | 3,487 | M | Later used on Intermediate service. Used during Boer War as a troopship. 1900: *Fiume* (Italy). 1902: Scrapped. |
| 1882 | | *Athenian* | 3,877 | M | 1887: Re-engined from single screw compound to triple expansion. 1897: Sold to Canadian Pacific for new service serving Klondyke Gold Rush. 12.2.1898: Sailed from Southampton for Vancouver via Cape Horn; subsequently made six voyages from Vancouver to Skagway with prospectors, then placed on trans-Pacific run. 1907: Scrapped Osaka. |
| 1882 | | *Moor* | 3,688 | M | See text. |
| 1883 | | *Mexican* | 4,661 | M | 4.4.1900: Sank 70 miles from Cape Town soon after sailing from the port and following collision in fog with ss *Winkfield* (British). |
| 1883 | | *Tartar* | 4,425 | M | 1889: Re-engined from single screw compound to triple expansion. 1897: Sold to Canadian Pacific for new service serving Klondyke Gold Rush. 5.2.1898: Sailed from Southampton for Vancouver via Cape Horn. 17.10.1907: Beached at English Bay, B.C., after collision with local coastal steamer *Charmer* (1887/1,081 gt.). Sold to Japanese shipbreakers. 1908: Scrapped Osaka. |

| Date acquired: Union Line | Date acquired: Castle Line | Name | Grt | Original service | History: |
|---|---|---|---|---|---|
| | 1883 | *Dolphin* | 49 | Tg | Used in service at East London. 1900: Sold to C. H. Knight, Cape Town. |
| | 1883 | *Dunbar Castle* | 2,837 | I | Intended to be named *Doune Castle.* Sometimes used in Mail service but primarily as an Extra steamer, serving Mauritius. 1895: *Olympia* (U.S.A.). 12.1910: Wrecked on coast of Alaska. |
| | 1883 | *Hawarden Castle* | 4,380 | M | Intended to be named *Ardtornish Castle*, but as a mark of respect to Prime Minister William Gladstone was renamed *Hawarden Castle*, after Gladstone's home in Wales. The ship was launched on the Clyde by Mrs. Gladstone. 1903: Sold to Booth Line, renamed *Cyril.* 9.1905: Lost in collision with Booth Line's *Anselm* in River Amazon. |
| | 1883 | *Methven Castle* | 2,681 | I | Intended to be named firstly, *Arundel Castle*, then *Cluny Castle*. Used occasionally on Mail service. 1897: *Columbia* (U.S.A.). 1903: Converted to a tanker, renamed *Rosecrans.* 1.1913: Wrecked. |
| | 1883 | *Norham Castle* | 4,240 | M | 1903: *Martinique* (France). 1933: Scrapped Italy. |
| | 1883 | *Pembroke Castle* | 3,946 | I | Acquired while still building on stocks. First 4-masted steamer of Castle Line. Replaced sailing ship of same name, being acquired same year as sailing ship was disposed of. Occasionally used on Mail Service. 1906: *Bezmi-Alem* (Turkey). 8.1915: Sunk by Russian Fleet near Samsoun, Turkey. |
| | 1883 | *Roslin Castle* | 4,267 | M | Intended to be named *Armadale Castle.* 1905: Sold to German buyers but fitted out as a storeship for Russian Baltic Fleet, renamed *Regina.* 3.1905: Ran aground off Mozambique. Refloated and towed to Durban. Sold to Italian buyers. 1908. Scrapped Genoa. |
| | 1883 | *Cluny Castle* (sailing vessel) | 1,934 | — | The last of Donald Currie's Indian Trade sailing ships. 1889: *Rowena* (British). 1913: *Rowena* (Finland). 1924: Scrapped. |
| 1884 | | *Carnarvon* | 104 | Tg | In service at Durban and Lourenco Marques. 1896: Sold (same name) to Lourenco Marques buyers. 11.1902: Lost at sea without trace. |

| Date acquired: Union Line | Date acquired: Castle Line | Name | Grt | Original service | History: |
|---|---|---|---|---|---|
| 1886 | | *African* | 1,372 | Co | 1893: *Graceful* (British). 1902: *Sovereign* (Norway). 1912: *Zeta* (Norway). 1931: Scrapped. |
| | 1886 | *Finland* | 1,363 | — | Laid down as *Cape Merchant* for Cape & Natal Merchants Line. Taken over by and completed for Donald Currie. 26.4.1887: Ran aground east of Kowie River while bound to Mauritius from Cape Town. Lost. |
| 1887 | | *Saxon* | 469 | Co | 1895: Sold Portuguese buyers (same name). 1.1896: Wrecked on coast of Zululand while on delivery voyage from Durban to new owners in Portuguese East Africa. |
| 1889 | | *Dane* | 3,666 | I | Built 1870 for P & O as *Australia*. 1893: Scrapped. |
| 1889 | | *Midge* | 64 | Tg | Used in service at East London. 1905: Withdrawn from service when replaced by tender/tug *Stork* (which see). 1906: Sold to African Fisheries Co. |
| 1890 | | *Norseman* | 938 | C | 1893: Sold British owners (same name). 1895: *Saint Antoine* (France). 26.5.1928: Wrecked 30 miles S.W. of Noumea, New Caledonia. |
| 1890 | | *Roman* | 3,021 | I | Built 1870 as *Nile* for R.M.S.P. Co. 1890: Proved to be unsuitable for Cape Intermediate service so placed on Hamburg-Southampton feeder service. 1891: Scrapped. |
| 1890 | | *Tyrian* | 1,455 | Co | 1894: Sold Australia (same name). 1914: *Kiodo Maru No. 16* (Japan). 1920: *Kyodo Maru No. 16* (Japan). 14.11.1938: Caught fire off Tsingtao. Towed in, wreck beached. |
| | 1890 | *Doune Castle* | 4,045 | I | 1904: Reverted to shipbuilders Barclay Curle in part-payment for new tonnage. 1904: Sold to Danish East Asiatic Co., renamed *Saint Domingo*. 1905: Resold to Russian subsidiary company, renamed *Curonia*. 1913: *Kaijo Maru* (Japan). 1919: *Susana II* (Philippines). 1936: Scrapped. |

| Date acquired: Union Line | Date acquired: Castle Line | Name | Grt | Original service | History: |
|---|---|---|---|---|---|
| | 1890 | *Dunottar Castle* | 5,625 | M | First Castle Line steamer fitted with two funnels. 1904: Withdrawn from service. 1907: Chartered to Panama Railroad Co. for New York/Panama run. 1909-12: Chartered for cruising service, including 1911 cruise to India for Delhi Durbar. 1913: Sold to R.M.S.P. Co., renamed *Caribbean.* 1914: Requisitioned by Admiralty and 27.9.1915: Foundered off Cape Wrath while bound for Scapa Flow. |

The *Dunottar Castle* of 1890 was the first Castle Line ship with two funnels.
*Tom Rayner collection*

| Date acquired: Union Line | Date acquired: Castle Line | Name | Grt | Original service | History: |
|---|---|---|---|---|---|
| 1891 | | *Scot* | 6,844 | M | 1896: Lengthened by 54 feet and tonnage increased to 7,815 gt. 1905: Sold to Hamburg Amerika Line, renamed *Oceana.* 1910: Sold to American buyers for service between New York and Bermuda. 1916: *Alfonso XIII* (Spain). 1923: *Vasco Nunez de Balboa* (Spain). 1927: Scrapped Italy. |
| | 1891 | *Lismore Castle* | 4,046 | I | 1904: Taken over by shipbuilders Barclay Curle in part-payment for new tonnage, renamed *Westmount.* 1905: *C. Lopez y Lopez* (Spain). 1931: Scrapped. |
| 1892 | | *Natal* | 158 | T | Used as a passenger tender at Durban. 1913: Sold to Cape Town buyers for Table Bay pleasure cruises, renamed *Sir Fred.* |

| Date acquired: Union Line | Date acquired: Castle Line | Name | Grt | Original service | History: |
|---|---|---|---|---|---|
| 1893 | | *Gaul* | 4,745 | I | 1906: Sold to R.M.S.P. Co., renamed *Sabor*. 1908: *Carmarthenshire* (Shire Line). 1913: *Chaleur*. 1927: Scrapped Holland. |
| 1893 | | *Goth* | 4,738 | I | 1913: Sold to R.M.S.P. Co., renamed *Cobequid*. 13.1.1914: Wrecked, Bay of Fundy. |
| 1893 | | *Greek* | 4,747 | I | 1906: Sold to R.M.S.P. Co., renamed *Segura*. 1908: *Pembrokeshire* (Shire Line). 1913: *Chignecto* (R.M.S.P. Co.). 1927: Scrapped Holland. |
| 1894 | | *Guelph* | 4,917 | I | Used on west coast service, then 1909: commenced east coast service to Durban via Suez. 1913: Sold to R.M.S.P. Co., renamed *Caraquet*. 6.1923: Wrecked off Bermuda. |
| 1894 | | *Norman* | 7,537 | M | See text. |
| | 1894 | *Harlech Castle* | 3,624 | I | 1904: Sold to Earl Fitzwilliam as a yacht for a treasure hunting expedition to Cocos Islands, renamed *Veronique*. 1915: *Iquitos* (Peruvian Navy transport). 1923: *Amazonas* (Peru). 1934: Scrapped. |
| | 1894 | *Tantallon Castle* | 5,636 | M | See text. |
| | 1895 | *Arundel Castle* | 4,588 | I | 1905: Sold to Danish East Asiatic Co., renamed *Birma*. 1909: Transferred to Russian subsidiary company, renamed *Mitau*. 1918: Reverted to parent company. 1921: *Jozef Pilsudski* (Poland). 1924: *Wilbo* (German). 1924: Scrapped Italy. |
| 1895 | | *Gascon* (intended to be) | 5,237 | — | Built 1891 as *Ruthenia*. 1892: *Mariposa*. In September, 1895, the Union Line agreed to purchase the vessel from Elder Dempster Line, advertising the ship to sail in the Intermediate service in October, 1895. But before delivery could be taken the vessel ran aground and was wrecked in Straits of Bellevue, St. Lawrence river. |
| 1896 | | *Falcon* | 41 | T | See text. |
| | 1896 | *Dunvegan Castle* | 5,958 | M | 1904: Used for cruising to Norway, the Mediterranean and round the U.K., then laid up at Netley. 1910: Placed on East African service. 1912: Used on Intermediate service, replacing *Guelph*, which was sold. 1914: Again laid up at Netley, but requisitioned on outbreak of |

| Date acquired: Union Line | Date acquired: Castle Line | Name | Grt | Original service | History: |
|---|---|---|---|---|---|
| | | | | | war, serving as a transport and then as a hospital ship. 1918: Used on Liverpool/ New York service under the management of the Shipping Controller. 1919: Chartered to French Government for repatriating French P.O.W's. 1919: Reverted to owners, placed on East African service. 1923: Scrapped Germany. |
| | 1896 | *Tintagel Castle* | 5,531 | I | 1912: *Liger* (France). 1923: Scrapped Genoa. |
| | 1897 | *Avondale Castle* | 5,531 | I | 1912: *Garonna* (France). 1923: Scrapped Bordeaux. |
| | 1897 | *Dunolly Castle* | 4,167 | I | 1905: Sold to Danish East Asiatic Co., renamed *Juliette*. 1905: Transferred to Russian subsidiary company, renamed *Arconia*. 1910: *Hittfeld* (Germany). 1913: *Ioannina* (Greece). 15.12.1917: Sunk by submarine torpedo off Azores. |
| | 1897 | *Raglan Castle* | 4,324 | I | Intended to be named *Dunluce Castle*. 1905: Sold for use as a storeship in Russian Navy and renamed *Hanna*, but after Russian collapse in Russo-Japanese war was promptly resold to Danish East Asiatic Co., renamed *Saint Domingo*. 1908: *Raglan Castle* (Union Castle). 1909: *Pythia* (Norway). 1917: Converted to tanker/whaling depot ship. 1931: *Ready* (Norway). 1937: Scrapped. |
| 1897 | | *Briton* | 10,248 | M | See text. |
| 1897 | | *Gaika* | 6,287 | I | 1928: Scrapped. |
| 1897 | | *Gascon* | 6,288 | I | 1910: Transferred from west coast to east coast service—the London/Durban route via Suez. 1914: the first Union-Castle liner to sail for South Africa after the start of World War I. 1914: Requisitioned for use as a hospital ship. 1920: Reverted to regular Intermediate service. 1.1926: Laid up at Netley but recommissioned later in same year. 5.1928: Laid up in East India Dock, London. 9.1928: Scrapped Inverkeithing. |
| 1897 | | *Goorkha* | 6,335 | I | 1926: Scrapped Italy. |

| Date acquired: Union Line | Date acquired: Castle Line | Name | Grt | Original service | History: |
|---|---|---|---|---|---|
| 1898 | | *German* | 6,763 | I | 1899: Used as a transport during Boer War. 1914: Renamed *Glengorm Castle*. Converted to a hospital ship. 1918: Used as a troopship. 1921: Made a special voyage in Cape Mail service while still under Government control. 1925: Reverted to owners' Intermediate service. 1930: Scrapped Holland. |
| 1898 | | *Sabine* | 3,809 | C | Built 1894 as *Marino*. 1921: Sold to Bullard, King & Co. (Natal Line) renamed *Umzinto*. 1925: Scrapped Holland. |
| 1898 | | *Sandusky* | 5,257 | C | See text. |
| 1898 | | *Susquehanna* | 3,702 | C | Built 1896 as *Mount Sephar*. 1921: Sold to Denaby & Cadeby Main Collieries Ltd., renamed *London City* and used as a coal hulk at Brixham, Devon. Later transferred to Torbay & Brixham Coaling Co. Ltd. 15.7.1940: Bombed by enemy aircraft and sunk in Brixham Harbour. Later refloated and repaired. 31.3.1942: Again bombed and sunk. Wreckage later removed. |
| 1898 | | *Titan* | 151 | Tg | Used in service at Durban. 1902: Sold to South African Boating Co. 1930: Scrapped. |
| | 1898 | *Braemar Castle* | 6,266 | I | Used on Cape run until 1909, then chartered by Government and used as a transport. 1915: Converted to a hospital ship. 23.11.1916: Struck a mine in Mykoni Channel, Mediterranean. Beached. Repaired at Spezia. 1918: Used as Allied Base Hospital, Murmansk. 1920: Made further intermediate sailing in owners' service, but 1921: Reverted to troopship service. 1924: Scrapped Italy. |
| | 1898 | *Carisbrook Castle* | 7,594 | M | See text. |
| | 1899 | *Kildonan Castle* | 9,692 | M | See text. |
| | 1899 | *Kinfauns Castle* | 9,664 | M | Used in the Mail service until 1914, then requisitioned and converted to an armed merchant cruiser. Later placed on trooping service. 1920: reverted to owners' mail service, but 1922: Laid up at Netley. Made some emergency voyages during a shipping strike. 1927: Scrapped Holland. |

| Date acquired: Union Line | Date acquired: Castle Line | Name | Grt | Original service | History: |
|---|---|---|---|---|---|
| | 1899 | *Penguin* | 123 | Tg | Used in service at East London. 1924: *Nyati* (African Wharfage & Lighterage Co., Mombasa). 1928: Dismantled. |
| 1899 | | *Galeka* | 6,772 | I | Last vessel built for the Union Line. 1914: Requisitioned for use as a transport. 1915: Converted to a hospital ship. 28.10.1916. Struck a mine 5 miles N.W. of Cape La Hague, Cherbourg Peninsula while on cross-Channel service. Abandoned. Drifted ashore on to rocks and wrecked. |

| Date acquired by Union-Castle Line: | Name | Grt | Original service | History: |
|---|---|---|---|---|
| 1900 | *Galician* | 6,575 | I | Laid down for the Union Line but completed after amalgamation. 1914: Captured near Canary Islands by German commerce raider *Kaiser Wilhelm der Grosse*, but later released due to number of passengers and children on ship. 1914: Renamed *Glenart Castle*. 1915: Requisitioned as a hospital ship. 1.3.1917: Torpedoed by submarine off Owers light vessel while on voyage from Havre to Southampton with wounded personnel. Towed to Portsmouth, repaired. 26.2.1918: Sunk by submarine torpedo 10 miles west of Lundy Island while bound from Newport, Mon., to Brest. |
| 1900 | *Saxon* | 12,385 | M | See text. |
| 1901 | *Alnwick Castle* | 5,893 | E | See text. |
| 1901 | *Aros Castle* | 4,460 | C | See text. |
| 1901 | *Bellona* (lighter) | 117 | — | 6.1912: Wrecked near Stoney Bay, Cape Hangklip. |
| 1901 | *Corfe Castle* | 4,592 | C | 1927: *Ostsee* (Germany). 1932: Scrapped. |
| 1901 | *Gordon Castle* | 4,406 | C | Bought while still building on stocks. 1924: Scrapped. |
| 1901 | *Lochgair* (lighter) | 111 | — | Built in 1888. Used at Port Elizabeth during Boer War to help discharge of ships loaded with war supplies and anchored in Algoa Bay. |
| 1901 | *Machrie* (Yawl-rigged steamer) | 251 | — | Built in 1900. 1905: Sold Spanish (same name). 1923: *Margarita* (Spain). 1924: *Anselmi* (Spain). 1932: *Margarita* (Spain). 1939: *Anselmi* (Spain). 1965: Scrapped. |
| 1901 | *York Castle* | 5,517 | C | 1924: *Terenzo* (Italy). 1932: Scrapped. |

| Date acquired by Union-Castle Line | Name | Grt | Original service | History: |
|---|---|---|---|---|
| 1902 | *Berwick Castle* | 5,883 | E | 10.1919: Gutted by fire in Kilindini Harbour, Mombasa. Later laid up in Durban Bay, reported renamed *Andorra Castle*. 1925: Scrapped Italy. |
| 1902 | *Cawdor Castle* | 6,235 | E | See text. |
| 1902 | *Newark Castle* | 6,224 | E | See text. |
| 1902 | *Walmer Castle* | 12,546 | M | See text. |
| 1903 | *Armadale Castle* | 12,973 | M | 1935: Withdrawn from service, and 1936: Scrapped. |
| 1903 | *Cluny Castle* | 5,152 | E | 1924: Sold to Bullard, King & Co. (Natal Line), renamed *Umkuzi*. 1939: Scrapped. |
| 1903 | *Comrie Castle* | 5,167 | E | Used on U.K./Mauritius service. Requisitioned during First World War for use as a troop transport. Reverted to owners' service after war. 1924: Sold to Bullard, King & Co. (Natal Line) renamed *Umvoti*. 29..7.1940: Requisitioned by Admiralty, scuttled as a blockship in Folkestone Harbour. 1943: Wreckage removed and cut up on beach. |
| 1904 | *Dover Castle* | 8,271 | I | See text. |
| 1904 | *Dunluce Castle* | 8,114 | I | 1939: Sold for scrapping but taken over by Admiralty. Used as an accommodation ship at Immingham and later as a depot ship at Scapa Flow. 1945: Transferred to M.O.W.T. for disposal. Sold and scrapped at Inverkeithing. |
| 1904 | *Durham Castle* | 8,217 | I | 1939: Sold for scrapping but taken over by Admiralty. 1.1940: Mined and sunk off Invergordon, while being towed to Scapa Flow. |
| 1904 | *Helius* | 4,579 | — | Built 1888 as *Dresden*. 1903: *Helius* (Houston Line passenger ship to South Africa). Acquired by Union-Castle Line but not used; laid up at Netley. 1906: *Tirimujghian* (Turkey). 1911: Name removed from ship registers. |
| 1904 | *Kenilworth Castle* | 12,975 | M | 1907: First vessel to use Natal coal (2,000 tons) for the long voyage to U.K. Previously this local coal had been found to be subject to regular spontaneous combustion and was not considered suitable for long-term bunker usage. 1936: Scrapped. |

| Date acquired by Union-Castle Line | Name | Grt | Original service | History: |
|---|---|---|---|---|
| 1905 | *Stork* | 278 | Tg | Used as passenger tender and tug at East London. Replaced the *Midge* (of 1889). 1942: Sold South Africa (same name). 1955: Name deleted from ship registers. |
| 1907 | *Hansa* | 880 | Co | Built 1904 for D. Currie's Liverpool & Hamburg Line. 1906: Chartered by Union-Castle, used on Southampton—Continental feeder service. Acquired the following year. 1937: *Stanray* (British). 1938: Scrapped. |
| 1910 | *Balmoral Castle* | 13,361 | M | See text. |
| 1910 | *Edinburgh Castle* | 13,330 | M | See text. |
| 1910 | *Firefly* (launch) | — | — | 1910: Shipped to East Africa on *Dunluce Castle* for service in local ports. |
| 1910 | *Garth Castle* | 7,612 | I | See text. |
| 1910 | *Glowworm* (launch) | — | — | Served in East African ports, mainly Mombasa. 1920: Sold. |
| 1910 | *Grantully Castle* | 7,617 | I | See text. |
| 1911 | *Galway Castle* | 7,988 | I | See text. |
| 1911 | *Gloucester Castle* | 7,999 | I | 16.7.1942: Sunk by German raider *Michel* 600 miles N.N.W. of St Helena while still on regular liner trade to South Africa. |
| 1911 | *Guildford Castle* | 7,995 | I | See text. |
| 1914 | *Glenart Castle* | 6,575 | — | Built 1900 as Union-Castle Line's *Galician* (which see). |
| 1914 | *Glengorm Castle* | 6,763 | — | Built 1898 as Union Line's *German* (which see). |
| 1914 | *Llandovery Castle* | 11,423 | I | See text. |
| 1914 | *Llanstephan Castle* | 11,346 | I | See text. |
| 1915 | *Chepstow Castle* | 7,494 | C | Built 1913 as *Anglo Brazilian* for Nitrate Producers Co. 1933: Scrapped. |
| 1915 | *Ipu* | 712 | Co | Built 1905 for Brazilian owners. 1923: *Choyo* (British). 1925: Wrecked. |
| 1916 | *Carlisle Castle* | 4,325 | C | Built 1913 as *Holtye*. 14.2.1918: Sunk by submarine torpedo 8 miles E. by N. from Royal Sovereign light vessel. |
| 1916 | *Polglass Castle* | 4,762 | — | Built 1903 as *Reichenfels*. See text. |

| Date acquired by Union-Castle Line | Name | Grt | Original service | History: |
|---|---|---|---|---|
| 1917 | *Carlow Castle* | 5,833 | C | 1930: Sold to Mitchell Cotts & Co., renamed *Cape St. Columba.* 1935: *Adelfotis* (Greece). 1.5.1943: Sunk by submarine (*U.182*) torpedo in South Atlantic. |
| 1917 | *Crawford Castle* | 4,264 | C | Built 1910 as *Hova.* 1930: *Victoria W. Kunstmann* (Germany). 1936: *Radbod* (Germany). 5.12.1944: Sunk by Allied air attack off Osternfjord, Norway. |
| 1917 | *Leasowe Castle* | 9,737 | — | See text. |
| 1919 | *Andorra Castle* | 5,883 | — | See *Berwick Castle* (built 1902). |
| 1919 | *Dromore Castle* | 5,242 | C | Laid down as *War Poplar.* See text. |
| 1919 | *Dundrum Castle* | 5,239 | C | Laid down as a "War standard" type. See text. |
| 1919 | *Ripley Castle* | 7,521 | C | Built 1917 as *War Soldier* in Japan. 1932: Scrapped Savona. |
| 1919 | *Rosyth Castle* | 4,328 | C | Built 1918 as *War Earl* in Canada. 1920: Sold to Bullard, King & Co. (Natal Line), renamed *Umlazi.* 1936: *Campden Hill* (British). 1937: *Hokuju (Hokuzyu) Maru* (Japan). 1966: Scrapped Japan. |
| 1920 | *Banbury Castle* | 6,430 | C | Built 1918 as *War Climax.* 1919: *Glenstrae* (British). 1931: *Rokos* (Greece). 23.12.1941: Struck mine off Harwich; grounded and sunk while in tow. |
| 1920 | *Bampton Castle* | 6,698 | C | 1932: *Atlantis* (Greece). 1932: *Mount Taygetus* (Greece). 23.12.1933: Grounded in English Narrows, Chile; refloated but abandoned to salvors. 1934: Sold and scrapped. |
| 1920 | *Bratton Castle* | 6,696 | C | 1931: *Proteus* (Greece). 1932: *Mount Taurus* (Greece). 17.11.1942: Sunk by submarine (*U.264*) torpedo in Atlantic. |
| 1921 | *Arundel Castle* | 19,216 | M | See text. |
| 1921 | *Sandown Castle* | 7,607 | C | See text. |
| 1922 | *Sandgate Castle* | 7,634 | C | See text. |
| 1922 | *Windsor Castle* | 18,967 | M | See text. |
| 1924 | *Koodoo* | 119 | Tg | Used in service at East London. 1937: Sold to South African Railways & Harbour Administration (same name). 1960: Scrapped South Africa. |

| Date acquired by Union-Castle Line | Name | Grt | Original service | History: |
|---|---|---|---|---|
| 1925 | *Llandovery Castle* | 10,639 | I | See text. |
| 1926 | *Carnarvon Castle* | 20,063 | M | See text. |
| 1926 | *Eider* | 1,236 | — | Built 1900 as *Eider* for R.M.S.P. Co. 1926: Acquired for feeder service between Southampton and Continent. 1936: *Stanhill* (British). 1937: Sold British buyers, name reverted to *Eider*. 1938: *Docilitas* (Italy). 9.1943: Seized by Germany. 5.1944: Sunk by air attack at Genoa. 1947: Salved and scrapped. |
| 1926 | *Llandaff Castle* | 10,786 | I | See text. |
| 1927 | *Rovuma* | 1,289 | Co | See text. |
| 1929 | *Llangibby Castle* | 12,039 | I | See text. |
| 1930 | *Dunbar Castle* | 10,002 | I | See text. |
| 1930 | *Winchester Castle* | 20,001 | M | See text. |
| 1931 | *Warwick Castle* | 20,445 | M | See text. |
| 1935 | *Roslin Castle* | 7,016 | C | 1968: Scrapped Taiwan. |
| 1935 | *Rothesay Castle* | 7,016 | C | See text. |
| 1936 | *Athlone Castle* | 25,567 | M | See text. |
| 1936 | *Dunnottar Castle* | 15,002 | I | See text. |
| 1936 | *Dunvegan Castle* | 15,007 | I | See text. |
| 1936 | *Stirling Castle* | 25,554 | M | See text. |
| 1936 | *Walmer Castle* | 906 | Co | Used on fast feeder ship service between Southampton and Continent. See text. |
| 1937 | *Rochester Castle* | 7,795 | C | See text. |
| 1937 | *Roxburgh Castle* | 7,801 | C | See text. |
| 1938 | *Capetown Castle* | 27,002 | M | See text. |
| 1938 | *Durban Castle* | 17,382 | I | See text. |
| 1939 | *Pretoria Castle* | 17,383 | I | See text. |
| 1939 | *Richmond Castle* | 7,798 | C | See text. |
| 1939 | *Rowallan Castle* | 7,798 | C | See text. |
| 1943 | *Rowallan Castle* | 7,950 | C | See text. |
| 1944 | *Richmond Castle* | 7,971 | C | See text. |
| 1945 | *Roxburgh Castle* | 8,003 | C | See text. |

| Date acquired by Union-Castle Line | Name | Grt | Original service | History: |
|---|---|---|---|---|
| 1946 | *Drakensberg Castle* | 9,904 | C | See text. |
| 1946 | *Good Hope Castle* | 9,879 | C | Built 1945 as *Empire Life*. 1959: Scrapped Hong Kong. |
| 1946 | *Kenilworth Castle* | 9,916 | C | See text. |
| 1946 | *Riebeeck Castle* | 8,322 | C | See text. |
| 1946 | *Rustenburg Castle* | 8,322 | C | See text. |
| 1946 | *Warwick Castle* | 17,383 | I | See *Pretoria Castle* (built 1939). |
| 1948 | *Braemar Castle* | 7,065 | C | Built 1943 as *Empire Duchess*. 1950: Transferred to King Line, renamed *King James*. See Appendix D. |
| 1948 | *Edinburgh Castle* | 28,705 | M | See text. |
| 1948 | *Pretoria Castle* | 28,705 | M | See text. |
| 1950 | *Bloemfontein Castle* | 18,400 | I | See text. |
| 1951 | *Rhodesia Castle* | 17,041 | I | See text. |
| 1952 | *Braemar Castle* | 17,029 | I | 1966: Scrapped Faslane. |
| 1952 | *Kenya Castle* | 17,041 | I | See text. |
| 1954 | *Tantallon Castle* | 7,432 | C | 1971: *Aris II* (Greece). 1972: *Aris* (Greece). 1978: Scrapped Japan. |
| 1954 | *Tintagel Castle* | 7,430 | C | 1971: *Armar* (Greece). 1978: Scrapped Kaohsiung. |
| 1958 | *Pendennis Castle* | 28,582 | M | See text. |
| 1959 | *Rotherwick Castle* | 9,650 | C | 1975: *Sea Fortune* (Liberia). 1980: *Silver Rays* (Panama). 1983: Scrapped Bangladesh. |
| 1960 | *Rothesay Castle* | 9,650 | C | 1975: *Laura* (Uruguay). 1980: Scrapped Pakistan. |
| 1960 | *Windsor Castle* | 37,640 | M | 1977: *Margarita L* (Greece). Converted at Piraeus to a luxury accommodation vessel for service at Jeddah, Saudi Arabia. |
| 1961 | *Transvaal Castle* | 32,697 | M | See text. |
| 1962 | *Kinnaird Castle* | 7,718 | C | Built 1956 as *Clan Ross*. 1961: *South African Scientist* (Safmarine). 1962: Reverted to Clan Line management but renamed *Kinnaird Castle*. 1967: Transferred to King Line management. 1975: *Nazeer* (Panama). 1978: Scrapped Pakistan. |

| Date acquired by Union-Castle Line | Name | Grt | Original service | History: |
|---|---|---|---|---|
| 1962 | *Kinpurnie Castle* | 8,189 | C | Built 1954 as *Clan Stewart.* 1961: *South African Sculptor* (Safmarine). 1962: Reverted to Clan Line management but renamed *Kinpurnie Castle.* 1967: Transferred to King Line management. 1967: *Hellenic Med* (Greece). 1978: Scrapped Pakistan. |
| 1965 | *Good Hope Castle* | 10,538 | M | See text. 1984: Scrapped Shanghai as *Paola.* |
| 1965 | *Southampton Castle* | 10,538 | M | See text. 1984: Scrapped China as *Franca.* |
| 1973 | *Reina Del Mar* | 20,225 | — | See text. |
| 1976 | *Balmoral Castle* | 7,952 | C | Built 1965 as *Clan Robertson* for Clan Line (British & Commonwealth Shipping Co.) but placed under Union-Castle management. 1976: Transferred to Union-Castle for Europe/Africa service; renamed. 1979: *Balmoral Universal.* 1982: *Psara Reefer* (Greece). 1984: Scrapped Bangladesh. |
| 1976 | *Dover Castle* | 7,955 | C | Built 1965 as *Clan Ranald* for Clan Line (British & Commonwealth Shipping Co.) but placed under Union-Castle management. 1976: Transferred to Union-Castle for Europe/Africa service; renamed. 1979: *Dover Universal.* 1981: *Golden Sea* (Greece). 1985: Scrapped Pakistan. |
| 1976 | *Kinpurnie Castle* | 7,952 | C | Built 1966 as *Clan Ross* for Clan Line (British & Commonwealth Shipping Co.) but placed under Houston Line management. 1976: Transferred to Union-Castle for Europe/Africa service; renamed. 1979: *Kinpurnie Universal.* 1982: *Syros Reefer* (Greece). 1984: Scrapped Bangladesh. |
| 1976 | *Winchester Castle* | 7,952 | C | Built 1965 as *Clan Ramsay* (British & Commonwealth Shipping Co.) but placed under Union-Castle management. 1976: Transferred to Union-Castle for Europe/Africa service; renamed. 1979: *Winchester Universal.* 1980: *Lady Madonna* (Greece). 1985: Scrapped Pakistan. |
| 1981 | *Caribbean Universal* | 9,996 | C | Built in 1979 as *Polar Costa Rica* for R. A. Oetker, Hamburg. 1981: Transferred to Safmarine control. |
| 1981 | *Edinburgh Universal* | 9,996 | C | Built 1979 as *Polar Honduras* for R.A. Oetker, Hamburg. 1985: *Caspian Universal.* Still in service. |
| 1981 | *Stirling Universal* | 9,073 | C | Built 1979 as *Hilco Speedster* for I. Larsen, Oslo, Norway. 1985: *Speedster Universal.* Still in service. |

Vessels under British Government jurisdiction and managed by Union-Castle Mail S.S. Co. Ltd. during the war years 1939-1945

Managed for Ministry of War Transport:

| Name: | Built: | Grt: | History until postwar disposal: |
|---|---|---|---|
| *Empire Arun* | 1922 | 5,490 | ex *Savoia* (Lloyd Triestino). 11.2.1941: Captured on voyage Kismayu/Diego Suarez. 1946: *Granlake* (British, Goulandris Bros.). |
| *Empire Success* | 1921 | 6,009 | *ex Ixia*—1940, *ex Hagen*—1940, (Hamburg Amerika Line). 9.1939: Seized by South African Navy at Durban. 22.8.1948: Scuttled with cargo of gas bombs in Bay of Biscay. |
| *Compiegne* | 1923 | 9,986 | (Messageries Maritimes). 11.1941: Taken into East London by R.N. Later used as a training ship. 1945: Returned to owners. |
| *Charles L.D.* | 1933 | 5,273 | (Louis Dreyfus & Cie). 3.1941: Seized at Mauritius. 9.12.1942: Sunk by submarine torpedo S.E. of Cape Farewell, 59.02N 30.45W. |
| *Jean L.D.* | 1935 | 5,794 | (Louis Dreyfus & Cie). 1.1941: Taken into Cape Town by R.N. 1945: Returned to owners, renamed *Betelgeuse*; later reverted to original name. |
| *Gerusalemme* | 1920 | 8,052 | (Adriatica). 1944: Taken as a prize by R.N. Fitted out as a hospital ship. 1947: Returned to owners. |
| *Sontay* | 1921 | 8,917 | (Union Maritime Mediterranee). 1.1941: Taken into Durban by R.N. 1946: Returned to owners. |
| *Ville de Majunga* | 1931 | 4,972 | (Nouvelle Cie Havraise Pen de Nav). 3.1941: Taken into Cape Town by R.N. 1945: Returned to owners. |
| *Ville de Strasbourg* | 1920 | 7,138 | (Messageries Maritimes). 3.1941: Taken into Durban by R.N. 1946: Returned to owners. |
| *Touareg* | 1924 | 5,135 | (Compagnie de Nav. Fraissinet). 1940: Taken over by Britain. Later used as a training ship in River Thames. 1945: Returned to owners. |

Managed for Ministry of War Transport (on bareboat charter from War Shipping Administration, U.S.A.):-

| Name: | Built: | Grt: | History until postwar disposal: |
|---|---|---|---|
| *Frank A. Vanderlip* | 1943 | 7,219 | ex *Sambuff*, ex *Frank A. Vanderlip*. 1947: Returned to U.S.A. |
| *Samflora* | 1943 | 7,219 | ex *Israel J. Merritt*. 1947: *Primrose Hill* (Counties Ship Management). |
| *Sampan* | 1943 | 7,219 | ex *William I. Kip*. 1950: *William I. Kip* (U.S.A.) |
| *Samsteel* | 1943 | 7,219 | ex *James H. Robinson*. 1947: *James H. Robinson* (U.S.A.) |
| *Samtrent* | 1943 | 7,219 | ex *Percy D. Houghton*. 1947: Returned to U.S.A. |

# BULLARD, KING & CO. LTD.

late Bullard, King & Co.

THE origin of this company dates back to 1850 when two sea captains, Samuel Bullard and Daniel King, became partners in running a fleet of small sailing ships from the Thames. Their enterprise so developed that within a decade they had formed the White Cross Line, trading to Morocco and the Mediterranean.

A barque, *Priscilla*, was despatched in 1858 with missionaries to Natal direct, and after some initial competition something of a joint service was conducted with John T. Rennie who had been operating his Aberdeen Direct Line since 1854.

The two fleets actually wore the Rennie houseflag—a blue background with a white eight-pointed star in the middle; the White Cross Line name was abandoned in 1869.

The working arrangement continued happily until both companies built their first steamers—Bullard, King the *Pongola* in 1879 and Rennie the *Dabulamangi* in 1882. With the *Pongola*, Bullard, King introduced their Natal Direct Line for, as with Rennie's Aberdeen Line, known for a long time as the Aberdeen Direct Line, they did not call at Cape Town or intermediate ports, but made straight for Durban and across the Bar there, which cut their times considerably.

As newbuildings increased in size they moved from their loading berth in London at St. Katharine Dock to the West India Dock. In 1886 the Rand Gold Fields were proclaimed as Public Diggings and the discovery of gold caused a great number of Europeans to emigrate to the Transvaal. And in 1889 came a contract for the carrying of field labourers from Calcutta, Madras and Colombo to work the sugar plantations of Natal and Transvaal. Larger and faster ships followed and burned local Natal coal in their boilers.

At the turn of the century, however, the increasing trade competition between Europeans and Indians caused the Union Government to undertake legislation in 1911 and further immigration from India was stopped.

In 1914 there occurred the Rand riots and General Smuts chose the *Umgeni* to dispatch nine deportees to England—a Bullard, King ship apparently being chosen because she would go direct, not calling at Cape Town, where a Supreme Court order might have detained her.

Bullard, King became a limited liability company in 1919 and was acquired by the Union-Castle Mail S.S. Company, although keeping its independent status and colours. Two Union-Castle ships, the *Cluny Castle* and *Comrie Castle*, were transferred to Bullard, King in 1924. At the time they were built in 1903 the Boer War had just ended and as it was thought that there would be a great surge of immigrants to South Africa their accommodation had been designed with great austerity, mainly to third class standards, although there were a few cabins amidships reaching a higher grade. The immigrant rush never really materialised and the two ships were removed to extra services—on to Mauritius and returning with sugar. Of unusual profile, they were of a three-island type with vertical masts and a rather short funnel.

To the time of the Second World War the services had been built up into a passenger/cargo run from London to Port Natal, Lourenco Marques and Beira with an "inducement" call at Cape Town. The other service was from Natal to Bombay, Calcutta and Madras, calling at Colombo, but this service ceased in 1933.

Six vessels were in the fleet in 1939 but four were lost in war service, *Umtata* of 1935, *Umvuma* (1914) and *Umona* (1910) by submarine and the *Umvoti* as a blockship. This left the *Umgeni* of 1938 and *Umtali* of 1936, to which was added the *Umtata*, built in 1944, to maintain the service which now included Port Elizabeth and East London as ports of call. In 1956 the *Clan Angus* (built 1942 as *Empire Prince*) joined the fleet and was renamed *Umkuzi*. She reverted to the Clan Line in 1959.

In 1957 the *Umgeni* and *Umtali* were sold to Elder Dempster & Company. These two ships, each carrying 108 passengers in one class, had provided the passenger service of the Natal Line. Twin-screw steamers of a comfortable 14 knots, they could also carry some 7,500 tons of cargo and had some refrigerated space in the 'tween decks. They were replaced by two "Clan" vessels renamed *Umvoti* and *Umtali*, and another three were transferred in 1959 so that by the summer of that year seven vessels were in the fleet, two of which, *Umgeni* (1942) and *Umgazi* (1940), had refrigerated space. Three "Clan" ships, however, were returned to the Clan Line and the remaining four, *Umtata* (1944), *Umzinto* (1954), *Umgeni* (1942) and *Umgazi* (1940), were taken into the Springbok Shipping Co. Ltd. In addition the *Clan Shaw* and the *Clan Sinclair* (both built 1950), previously managed by Bullard, King & Company, also joined the Springbok fleet.

The colours of the Bullard, King ships were grey hulls; upperworks, boats and davits, white; vents, white with red inside cowls. The funnel was buff with black top and a chocolate band. The flag was red with a white cross and rectangle and the letters B.K. & Co. in red on the centre. Ships names were Zulu, beginning with 'Um'.

See Appendices C and E

The *Umkuzi*, seen here leaving Cape Town, was built at Dundee in 1942 as the B-type war standard ship *Empire Prince*. *Fotoship*

Fleet:

| Name: | Acquired: | Grt: | History: |
|---|---|---|---|
| *Pongola* | 1879 | 1,449 | 1907: *Mitidja* (France). 1912: *Provvidenza* (Italy). 1924: *Gabriella* (Persia). 1926: *Selam* (Turkey). 1930: Scrapped. |
| *Limpopo* | 1880 | 1,174 | (owned by Wm. Gray, London, but operated by Natal Line). 1892: Wrecked off Reunion. |
| *Congella* | 1881 | 1,585 | 1910: *Douro* (Ellerman). 5.9.1915: Sunk by submarine gunfire 79 miles S.W. by W. from Bishop Rock. |
| *Umtata* | 1883 | 1,789 | 1891: Wrecked near Madras. |
| *Palala* | 1885 | 1,144 | 1886: Wrecked, Kimmeridge Ledge, Dorset. |
| *Umzinto* | 1886 | 1,802 | 1912: *Rapide* (Algeria). 14.10.1912: Ashore in Lynn Channel (Sfax/Lynn—phosphate). Refloated, towed to Tyne and scrapped. |
| *Umlazi* | 1888 | 1,793 | 1913: *Concadore* (Italy). 1916: *Obell* (British). 28.12.1916: Stranded, Bashee River, Cape Province. |
| *Umvolosi* | 1889 | 1,775 | 1890: Wrecked, Kowie River, Eastern Province. |
| *Umbilo* | 1890 | 1,923 | 1909: *Castilian* (Ellerman). 18.4.1917: Sunk by submarine torpedo 110 miles N.W. by W. from Torry Island. |
| *Umhloti* | 1890 | 2,204 | 1922: Scrapped, Germany. |
| *Umkuzi* | 1890 | 2,057 | 1923: *Tilde* (Germany). 1925: Scrapped. |
| *Umona* | 1890 | 2,031 | 5.1903: Wrecked on coral reef, Maldive Islands. |
| *Umfuli* | 1893 | 2,370 | 1924: Scrapped, River Tees. |
| *Umtali* | 1896 | 2,641 | 1925: *Solun* (Yugoslavia). 1927: converted to submarine depot ship *Hvar.* |
| *Umvoti* | 1896 | 2,626 | 8.4.1917: Sunk by submarine torpedo 200 miles N.W. by W. from Ushant. |
| *Umgeni* | 1898 | 2,662 | 12.1916: Lost in heavy weather while in convoy. |
| *Umtata* | 1898 | 2,655 | 1924: Scrapped, Savona. |
| *Umsinga* | 1901 | 2,958 | 1928: Scrapped. |
| *Umvolosi* | 1902 | 2,986 | 1930: Scrapped, Stavanger. |
| *Umhlali* | 1904 | 3,380 | 16.9.1909: Wrecked in fog near Cape Point. |
| *Umzumbi* | 1904 | 3,379 | 1932: Scrapped. |
| *Umona* | 1910 | 3,759 | 30.3.1941: Sunk by submarine (*U.124*) torpedo 90 miles S.W. of Freetown. |
| *Umvuma* | 1914 | 4,419 | 7.8.1943: Sunk by submarine (*U.181*) torpedo in Indian Ocean, off Mauritius. |

| Name: | Acquired: | Grt: | History: |
|---|---|---|---|
| *Umlazi* | 1920 | 4,276 | Built in Canada in 1918 as *War Earl*. 1919: *Rosyth Castle*. 1936: *Campden Hill* (British). 1937: *Hokuju (Hokuzyu) Maru* (Japan). 1966: Scrapped Japan. |
| *Umzinto* | 1921 | 3,809 | Built 1894 as *Marino*. 1898: *Sabine* (Union Line). 1925: Scrapped Holland. |
| *Umvoti* | 1924 | 5,183 | Built 1903 as *Comrie Castle*. 29.7.1940: Sunk as a blockship, Folkestone Harbour. 1943: Wreck removed and cut up on beach. |
| *Umkuzi* | 1924 | 5,175 | Built 1903 as *Cluny Castle*. 1939: Scrapped. |
| *Umtata* | 1935 | 8,147 | 9.3.1942: Damaged by submarine (*U.161*) torpedo while at anchor in Castries Harbour, St. Lucia, W. Indies. Repaired. 7.7.1942: Sunk by submarine (*U.571*) torpedo off Miami while on Admiralty service. |
| *Umtali* | 1936 | 8,135 | 1957: *Calabar* (Elder Dempster). 1963: Scrapped Inverkeithing. |
| *Umgeni* | 1938 | 8,149 | 1957: *Winneba* (Elder Dempster). 1963: Scrapped Antwerp. |
| **Umtata* | 1944 | 7,288 | 1960: Transferred to Springbok Line, renamed *Klipbok*. |
| *Umzinto* | 1948 | 6,751 | Built 1942 as *Empire Kinsman*. 1956: *Vastric* (Costa Rica). 1966: Scrapped Japan. |

*Umtali*, built 1936, in the River Thames in 1955.

*Umtata,* built in 1944 and transferred to Springbok Line in 1960.

| Name: | Acquired: | Grt: | History: |
|---|---|---|---|
| *Umkuzi* | 1956 | 7,015 | Built 1942 as *Empire Prince.* 1945: *Clan Angus.* 1959: Reverted to Clan Line and old name. 1962: Scrapped Hirao. |
| *Umvoti* | 1957 | 7,103 | Built 1942 as *Empire Barrie.* 1945: *Clan Alpine.* 1959: Reverted to Clan Line and old name. 31.10.1960: Grounded in cyclone at Chittagong. Sold to Pakistan shipbreakers. |
| *Umtali* | 1958 | 7,025 | Built 1942 as *Empire Forest.* 1947: *Clan Allan.* 1959: Reverted to Clan Line and old name. 1961: *Ardsirod* (Hong Kong). 1966: Scrapped Taiwan. |
| **Umgazi* | 1959 | 8,167 | Built 1940 as *Lanarkshire.* 1960: Transferred to Springbok Line, renamed *Grysbok.* |
| **Umgeni* | 1959 | 9,184 | Built 1942 as *Empire Might.* 1946: *Clan Macrae.* 1960: Transferred to Springbok Line, renamed *Gemsbok.* |
| **Umzinto* | 1959 | 7,878 | Built 1954 as *Clan Robertson.* 1960: Transferred to Springbok Line, renamed *Rooibok.* |

The following two Clan Line vessels were managed by Bullard, King & Company after the formation of the British & Commonwealth group:

| | | | |
|---|---|---|---|
| **Clan Shaw* | 1959 | 8,101 | (Not renamed). 1960: Transferred to Springbok Line, renamed *Steenbok.* |
| **Clan Sinclair* | 1959 | 8,386 | (Not renamed). 1960: Transferred to Springbok Line, renamed *Bosbok.* |

*See Appendix C.

# SPRINGBOK SHIPPING CO. LTD.

TOWARDS the end of 1958 it was announced that the British & Commonwealth group was considering the establishment of a new shipping company in South Africa and in 1959 the Springbok Shipping Company Limited was formed to take over the services of Bullard, King & Company Limited (Natal Line). There were several additions and disposals of ships of the Bullard, King fleet in 1959 and eventually the four ships remaining were transferred and another two were moved from Clan Line ownership. Thus by 1960 a total of six ships continued the Bullard, King service between U.K. East Coast ports, the Continent and South and East Africa. The move seems to have been a precautionary measure in case of discrimination against British-flag ships in the South African trade.

The funnel colouring remained almost the same except that an addition was a brown leaping Springbok in a white diamond, the upper edges blue and with six horizontal blue lines in the lower part covering the buff/chocolate bands. The houseflag had a similar Springbok and diamond with a light blue background.

The *Gemsbok* was built at Greenock in 1942 as the fast refrigerated ship *Empire Might*.

The *Bosbok* was built in 1950 as *Clan Shaw*.

| Fleet: | Built: | grt: | | |
|---|---|---|---|---|
| *Grysbok* | 1940 | 8,167 | ex *Umgazi*,<br>ex *Lanarkshire*. | 1961: *South African Farmer*. |
| *Gemsbok* | 1942 | 9,184 | ex *Umgeni*,<br>ex *Clan Macrae*,<br>ex *Empire Might*. | 1961: *South African Financier*. |
| *Klipbok* | 1944 | 7,280 | ex *Umtata*. | 1961: Scrapped Japan. |
| *Rooibok* | 1954 | 7,878 | ex *Umzinto*,<br>ex *Clan Robertson*. | 1961: *South African Shipper*. |

Added to this quartet in 1959 were the two Clan Line ships previously managed by Bullard, King & Company.

| | | | | |
|---|---|---|---|---|
| *Steenbok* | 1950 | 8,101 | ex *Clan Shaw* | 1961: *South African Seafarer*. |
| *Bosbok* | 1950 | 8,386 | ex *Clan Sinclair* | 1961: *South African Statesman*. |

In March, 1961, the British & Commonwealth group and the Industrial Development Corporation, which controlled Safmarine, came to terms by which from July, 1961, the Springbok Shipping Company became a totally owned subsidiary of Safmarine and its ships passed to that company. This acquisition not only augmented the Safmarine fleet but included the old Bullard, King Line U.K., East Coast and Continental rights.

See Appendices B and E

# KING LINE LTD.

THIS company, which dates back to 1889, was founded by a 26-year-old man, Owen Cosby Philipps. The title of the company, as managers of the King Alfred S.S. Company (from 1893 King Line) was Philipps & Company, although this was altered to become Philipps, Philipps & Company Limited in 1900. The first steamship was the "name" ship of the company, being the *King Alfred*, built in 1889 and of some 1,100 gross tons. She was wrecked only five years later.

The formation of the company was O. C. Philipps' first attempt at shipowning but certainly not his last, for in 1903 he was appointed chairman of the already-huge Royal Mail Steam Packet combine. He went on to become Sir Owen Philipps in 1908 and then Lord Kylsant.

The RMSP empire had not yet reached its zenith and took over several companies before acquiring control of the Union-Castle Mail S.S. Company Limited in 1912, when Sir Owen Philipps became chairman of both King Line and Union-Castle.

But from the Philipps, Philipps company another personality was to emerge, Francis Vernon Thompson, later destined to become Sir Vernon Thompson, chairman of the Union-Castle Line. It was he who formed a company in 1923 to merge with George Dodd & Company Limited, the resultant title becoming Dodd, Thompson & Company Limited, and management of the King Line (and its associated Scottish S.S. Company, formed in 1896 to manage the *King Edgar* of 2,552 grt) was transferred from Philipps, Philipps & Company Limited to the new concern. At about this time two interesting sisterships were ordered for the British Motorship Company (Scottish S.S. Co.) from the Glasgow yard of D. & W. Henderson & Co. They were the *King James*, completed in November, 1925, and the *King Malcolm*, delivered the following month. Shelter deck ships, they were constructed to the

The King Line bulk carrier *King James*, built in 1970, is seen here under charter. *Skyfotos*

corrugated "Monitor" system, each vessel having two large corrugation "ridges" along each side from bow to quarter. This system, first patented in 1906, was intended to provide greater stability, increased cargo space, reduction of vibration and better seaworthiness.

Following the great depression of 1929-30 the Royal Mail Steam Packet group fell into difficulties, and one of the results was that Union-Castle regained independence.

Thus the King Line and Union-Castle had common roots even before November, 1948, when Union-Castle acquired a controlling interest in King Line, completing the purchase in the following year. In 1950 the Scottish S.S. Company ceased to function when its last vessel, *King James* (built 1925), was sold to Liberian-flag buyers.

Over the years the King Line ships have been engaged in world-wide tramping, while during the Second World War seventeen war-built standard-type ships were managed on behalf of the British Ministry of War Transport.

All King Line ships (except three small vessels built 1893/4) had the prefix "King" to their name. Six vessels were constructed in the late 1950s but transferred to the Clan Line in 1959. Later, some went to another associated company—Hector Whaling Limited. Of these six, the *King Henry* (delivered in 1958) was the last vessel built for the King Line before its absorption into the British & Commonwealth Group.

In the 1960-1970's there were numerous transfers of "Clan" ships and "King" ships between the two companies, while in 1966-68 two "Castle"-named ships were placed under King Line management. Gradually, however, the fleet was turned into bulk carrier operation and in 1977 consisted of six bulk carriers.

In 1981 the King Line operated two bulk carriers and two tankers, the Scottish Tanker Company managed two "King"-named bulk carriers and the Clan Line managed one. By the latter part of 1982 three of the bulk carriers had been sold and the remaining two, the *King Charles* and the *King Alfred*, had transferred to the management of the British & Commonwealth's subsidiary, Cayzer, Irvine & Company.

| Fleet: Name: | Acquired: | Grt: | History: |
|---|---|---|---|
| *King Alfred* (King Alfred SS Co.) | 1889 | 1,137 | 4.1894: Wrecked on South Uist. |
| *King Bleddyn* | 1894 | 2,351 | 1901: *Eleni Jean Sifneo* (Greece). 1906: *Anargyros Simopoulos* (Greece). 3.1909: Wrecked off Imbros. |
| *King Cadwallon* | 1894 | 2,380 | Built 1892 as *Auriga*. 1898: *Bakio* (Spain). 1.1902: Wrecked on north pier, Hook of Holland. |
| *King Arthur* | 1895 | 1,229 | Built 1891 as *Silvia*. 1900: *Gyptis* (France). 1923: Sold Belgium (Same name). 28.11.1924: Wrecked at La Coubre. |
| *King David* | 1895 | 2,555 | 1905: *Acuario* (Spain). 1910: *Teresa Pamies* (Spain). 1932: *Sac 9* (Spain). 1949: *Sac Santander* (Spain). 1963: Scrapped Spain. |
| *King Edgar* (Scottish SS Co.) | 1896 | 2,552 | 1901: *Elorrio* (Spain). 1917: *Begona No. 1* (Spain). 1919: *Santofirme* (Spain). 1931: *Vicente Figaredo* (Spain). 1934: Scrapped. |
| *King Frederick* | 1897 | 2,577 | 1905: *Leo* (Honduras). 4.1907: Sunk in collision off Finisterre. |
| *King Gruffydd* | 1898 | 2,994 | 1906: *Michael* (Greece). 6.1908: Sunk in collision off Lisbon. |

| Name: | Acquired: | Grt: | History: |
|---|---|---|---|
| *Barnstaple* | 1900 | 1,356 | Built 1894 (R. Craggs & Sons). 1913: Scrapped Briton Ferry. |
| *Brookline* | 1900 | 1,356 | Built 1894 (R. Craggs & Sons). 1913: Scrapped Morecambe. |
| *Mexico* (tanker) | 1900 | 1,973 | Built 1893 (R. Craggs & Sons). 9.1903: Sank in Atlantic during a hurricane. |
| *King Cadwallon* | 1904 | 3,275 | Built 1900 as *Edderton*. 7.1906: Wrecked on Scilly Isles. |
| *King Arthur* (Scottish SS Co.) | 1905 | 3,968 | 5.1912: Wrecked off South America. Salved, repaired and 1912: *Merity* (Brazil). 1915: *Hassel* (Norway). 1929: *Maize* (Norway). 1934: Scrapped U.K. |
| *King Bleddyn* | 1905 | 4,387 | 1.12.1916: Scuttled after capture by German submarine S. by W. from Ushant. |
| *King David* | 1906 | 3,680 | 10.7.1917: Sunk by submarine gunfire 360 miles from Fastnet. |
| *King Edward* | 1906 | 4,357 | 1924: *Marchioness of Bute* (Britain). 1932: Scrapped Savona. |
| *King Frederick* | 1906 | 3,756 | 1915: *Niritos* (Greece). 12.4.1917: Sunk by submarine off Augusta, Sicily. |
| *King Howel* | 1906 | 4,343 | 1916: *Bayhowel* (Britain). 1921: *Hohneck* (France). 1922: *Artemissia* (Greece). 1935: *Alexandros* (Greece). 15.9.1940: Sunk by submarine torpedo in Atlantic, N.W. of Ireland. |
| *King Idwal* | 1906 | 3,631 | 22.11.1917: Sunk by submarine torpedo 29 miles S.E. from Buchan Ness. |
| *King John* | 1906 | 3,664 | 1919: *Carlo Victoria* (Britain). 1923: *Lydia M* (Brazil). 1952: *Antonio Castro* (Brazil). 2.1970: On fire in boiler room. Repairs uneconomic; sold and 1970: Scrapped Rio de Janeiro. |
| *King Lud* | 1906 | 3,650 | 25.9.1914: Scuttled after capture by German cruiser *Emden* 25 miles S.S.W from Point de Galle, Indian Ocean. |
| *King Malcolm* (Scottish SS Co.) | 1906 | 4,351 | 28.11.1916: Sunk by submarine torpedo 144 miles N.W. from Alexandria. |
| *King Arthur* (Scottish SS Co.) | 1912 | 2,848 | Built 1905 as *Kingsland*. 1913: *Heina* (Norway). 1921: *Strudsholm* (Norway). 1922: *Atsuta Maru No. 1* (Japan). 27.8.1926: Wrecked at Tsuchisaki, Japan. |
| *King Alfred* | 1919 | 5,275 | Laid down as *War Azalea*; completed as *King Alfred*. 4.8.1940: Torpedoed by submarine (*U.52*) in N. Atlantic. Broke in two, bow sank. Stern sunk by gunfire of H.M. ship. |
| *King Bleddyn* | 1920 | 6,498 | Built 1918 as *War Music*. 1919: *Glenspey*. 1937: *Stad Maassluis* (Holland). 1950: *Fransescu* (Italy). 6.4.1954: Stranded off Bats, River Schelde. Broke in two. Sold and scrapped. |
| *King David* | 1921 | 3,721 | Built 1912 as *Gundomar*. 1939: *Hortensia Bertin* (France). 1941: *Nicaragua* (Panama). 1946: *Greater Shanghai* (China). 1950: *Miramar* (Panama). 1951: *Hoping Err* (China). 1962: Name removed from shipping registers. |

| Name: | Acquired: | Grt: | History: |
|---|---|---|---|
| *King Cadwallon* | 1923 | 5,119 | Laid down in Hong Kong as *War Piper.* Completed in 1920 as *Stathis.* 12.7.1929: Abandoned on fire south of Madagascar. Salved, towed to East London. 12.9.1929: Broke from moorings and wrecked. |
| *King Frederick* | 1923 | 5,106 | Laid down in Hong Kong as *War Sceptre.* Completed in 1920 as *Trialos.* 19.7.1944: Sunk by submarine (*U.181*) torpedo in Indian Ocean. |
| *King Gruffydd* | 1923 | 5,063 | Laid down in Hong Kong as *War Trooper.* Completed in 1919 as *Ambatielos.* 17.3.1943: Sunk by submarine (*U.338*) torpedo in N. Atlantic. |
| *King Howel* | 1923 | 5,102 | Laid down in Hong Kong as *War Miner.* Completed in 1919 as *Stathis.* 1920: *Cephalonia* (Greece). 1937: *Rowanbank* (Britain). 31.1.1941: Sunk by air attack 300 miles N.W. of Ireland. |
| *King Idwal* | 1923 | 5,115 | Laid down in Hong Kong as *War Coronet.* Completed in 1920 as *Keramies.* 23.11.1940: Sunk by submarine (*U.123*) torpedo in N. Atlantic. |
| *King Edward* | 1924 | 5,224 | Laid down as *War Terrier.* Completed in 1919 as *Gorala* (Britain). 27.12.1942: Sunk by submarine (*U.356*) torpedo in N. Atlantic. |
| *King James* (Scottish SS Co.) | 1925 | 5,066 | Laid down as *River Ottawa.* Completed as *King James.* 1950: *Sophoclyve* (Liberia). 8.8.1960: Sprang leaks, abandoned and sank in Indian Ocean. |
| *King Malcolm* (Scottish SS Co.) | 1925 | 5,064 | Laid down as *River St Lawrence.* Completed as *King Malcolm.* 31.10.1941: Sunk by submarine (*U.374*) torpedo N.E. of Newfoundland. |
| *King Robert* (Scottish SS Co.) | 1926 | 5,886 | Built 1920 as *Citta di Messina.* 29.1.1941: Sunk by submarine (*U.93*) torpedo N.W. of Ireland. |
| *King Edgar* | 1927 | 4,536 | 2.3.1945: Sunk by submarine (*U.1302*) torpedo in Irish Sea. |
| *King Edwin* | 1927 | 4,536 | 14.4.1943: On fire, sank, at Grand Harbour, Valletta, Malta. 1945: Wreck raised, towed to sea and scuttled. |
| *King Arthur* | 1928 | 5,224 | 15.11.1942: Sunk by submarine (*U.67*) torpedo off Barbados. |
| *King Egbert* | 1928 | 4,535 | 12.12.1939: Mined and sunk 4 miles S.W. of Haisboro' L.V., North Sea. |
| *King John* | 1928 | 5,228 | 13.7.1940: Sunk by raider *Widder* in Atlantic. |
| *King Lud* | 1928 | 5,224 | 8.6.1942: Sunk by Japanese submarine (*I.10*) torpedo in Indian Ocean. |
| *King Neptune* | 1928 | 5,224 | 1957: *Wing On* (Hong Kong). 1968: Scrapped Taiwan. |
| *King Stephen* | 1928 | 5,274 | 1957: *Golden Delta* (Hong Kong). 1965: Scrapped Hong Kong. |
| *King William* | 1928 | 5,274 | 1959: Scrapped Japan. |
| *King Alfred* | 1945 | 6,919 | Built 1941 as *Empire Ray.* 1963: Scrapped Hamburg. |

| Name: | Acquired: | Grt: | History: |
|---|---|---|---|
| *King David* | 1945 | 7,250 | Built 1941 as *Empire Mist.* 1962: *Hong Kong Venture* (Liberia). 1969: Scrapped Hong Kong. |
| *King Edgar* | 1946 | 7,058 | Built 1945 as *Empire Gambia.* 1959: Scrapped Japan. |
| *King Robert* | 1946 | 6,981 | Built 1943 as *Empire Grange.* 1961: *Ardgem* (Hong Kong). 1967: *Kelso* (Gibraltar). 1969: Scrapped Taiwan. |
| *King James* | 1950 | 7,065 | Built 1943 as *Empire Duchess.* 1948: *Braemar Castle* (Union-Castle). 1958: *Tyne Breeze* (Hong Kong). 1963: *Cathay Trader* (Hong Kong). 1964: *Pearl Light* (Hong Kong). 1966: *Habib Marikar* (Hong Kong). 4.11.1967: Drifted aground after engine failure and wrecked on Paracel Islands. |
| *King Alexander* | 1952 | 5,883 | First vessel built for King Line after company was taken over by Union-Castle in 1948. 1959: Transferred to Clan Line (same name). 1963: Transferred to the associated Hector Whaling Ltd. 1972: *Elli 2* (Cyprus). 1980: *Bangkok 2* (Panama). 1982: Sold Pakistan shipbreakers. |
| *King Malcolm* | 1952 | 5,883 | 1959: Transferred to Clan Line (same name). 1963: Transferred to associated Hector Whaling Ltd. 1972: *Kanaris* (Cyprus). 1980: *Dimitra K* (Greece). 1981: Arrived Chittagong for scrapping. |
| *King Arthur* | 1953 | 5,883 | 1959: Transferred to Clan Line (same name). 1963: Reverted to King Line. 1972: *Toulla* (Cyprus). 1980: *Despo* (Cyprus). 1980: *Pearl Rainbow* (Panama). 1981: *Greenleaf* (Panama). 1983: Scrapped Bangladesh. |
| *King Charles* | 1957 | 5,993 | 1959: Transferred to Clan Line (same name). 1970: Transferred to associated Houston Line. 1973: *Aegis Might* (Greece). 1979: Scrapped Taiwan. |
| *King George* | 1957 | 5,989 | 1959: Transferred to Clan Line (same name). 1970: Transferred to associated Houston Line. 1972: *Eleni 2* (Cyprus). 1980: *Taichung 2* (Panama). 1982: Scrapped Taiwan. |
| *King Henry* | 1958 | 6,133 | 1959: Transferred to Clan Line (same name). 1970: Transferred to associated Houston Line. 1972: *African Lion* (Greece). 1981: *Kladitis Emmanuel* (Greece). 1983: *Verbier* (Malta). 4.1983: Scrapped Karachi. |
| *Kinnaird Castle* | 1968 | 7,718 | Built 1956 as *Clan Ross.* See Union-Castle fleet list and Appendix E. |
| *Kinpurnie Castle* | 1966 | 8,189 | Built 1954 as *Clan Stewart.* See Union-Castle fleet list and Appendix E. |

After this the fleet consisted of the following bulk carriers and tankers:

| | | | |
|---|---|---|---|
| *King Alfred* | 1968 | 29,419 | Launched 1968 as *Angelus* (Norway). Sold while fitting out, renamed *Hemsefjell.* Sold again and completed as *King Alfred.* 1977: Transferred to associated Houston Line. 1980: To Clan Line management. 1981: To Cayzer, Irvine & Co. management. 1983: *Luo Fu Shan* (China). Still in service. |

| Name: | Acquired: | Grt: | History: |
|---|---|---|---|
| *King James* | 1970 | 30,289 | Launched 1970 as *Aralar* (Spain). Sold and completed as *King James.* 1978: *Number Four* (Liberia). 1982: *Tyne* (Liberia). 9.1982: Arrived Spezia for scrapping. |
| *King William* | 1974 | 43,742 | (Managed by associated Scottish Tanker Co.). 1982: *Panamax Sun* (Panama). 1986: *Blooming Orchid* (Taiwan). 1986: *King William* (British). 1986: *Pacifico* (Italy). Still in service. |
| *King Charles* | 1974 | 30,276 | 1982: To Cayzer, Irvine & Co. management. 1983: *Cypress* (Liberia). Still in service. |
| *King George* | 1975 | 43,742 | 1982: *Atlantico* (Italy). Still in service. |
| *King Richard* | 1974 | 42,725 | Built 1966 as *Elbe Ore* (Liberia). 1967: Purchased by British & Commonwealth Shipping Co. (managed by Scottish Tanker Co.), chartered out and name unchanged, but ship re-registered in London. 1974: Transferred to King Line and renamed. 1978: Transferred to Scottish Tanker Co. 1982: *Panamax Moon* (Panama). 1984: Scrapped Taiwan. |
| *Scottish Lion* (tanker) | 1979 | 32,995 | 1985: *Leon* (Greece). 1986: *Kappa-Due* (Italy). 1986: *Da Quing* (China). Still in service. |
| *Scottish Eagle* (tanker) | 1980 | 32,995 | 1986: *Seamagic* (Cyprus). Still in service. |

*Scottish Lion.*

# SOUTH AFRICAN MARINE CORPORATION LTD. (SAFMARINE)

SOUTH AFRICA'S merchant marine is relatively young. Ships have used Cape Town as a port of call for centuries. Early pioneers, ships calling for water, food and stores on their way to the East or to the West, early traders and settlers—all have helped to build the port. And as the economy of South Africa grew, more and more ships used the coastal ports and demanded greater facilities. The trade grew and so did the ports. But, apart from ships showing the common Red Ensign, a very high percentage were of foreign nationality. During the Second World War, with many Red Ensign ships requisitioned for war use, it was realised just how much reliance had been and was being put on foreign-flag ships for the movement of South Africa's imports and exports. And coupled with this was the realisation of the huge amount of freight revenue paid to foreign owners.

So came the belief that a fair share of South African cargoes should be carried in South African-flag ships, not only for economic progress or profit but for the importance of national security in possessing a fleet under its national flag.

In 1946 came the formation of the South African Marine Corporation (quickly to be known as Safmarine) in which the American concern States Marine Corporation had a 40% interest. By June of that year enough capital had been raised to purchase from the United States Government three war standard Victory-type ships, which had been used as transports, and they were converted into dry cargo ships with accommodation for twelve passengers, being renamed after famous South African homesteads. The inaugural sailing of a monthly service from the United States to South Africa was made when the *Constantia* left New York on 1st August, 1947.

In 1950 Safmarine was admitted to the U.K.—S. & E. Africa Conference and in May of that year inaugurated a monthly service from the U.K. west coast ports of Newport, Liverpool and Glasgow to S. & E. Africa, the three Victory-type ships taking over this service and the company having to charter other ships to fulfil other service commitments. At this time (1950-51) the States Marine Corporation became the biggest shareholder and control of the company went to the U.S.A.

The tonnage shortage was relieved when four Norwegian ships (one on the stocks) were acquired from Gorrissen & Klaveness A/S of Oslo in 1955-56. Soon after, two Japanese-built sisterships were acquired from the same source, being placed under the subsidiary title of Cape Ocean Transport (Pty) Limited. They reverted to their original owner some three years later.

At the end of the decade, in April, 1959, the States Marine Corporation surrendered its interests in Safmarine, the equities being purchased by the Industrial Development Corporation. Safmarine was now fully South African, and some two years later terms were agreed with the British & Commonwealth Shipping Company for the Springbok Line to be transferred to Safmarine. Five ships were transferred but two, partly refrigerated, were soon sold for breaking up. With increased trading operations in Europe the South African Marine Corporation (U.K.) Limited was formed as a wholly-owned subsidiary of Safmarine.

With fruit as one of the country's main exports, shipped out over nine months of each year, it was logical that the development of the merchant marine should include refrigerated fruit ships. The first, *Langkloof*, was launched at Rotterdam on 10th August, 1963. This ship was to have perpetuated the name of *South African Farmer* (broken up in January, 1963) and the name had already been fitted to the stern in the builder's yard where the hull was being built in sections. A change of policy, however, led to the company deciding to name the new fruit ships after fruit-growing districts. Three other ships, *Letaba*, *Drakenstein* and *Tzaneen*, followed, although they were built for the British & Commonwealth Shipping Company and taken on bareboat charter, with arrangements to acquire in a short time.

Another major export from South Africa being sugar, the bulk carrier *S.A. Sugela* (24,000 tdw) entered service in December, 1965, for the South African Sugar Carriers (Pty) Limited, primarily carrying Natal sugar to Japan. A further acquisition in 1965, taking effect from January, 1966, was Safbulk (Pty) Limited, a joint company set up in 1964 by A. P. Moller, Denmark, and the Industrial Development Corporation. Two ships were involved, the *Safdan Helene* (ex *Olivia Maersk*) and the *Safdan Yvonne* (ex *Brigit Maersk*), both of which were to carry pig iron. They were 12,000 grt tankers converted and lengthened to bulk carriers of 16,000 grt; both were disposed of in 1968.

With increased competition from the U.S.-flag companies, Farrell, Robin and Lykes Lines, helped by subsidies, and coupled with the fact that the three old Victory ships were getting towards the end of their lives, it was decided in 1964 to order five 20-knot partly-refrigerated cargo ships. Shortly afterwards three more were also ordered from Japan, resuscitating the original three names given to the Victory ships with the addition of the initials S.A., which now became a standard prefix of the Safmarine fleet.

The biggest acquisition of 1965, however, was the purchase of the Union-Castle liners *Transvaal Castle* and *Pretoria Castle*, the former being the most modern ship of the fleet. They continued on the Southampton—South Africa mail service with Safmarine colouring and name changes to *S.A. Vaal* and *S.A. Oranje* respectively, under the subsidiary company South African Marine Corporation (U.K.) Limited, London. They did not change their nationality until early in 1969 when the South African flag was raised on the mainmast of the ships at Cape Town. The flag changing ceremony on *S.A. Vaal* was attended by State President J. J. Fouche on 12th February and that on *S.A. Oranje* by Prime Minister the Hon. B. J. Vorster on 17th March.

It was also agreed at the time that the next mailship replacement would be a Safmarine ship, thus giving a three-sevenths participation in the mail service. The two mailships were named after the country's two most important rivers, in recognition of their importance to South Africa's economic development.

Meanwhile the final two of the six refrigerated ships that had commenced with the *Langkloof* were completed, the *Hexrivier* in 1967 and the *Zebediela* in 1968.

By 1972 the Safmarine fleet consisted of two large passenger liners, fourteen dry cargo and six fruit ships and a bulk sugar carrier. They were also managing the country's seven-ship tanker fleet under a London subsidiary, Safcover (U.K.) Limited. These ships were under one-ship companies, registered in Panama or Bermuda and on long-term charter to the oil companies. Only ten years previously Safmarine had owned only seven freighters, and this phenomenal growth had been achieved without subsidy or government grants.

By 1973 Safmarine was operating supertankers, with most of the smaller units phased out. Their first VLCC was *Kulu* (103,291 grt., 218,290 tdw), delivered in October, 1971, and operating under the Panamanian flag. The second, *Gondwana*, with similar tonnages, came in 1972. These two ships were managed by Safiran Tanker Company, formed jointly by Safmarine and the National Iranian Tanker Company. In 1979 both vessels were sold, for South African-owned tankers were then becoming increasingly undesirable in certain countries due to the political situation. A third giant tanker, *Sinde*, even bigger at 125,422 grt., 271,686 tdw, was completed in March, 1973, but was sold four months later to Holland Bulk Transport N.V., and renamed *Maasbree*.

The next big acquisition also came in 1973 when South African Lines were taken over. This company and Safmarine formed the South African flag group of the Europe/South African Conference. The company had been formed in 1946 for trade between South Africa, West Africa, Brazil and Europe and the first ship was bought in 1947. Two more were acquired in 1949, but by 1954 all three had been sold and the company continued with chartered tonnage; in the mid-1950's they were working in association with a German company. Several vessels were purchased from Germany in the late 1960's, and in 1973 a controlling interest was acquired in Globus Reederei GmbH., operating three ships.

At this date these three vessels, plus four from South African Lines, were transferred to Safmarine and absorbed into their fleet.

Fleet:

| Acquired by South African Lines: | | Built: | Grt: | |
|---|---|---|---|---|
| 1947 | *Kaapland* | 1934 | 2,709 | ex *Aeolo*, ex *Vasaland. 1954: Harma* (Panama). 1956: *Mykinai* (Greece). 1972: *Ilkon Polly* (Greece). 1972: *Vivi* (Greece). 1978: Scrapped Karachi. |
| 1949 | *Damaraland* | 1924 | 5,704 | ex *Marlene*, ex *Historian*. 1951: *Semiramis* (Turkey). 1952: *Semiramis I* (Panama). 29.5.1955: Grounded and abandoned on Landfall Island, Bay of Bengal. Salved and re-entered service. 1960: Scrapped Japan. |
| 1949 | *Namaqualand* | 1919 | 3,107 | ex *Gloucester City*, ex *Cyprian Prince*. 1951: *Kaderbaksh* (Pakistan). 1961: Scrapped Pakistan. |
| 1959 | *Table Bay* | 1954 | 4,862 | ex *Tanganjika*. 1970: *Kostis* (Greece). 1971: *Costis* (Greece). 1980: Scrapped Taiwan. |
| 1962 | *Walvis Bay* | 1956 | 7,805 | ex *Usambara*. 1971: (To Globus Reederei). |
| *1977 | *Kaapland* | 1960 | 8,482 | |
| *1968 | *Krugerland* | 1962 | 8,383 | |
| *1971 | *Komatiland* | 1956 | 9,393 | ex *Geestemunde.* |
| *1971 | *Kuneneland* | 1956 | 9,312 | ex *Cuxhaven.* |
| from Globus Reederei GmbH: | | | | |
| | **Tugelaland* | 1966 | 10,527 | ex *Concordialand, ex Tugeland* |
| | **Oranjeland* | 1969 | 11,372 | |
| | **Walvis Bay* | 1956 | 7,805 | (ex South African Lines—1971). |

*to Safmarine.

Diverse activities of Safmarine include the operation of five oil pollution control ships named *Kuswag I-V* (built 1974, 150 grt.), interests in the South African coasting trade operating under the Unicorn Shipping Lines banner, and interests in bulk carriers. Bulk ship interests include a 50% share in the *Vanguard* of 78,120 grt., 154,000 tdw, and a slightly larger bulker, the *Sishen*, of 91,750 grt., 167,500 tdw, delivered in the latter part of 1977. These vessels load high-grade iron ore for the Far East at Saldhana Bay. The ore is brought by rail from mines at Sishen, northwest of Kimberley.

Two very large salvage tugs are also controlled by Safmarine, the Durban-built *John Ross* and the British-built sistership *Wolraad Woltemade*, both 2,822 grt. and completed in 1976. When built both had the "S.A." prefix to their names. These two tugs were so named to honour two men who figured prominently in early South African history.

On 31st May, 1773, the ship *De Jonge Thomas*, owned by the Dutch East India Company, dragged her anchor and was blown ashore near the mouth of the Salt River in Table Bay, soon beginning to break up. Among many onlookers was 65-year-old Wolraad Woltemade, who farmed on the slopes of Table Mountain. He saw that although people were still clinging to the wrecked ship, no one was concerned for their safety. So he mounted his horse and urged it through the raging surf to the ship. Two survivors leaped into the sea and, clinging to the horse, were towed back to the beach. In this way by repeated forays into the sea he saved fourteen lives, but on his next return to the ship several people jumped into the sea at once and clung to the horse, which by now was exhausted. All were overwhelmed by the sea and drowned. From the ship's complement of 207 persons only sixty-seven were saved—fourteen of them by the heroic efforts of one man and his horse.

The young Scot, John Ross, was one of the crew of the schooner *Anne* wrecked in 1826 at the entrance to Durban harbour. He settled in the Port Natal district, becoming friendly with a Zulu chief, Chaka. When the settlers in the area began to suffer badly from sickness and were without medical supplies, John Ross, because of his friendship with the Zulus and his knowledge of their language, was chosen to walk 300 miles through wild, hostile country to the Portuguese settlement at Delagoa Bay to seek essential medicines. This he did, with an escort of friendly Zulus, in eighteen days. Obtaining supplies, he returned to Port Natal without incident. John Ross eventually returned to Britain, becoming master of his own ship. His real name was Charles Rawdon Maclean, but he had adopted his new name to hide his real identity when he ran away to sea, and the name John Ross remained with him for the rest of his life.

Other Safmarine interests include air transportation and management of the South African cableship *Cable Restorer.*

After six years of investigation and study by the Europe/South and East Africa Conference and the Shipping Board of South Africa, the decision that a fully cellular container service was to be introduced was announced in March, 1974. The Safmarine contribution to this service was to be four large ships for the U.K. and North Europe to South Africa route and one Mediterranean trade vessel. However, these new ships would not be ready before 1977-78, and in November, 1973, contracts were placed to lengthen four of Safmarine's newer cargo ships by the inclusion of a partially cellularised hatch to enable each to carry two hundred 20-foot containers. A further contract to lengthen another four ships was made in August, 1974. These ships were intended to be used until the large container ships were delivered and would then continue to operate as back-up ships to the service.

The six refrigerated fruit carriers not lengthened were transferred to the associated Universal Bulk Carriers Limited, Bermuda, in 1977 under the British (Bermuda) flag. The only change of ships' names was the deletion of the "S.A." prefix. Later, this company title became Alltrade Bulk Carriers Limited, remaining registered in Bermuda.

In 1978 two new Japanese-built bulk carriers joined the Safmarine fleet, under the management of Sukumbi Shipping Inc. In 1979 the *Langkloof*, *Letaba*, *Drakenstein* and *Tzaneen* were placed under the newly-formed Monsone Reefers Limited, the *Hexrivier* passed to Zephyr Reefers Limited, and the *Zebediela* to Meltem Reefers Limited. All these companies were registered in Bermuda; all six vessels underwent name change. Two more reefer vessels were acquired in 1979, the *Bora Universal* passing to Alltrade Bulk Carriers and the *Scirocco Universal* to Kildare Limited, Bermuda, and in 1981 a further two were acquired, one from the Union-Castle fleet and one from Norwegian owners. During 1983 three more bulk carriers joined the Safmarine fleet.

In the summer of 1983 the South African government ordered the state-owned Industrial Development Corporation to sell its half-share in Safmarine because of Safmarine's decision to invest in a casino monopoly. Gambling is banned in South Africa, so the new casino company's thirteen resorts will be based outside the country's borders on the South African mainland and on the Indian Ocean island of Mauritius.

For some time there had been speculation in shipping circles that Safmarine were considering re-starting a passenger ship service to and from Europe and in September, 1983, negotiations began for the purchase of HADAG's West German cruise ship *Astor*, 18,834 gt., accommodating 638 passengers. The deal was agreed in October for delivery of the ship to Safmarine in February, 1984.

Safmarine then announced that the new service to reopen the blue-water passenger route down the west coast of Africa to Cape Town, which they once worked jointly with Union-Castle, would begin in April, 1984, the ship arriving at Southampton and sailing at 1300 hours on the 4th, with arrival at Cape Town on 19th April. The service took in a call at Las Palmas. Apart from the Cape-Southampton run, *Astor* cruised from South Africa to the Indian Ocean islands of Reunion, Mauritius and Seychelles; across the South Atlantic to Rio de Janeiro and along the shorter South African coastal route from Cape Town to Port Elizabeth and Durban.

The *Astor* was launched on 16th December, 1980, at the Howaldtswerke yard at Hamburg. Trials were made in November, 1981, and she began cruising for HADAG (Hadag Seetouristik und Fahrdienst A.G.). She is propelled by four six-cylinder diesel engines driving twin screws and has a speed of 20.5 knots. But in late summer 1985 she was sold, a new liner for Safmarine having been ordered from the Howaldtswerke-Deutsche Werft A.G. yard at Kiel for delivery in 1987.

The 1981-built *Astor* at Southampton while cruising for HADAG.

Safmarine fleet:

| Acquired: | | Built: | Grt: | |
|---|---|---|---|---|
| | ex U.S.A Victory-type ships | | | |
| 1947 | *Constantia* | 1945 | 7,607 | ex *New Bern Victory*. 1961: *South African Vanguard*. 1966: *S.A. Vanguard*. 1969: *Isabena* (Panama). 7.1972: Capsized and sank off Karachi while transhipping a wheat cargo. |
| 1947 | *Morgenster* | 1945 | 7,607 | ex *Westerly Victory*. 1961: *South African Venture*. 1966: *S.A. Venture*. 1968: *Hongkong Weaver*. (Hong Kong). 1972: Scrapped Taiwan. |
| 1947 | *Vergelegen* | 1945 | 7,607 | ex *Westbrook Victory*. 1961: *South African Victory*. 1966: *S.A. Victory*. 1969: Scrapped Taiwan. |
| | ex Norway (built Glasgow) | | | |
| 1955 | *South African Merchant* | 1955 | 9,866 | Taken over on stocks, unnamed. 1966: *S.A. Merchant*. 1977: Scrapped Taiwan. |
| 1957 | *South African Pioneer* | 1953 | 9,684 | ex *Sira*. 1966: *S.A. Pioneer*. 20.4.1972: Damaged in collision with tanker *Silver Castle* (1953, 12,174 grt.) off Port Elizabeth. Sold and scrapped Taiwan. |
| 1957 | *South African Trader* | 1954 | 9,826 | ex *Sjoa*. 1966: *S.A. Trader*. 13.5.1972: Caught fire after explosions in engine room off Delagoa Bay. Towed to Lourenco Marques. Sold and scrapped Taiwan. |
| 1958 | *South African Transporter* | 1953 | 9,603 | ex *Simoa*. 1966: *S.A. Transporter*. 1972: Scrapped Taiwan. |
| | ex Norway (Cape Ocean Transport (Pty) Ltd.) | | | |
| 1959 | *Cape Agulhas* | 1959 | 9,677 | Launched as *Sira* (Norway). 1960: Intended for transfer to States Marine Corp., to be renamed *Tarheel State*, but transfer not completed. 1961: *Surna* (Norway). 1965: *Ocean Prosper* (Panama). 1968: *Prometheus* (Panama). 1974: (Sold Greece—same name). 1985: *Amesa Ena* (Gibraltar). 1985: Scrapped India. |
| 1959 | *Cape of Good Hope* | 1959 | 9,677 | 1960: Intended for transfer to States Marine Corp., to be renamed *Beehive State*, but transfer not completed. 1961: *Sefra* (Norway). 1976: *Artemidi III* (Greece). 1976: *Bolmaren* (Sweden). 1979: *Kusu Island* (Singapore). 1984: Scrapped Taiwan. |
| | ex Springbok Shipping Co. (see Appendix C) | | | |
| 1961 | *South African Farmer* | | | ex *Grysbok*. 1963: Scrapped Japan. |

| Aquired: | | Built: | Grt: | |
|---|---|---|---|---|
| 1961 | *South African Financier* | | | ex *Gemsbok*. 1962: *Santa Maria de Ordaz* (Holland) resold and scrapped Spain. |
| 1961 | *South African Seafarer* | | | ex *Steenbok*. 1966: *S.A. Seafarer*. 1.7.1966: Grounded and broke in three off Cape Town, on voyage Glasgow/Beira. |
| 1961 | *South African Shipper* | | | ex *Rooibok*. 1966: *S.A. Shipper*. 1975: Scrapped Taiwan. |
| 1961 | *South African Statesman* | | | ex *Bosbok*. 1966: *S.A. Statesman*. 1972: Scrapped Taiwan. |
| | (see Union-Castle Line and Appendix D) | | | |
| 1961 | *South African Scientist* | | | ex *Clan Ross*. 1962: *Kinnaird Castle*, managed by Clan Line and later by King Line. |
| 1961 | *South African Sculptor* | | | ex *Clan Stewart*. 1962: *Kinpurnie Castle*, managed by Clan Line and later by King Line. |
| | First fully-refrigerated ship (built Verolme, Holland) | | | |
| 1963 | *Langkloof* | 1963 | 6,907 | 1966: *S.A. Langkloof*. 1977: *Langkloof*. 1979: *Monsone Universal*. 1982: *Aegean Pride* (Greece). 1985: Scrapped Bangladesh. |
| | The following three refrigerated ships were built for the British & Commonwealth Shipping Co. by Greenock Dockyard and bareboat chartered to Safmarine. | | | |
| 1969 | *Letaba* | 1963 | 6,827 | 1966: *S.A. Letaba*. 1977: *Letaba*. 1979: *Passat Universal*. 1982: *Africa Freezer* (Panama). 1985: Scrapped Pakistan. |
| 1969 | *Drakenstein* | 1964 | 6,837 | 1966: *S.A. Drakenstein*. 1977: *Drakenstein*. 1979: *Pampero Universal*. 1980: *Aegean Wave* (Greece). 1985: Scrapped Bangladesh. |
| 1969 | *Tzaneen* | 1964 | 6,837 | 1966: *S.A. Tzaneen*. 1977: *Tzaneen*. 1978: *S.A. Tzaneen*. 1978: *Tzaneen*. 1979: *Papagayo Universal*. 1982: *Asia Freezer* (Panama). 1985: Scrapped Bangladesh. |
| | The following two ships acquired from Union-Castle were, until early 1969, placed under South African Marine (U.K.) Ltd., London. | | | |
| 1965 | *S.A. Oranje* | 1948 | 28,625 | ex *Pretoria Castle*. 17.3.1969: Re-registered at Cape Town. 1975: Scrapped Taiwan. |
| 1965 | *S.A. Vaal* | 1961 | 30,212 | ex *Transvaal Castle* 12.2.1969: Re-registered at Cape Town. 1977: *Festivale* (Panama). Still in service. |
| | Bulk sugar carrier (built Japan) (South African Sugar Carriers (Pty) Ltd.) | | | |
| 1965 | *Sugela* | 1965 | 16,405 | 1966: *S.A. Sugela*. 1977: *Sugela*. 1982: *Erinio* (Greece). Still in service. |

The *Langkloof* leaving her builder's yard in Holland in 1963.

| Acquired: | | Built: | Grt: | | |
|---|---|---|---|---|---|

Dry cargo ships "Van der Stel" class (built Verolme, Holland and Cork).
(Lengthened in 1975, now with capacity for 20-foot containers)

| Acquired | Ship | Built | Grt | | |
|---|---|---|---|---|---|
| 1966 | *S.A. Van der Stel* | 1966 | 9,502<br>12,402 | (old)<br>(new) | 1984: Scrapped Taiwan. |
| 1966 | *S.A. Weltevreden* | 1966 | 9,496<br>12,371 | (old)<br>(new) | 1977: *Safocean Weltevreden.* 1981: *S.A. Weltevreden.* 1982. *Agia Marina* (Malta). Still in service. |
| 1967 | *S.A. Nederburg* | 1967 | 9,535<br>12,363 | (old)<br>(new) | 1980: *Safocean Nederburg.* Still in service. |

Refrigerated ships (built Verolme, Holland) (sisterships to *Langkloof*)

| Acquired | Ship | Built | Grt | | |
|---|---|---|---|---|---|
| 1967 | *S.A. Hexrivier* | 1967 | 6,396 | | 1977: *Hexrivier.* 1978: *S.A. Hexrivier.* 1978: *Hexrivier.* 1979: *Mistral Universal.* 1982: *Kaw Kab-1* (Saudi Arabia). 1985: *Mistral* (Bahamas). Still in service. |
| 1968 | *S.A. Zebediela* | 1968 | 6,361 | | 1977: *Zebediela.* 1979: *Meltem Universal. Al Mareekh* (Saudi Arabia). 1985: *Meltem* (Bahamas). Still in service. |

Dry cargo ships (built Fujinagata S.B. Co., Japan)
(Lengthened in 1974, now with capacity for 20-foot containers).

| Acquired | Ship | Built | Grt | | |
|---|---|---|---|---|---|
| 1966 | *S.A. Alphen* | 1966 | 10,571<br>12,251 | (old)<br>(new) | 1984: *Kota Agung* (Singapore). Still in service. |

Built at St Nazaire in 1978, the *S.A. Winterberg* is seen in the English Channel. *Skyfotos*

| Acquired: | | Built: | Grt: | | |
|---|---|---|---|---|---|
| 1966 | *S.A. Huguenot* | 1966 | 10,571<br>12,259 | (old)<br>(new) | 1982: *Nela* (Malta). Still in service. |

Dry cargo ships (built Mitsui S.B. Co., Japan)
(Lengthened in 1975, now with capacity for 20-foot containers)

| | | | | | |
|---|---|---|---|---|---|
| 1968 | *S.A. Constantia* | 1968 | 10,592<br>12,239 | (old)<br>(new) | 1969: Transferred to Safbulk (Pty) Ltd. 1985: *Constantia.* Still in service. |
| 1969 | *S.A. Morgenster* | 1969 | 10,596<br>12,239 | (old)<br>(new) | 1985: *Morgenster*. Still in service. |
| 1969 | *S.A. Vergelegen* | 1969 | 10,608<br>12,337 | (old) | 1985: *Vergelegen*. Still in service. |

The following ships were acquired from South African Lines Ltd.

| | | | | |
|---|---|---|---|---|
| 1973 | *S.A. Kaapland* | 1960 | 9,773 | ex *Kaapland*. 1978: *Kaaplan* (Cyprus). 1978: *Hamburg Express* (Greece). 1980: *Express* (Panama). 1980: *Alhana* (Panama). 1981: *Alhana* (Kuwait). 1984: Scrapped Taiwan. |
| 1973 | *S.A. Komatiland* | 1956 | 9,312 | ex *Komatiland*, ex *Geestemunde*. 1977: *Mati* (Cyprus). 1979: Scrapped Pakistan. |
| 1973 | *S.A. Krugerland* | 1962 | 9,771 | ex *Krugerland*. 1978: *Rini* (Greece). 1982: *Saria* (Saudi Arabia). 1984: Scrapped Pakistan. |
| 1973 | *S.A. Kuneneland* | 1956 | 9,312 | ex *Kuneneland*, ex *Cuxhaven*. 1977: *Nela* (Cyprus). 1978: *Grigorios D* (Greece). 1982: Scrapped Pakistan. |

| Acquired: | | Built: | Grt: | |
|---|---|---|---|---|
| | The following ships were acquired from Globus Reederei GmbH | | | |
| 1973 | *S.A. Tugelaland* | 1966 | 10,527 | ex *Concordialand*, ex *Tugelaland.* 1976: (To Globus Reederei GmbH). 1978: *Lu Cheng* (China). Still in service. |
| 1973 | *S.A. Oranjeland* | 1969 | 11,372 | ex *Oranjeland.* Renamed but remained on German registry, (Globus Reederei (Capesal Co. Inc., Panama)). 13.8.1974: Aground and wrecked in heavy weather off East London. |
| 1973 | *S.A. Walvis Bay* | 1956 | 7,720 | ex *Walvis Bay*, ex *Usambara.* 1976: *Athen Sky* (Greece). 1984: *Rose* (Greece). 1984: Scrapped Taiwan. |
| | Bulk carriers (built Mitsui S.B. Co., Japan) | | | |
| 1973 | *S.A. Sukumbi* | 1973 | 16,459 | ex *Sukumbi.* A sugar carrier for South African Sugar Carriers (Pty) Ltd. 1983: *Kertis* (Greece). 1985: *Sunbeam* (Cyprus). 1986: *Lark Barrow* (Liberia). Still in service. |
| 1974 | *S.A. Skukuza* | 1974 | 16,315 | ex *Skukuza.* 1983: *Perast* (Switzerland). Still in service. |
| 1976 | *S.A. Sabie* | 1976 | 15,714 | 1976: (to Globus Reederei GmbH., German registry). 1977: *Sabie.* 1981: (To Skukuza Shipping Corp., (Safmarine), Panama registry). Still in service. |
| | Container ship (built Italcantieri SpA., Genoa) | | | |
| 1977 | *S.A. Langeberg* | 1977 | 28,259 | Still in service. |
| | Container ships (built At. & Ch. de Dunkerque & Bordeaux, Dunkirk) | | | |
| 1977 | *S.A. Heldeberg* | 1977 | 53,023 | Still in service. |
| 1978 | *S.A. Sederberg* | 1978 | 53,023 | Still in service. |
| | Container ship (built Chantiers de L'Atlantique, St. Nazaire) | | | |
| 1978 | *S.A. Winterberg* | 1978 | 53,050 | Still in service. |
| | Container ship (built Ch. Nav. de la Ciotat, La Ciotat) | | | |
| 1979 | *S.A. Waterberg* | 1979 | 53,050 | Still in service. |
| | Refrigerated ships (built Mitsubishi Heavy Industries, Japan) | | | |
| 1979 | *Bora Universal* | 1979 | 7,935 | Still in service. |
| 1979 | *Scirocco Universal* | 1979 | 7,933 | Still in service. |
| | Bulk carriers (built Nippon Kokan K.K., Japan) | | | |
| 1978 | *Venture* | 1978 | 18,575 | Still in service. |
| 1978 | *Victory* | 1978 | 18,297 | Still in service. |

## THE CAPE RUN

| Acquired: | | Built: | Grt: | |
|---|---|---|---|---|
| | Refrigerated ship transferred from Union-Castle Line | | | |
| 1981 | *Caribbean Universal* | 1979 | 9,996 | (Caribbean Reefers Ltd., Bermuda). Still in service (Gateway Shipping Ltd., London). |
| | Refrigerated ship acquired from Norwegian owners | | | |
| 1981 | *Scamper Universal* | 1980 | 9,065 | Built 1980 as *Hilco Scamper* for I. Larsen, Oslo, Norway. Still in service (Gateway Shipping Ltd., London). |
| | Container ship (built Ishikawajima-Harima Heavy Industries, Japan) | | | |
| 1982 | *S.A. Vaal* | 1982 | 31,225 | Still in service. |
| | Bulk carriers (Nippon Kokan, Shimizu, Japan) | | | |
| 1983 | *Sea Transporter* | | 21,308 | Still in service (Gateway Shipping Ltd., London). |
| 1983 | *Sea Pioneer* | | 20,970 | Still in service (Gateway Shipping Ltd., London). |
| 1983 | *Sea Merchant* | | 20,970 | Still in service (Gateway Shipping Ltd., London). |
| | Passenger ships | | | |
| 1984 | *Astor* | 1981 | 18,834 | 1985: *Arkona* (East Germany). Still in service. |
| 1987 | *Astor* | 1987 | 20,159 | Still in service. |

The cruising liner *Astor* arriving at Southampton on 22nd January, 1987. Launched by Howaldtswerke-Deutsche Werft A.G. at Kiel on 30th May, 1986, she has a length of 580 feet, a breadth of 74 feet and ten decks, with accommodation for 650 passengers. Registered under the flag of Mauritius, her cruises are marketed by Astor Cruises' parent company, Morgan Leisure Ltd., Colchester. *W. Sartori*

# FOR THE RECORD—THE BRITISH SEAMEN'S STRIKE OF 1966

AT MIDNIGHT on Friday, 1st July, 1966, the Seamen's strike ended and the greatest seize-up of British ships of all time was over.

Peculiarly, the strike did not affect the man in the street very much, except for those whose holidays were booked afloat. The worst congestion was at Dover, where unbooked motorists arrived in hundreds but of course could not be taken by British flag ships. Some were absorbed in the Belgian Marine service to Ostend, while others drove to Newhaven, where half the service was run by French Railways. Others went on to Southampton, where the Norwegian ferries operated to Havre and Cherbourg.

The shipping companies, however, suffered great losses and on this day a look round Southampton Docks showed the cream of Britain's great liner fleet, lifeless alongside the great quays of the port. This was the biggest accumulation of liners ever gathered there, and companies whose houseflags had flown on the oceans of the world for a hundred years or more watched their great ships arrive, one by one, week by week, until their fleets were completely immobilised.

The Eastern Docks group at Southampton during the seamen's strike of 1966.
*Southern Evening Echo*

Before the end of the strike the Union-Castle—Safmarine saw all passenger ships of their South African mail service in port, and to these were added the *Capetown Castle*, the *Roxburgh Castle* and the *Rowallan Castle* as well as the cruising liner *Reina del Mar*.

Cunard were in a similar plight, their giant "*Queens*", *Caronia*, *Franconia* and *Carmania* losing huge sums of money for the company. One of the two major units of Shaw, Savill, the *Southern Cross*, was an early victim when she arrived on 24th May, but the *Northern Star* was fortunate to miss the strike completely, not arriving at Southampton until 4th July. To complete the big-ship picture were two of the P & O-Orient fleet, *Canberra* and *Arcadia*, and Royal Mail Line's cruising liner *Andes*.

With such a gathering as this there had to be doubling up on berths, and at one berth three Union-Castle ships lay treble-banked for a time. This was necessary as it was essential that a number of berths should be kept for foreign-flag callers.

During the weeks of the strike many thousands of sightseers came to the city, small fortunes being made by the local small-boat men who could truly advertise "a review of Britain's Merchant Navy"—and they did.

For the record, the Dock list is of ships in Southampton Docks on Friday 1st July, 1966: such an armada will never be seen like that again.

EASTERN DOCKS GROUP

| Berth | Ship/owner | Movements | gt. |
|---|---|---|---|
| 7 | *Viking I* (Thoresen Car Ferries) | for Cherbourg from Havre | 3,608 |
| 7 | *Viking II* (TCF) | from Havre for Cherbourg (am) | 3,611 |
| 7 | *Viking II* (TCF) | from Cherbourg for Havre (pm) | 3,611 |
| 7 | *Viking III* (TCF) | for Havre from Cherbourg | 3,821 |
| 20 | *Nordholm* (Oldendorff) | | 956 |
| 22 | **Lune Fisher* (Fisher) | | 1,200 |
| 23 | **Elk* (British Rail) | | 795 |
| 25 | *Leon* (Empresa Hondurena) | from Port Antonio | 3,346 |
| 26 | *Rio San Juan* (ELMA) | from Santos | 2,308 |
| 29 | **Twyford* (Risdon Beazley) | | 1,104 |
| 29 | **Moose* (British Rail) | | 795 |
| 30/31 | **Southern Cross* (Shaw Savill) | | 20,204 |
| | **Franconia* (Cunard) | | 22,637 |
| 32/33 | **Capetown Castle* (Union-Castle) | | 27,002 |
| | **S.A. Oranje* (Safmarine) | | 28,625 |
| 34/35 | **Clan Robertson* (Clan) | | 10,541 |
| 36 | **Good Hope Castle* (Union-Castle) | | 13,152 |
| 37 | **Chicanoa* (Elders & Fyffes) | | 6,283 |
| 38/39 | **Caronia* (Cunard) | | 34,274 |
| 40 | **Andes* (Royal Mail Lines) | | 26,435 |
| 41 | *Lions Gate* (Johnson) | for Honolulu | 9,173 |
| 43 | **Roxburgh Castle* (Union-Castle) | | 7,996 |
| | **Rowallan Castle* (Union-Castle) | | 7,943 |
| 43/44 | **Queen Mary* (Cunard) | | 81,237 |
| 46 | **Carmania* (Cunard) | | 22,592 |
| | **Port Lyttelton* (Port Line) | | 7,413 |
| 47 | **Reina del Mar* (Union-Castle) | | 21,495 |
| 49 | *Bess* (Wallenius) | | 1,600 |
| 50 | HM ships *Venturer*, *Thames* and *Warsash* | | |
| 50 | (dolphins) | | |
| | **Camito* (Elders & Fyffes) | | 8,687 |
| | **Golfito* (Elders & Fyffes) | | 8,740 |

WESTERN DOCKS

| | | | |
|---|---|---|---|
| 101 | **Edinburgh Castle* (Union Castle) | | 28,629 |
| 102 | **Canberra* (P & O-Orient) | | 45,733 |
| 102/3 | *Alexandra K* (Merabello SA) | | 2,908 |
| 104 | **S.A. Vaal* (Safmarine) | | 32,677 |
| 105 | *Willemstad* (KNSM) | from Amsterdam for Madeira | 5,088 |
| 106 | **Queen Elizabeth* (Cunard) | | 83,673 |
| 107 | *Rotterdam* (Holland America) | from New York for Rotterdam | 38,645 |
| 107 | *France* (CGT—French Line) | from Havre for New York | 66,348 |
| 107/8 | **Arcadia* (P & O-Orient) | | 29,664 |
| 110 | **Bay Fisher* (Fisher) | | 1,289 |
| 110 | **Dorset Coast* (Coast Lines) | | 1,167 |

DRY DOCKS

| | | | |
|---|---|---|---|
| 5 | **Southampton Castle* (Union-Castle) | | 13,152 |
| 6 | **Pendennis Castle* (Union-Castle) | | 28,582 |
| 7 | **Windsor Castle* (Union-Castle) | afloat | 37,647 |
| | *Strikebound | | 806,386 |

Summary

| | | | |
|---|---|---|---|
| 17 | British liners of over 10,000 gt. strikebound | 546,649 | |
| 2 | South African liners of over 10,000 gt. strikebound | 61,302 | |
| 12 | British ships under 10,000 gt. strikebound | 53,412 | |
| 2 | Foreign liner movements | 105,244 | |
| 11 | other foreign ships | 39,779 | 806,386 |

## FLAGS AND FUNNELS

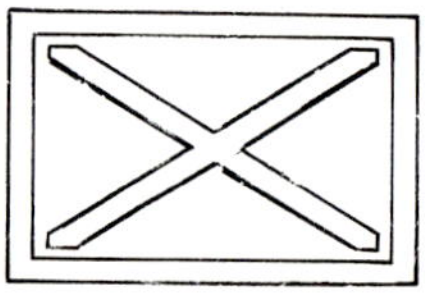

1

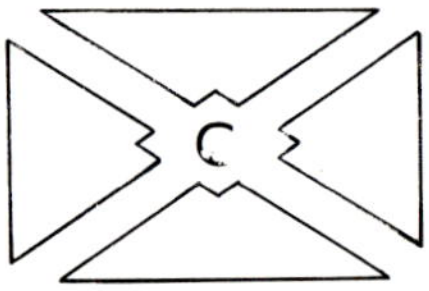

2

3

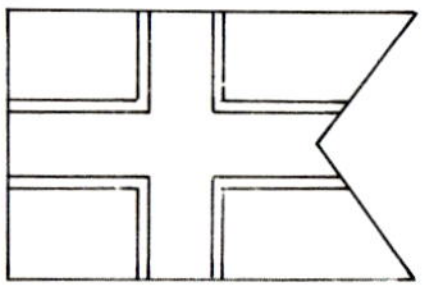

4

5

6

### FLAGS

1. Union Line
   white ground, blue edge, red saltire

2. Castle Line
   blue ground, white saltire with white diamond at centre bearing a red "C"

3. Union-Castle Line
   adaptation from Union and Castle flags i.e. blue ground, white saltire with white diamond and, superimposed, a red saltire

4. South African Marine Corporation (Safmarine)
   broad orange cross edged with blue on white ground

5. Clan Line
   red ground, white diamond, red lion

6. British & Commonwealth Shipping Group—burgee
   blue ground, red saltire over white saltire; white diamond with red lion

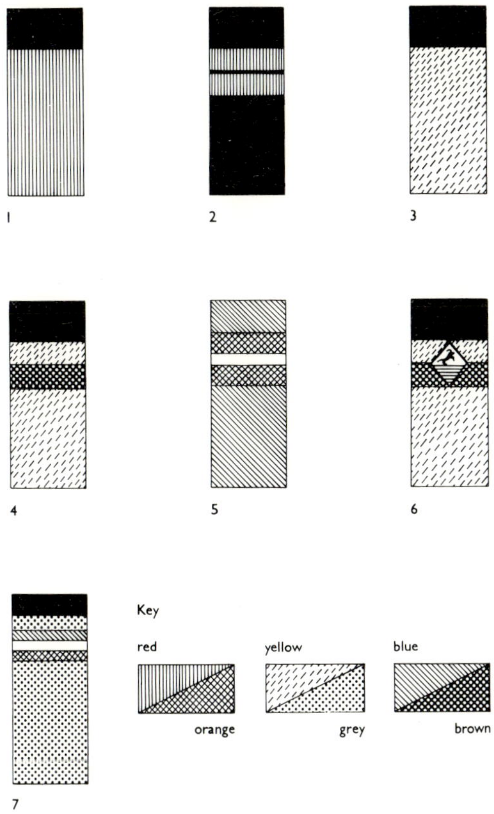


1. Castle Line
   Union-Castle Line

   Note: Union Line 1858 — black
   c. 1863 — buff, black top
   1870 — black
   1891 — buff

2. Clan Line

3. King Line

4. Bullard, King & Co. (Natal Line)

5. ) Springbok Shipping Co.
6. ) Springbok Shipping Co. "springbok" is brown; upper edges of diamond and lower horizontal lines are blue

7. South African Marine Corporation (Safmarine)

# General Index

# Index

of ships of the Union Line, Castle Line, Union-Castle Line and associated companies.

Where there is more than one ship of the same name acquisition dates are shown.

*Illustrations in bold type*

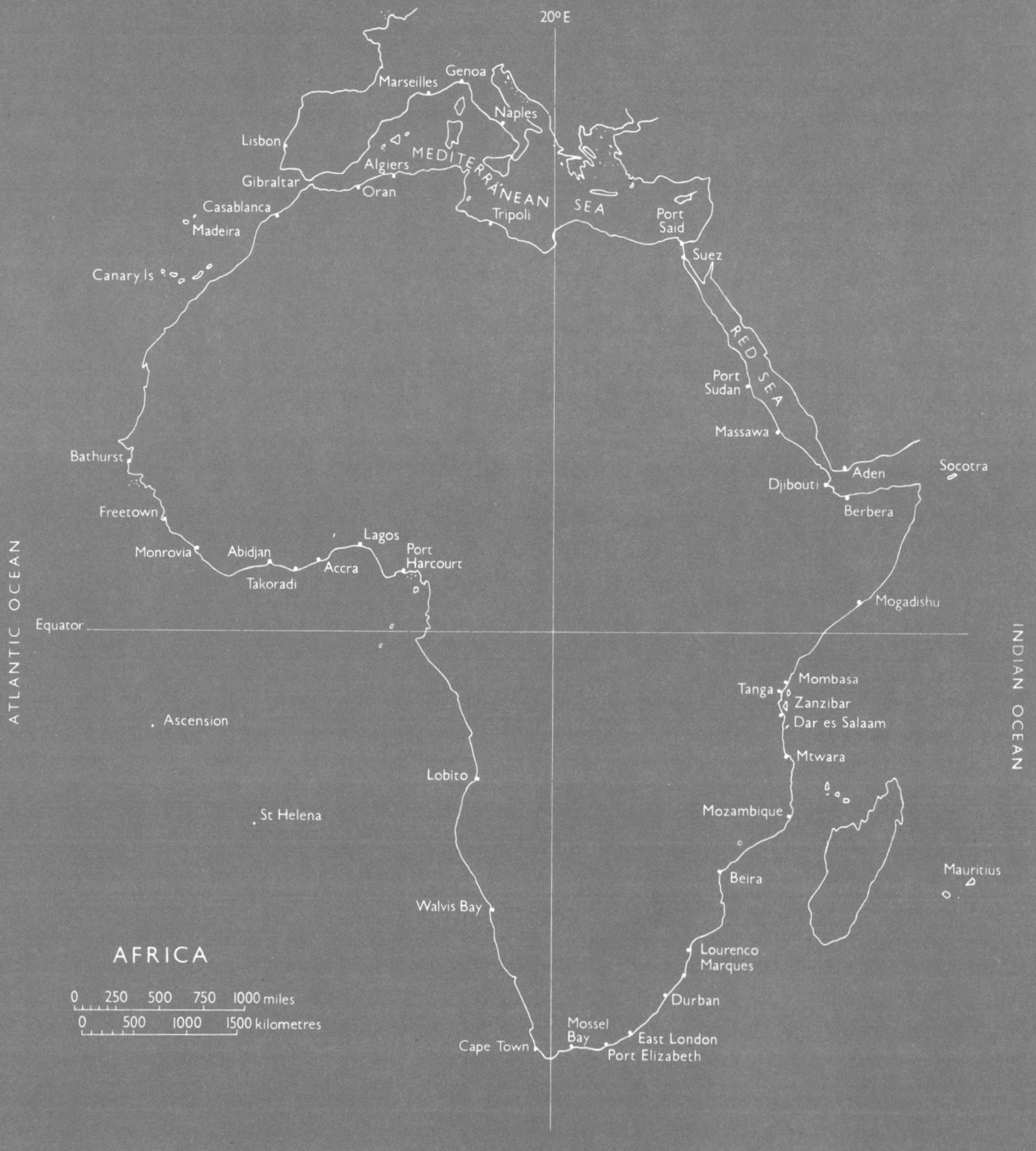
20° E
Marseilles
Genoa
Naples
Lisbon
MEDITERRANEAN SEA
Algiers
Gibraltar
Oran
Casablanca
Madeira
Tripoli
Port Said
Suez
Canary Is
RED SEA
Port Sudan
Massawa
Bathurst
Aden
Socotra
Djibouti
Berbera
Freetown
Lagos
Port Harcourt
Monrovia
Abidjan
Accra
Takoradi
Mogadishu
ATLANTIC OCEAN
Equator
INDIAN OCEAN
Mombasa
Tanga
Zanzibar
Dar es Salaam
Ascension
Mtwara
Lobito
St Helena
Mozambique
Beira
Mauritius
Walvis Bay
Lourenco Marques
AFRICA
Durban
0 250 500 750 1000 miles
0 500 1000 1500 kilometres
Mossel Bay
East London
Cape Town
Port Elizabeth